Hotel Contract Negotiation
Tips, Tricks, and Traps

Stephen R. Guth

This book is dedicated to you know who.

First Edition

DISCLAIMER: THIS BOOK, IT'S CONTENTS, AND THE INCLUDED CONTRACT TEMPLATE SHOULD IN NO WAY BE CONSTRUED AS A SUBSTITUTE FOR LEGAL ADVICE. READERS ARE ENCOURAGED TO SEEK COMPETENT LEGAL ADVICE REGARDING CONTRACTS AND OTHER LEGAL MATTERS RELATING TO HOTEL CONTRACTING.

Published in the United States by Guth Ventures LLC, Alexandria, Virginia.

ISBN: 978-1-4583-5033-6

Library of Congress Control Number: 2011900516

Printed in the United States of America

10 9 8 7 6 5 4 3 2 1

About the Author

Stephen R. Guth has over 15-years of multinational supply management experience, representing companies such as Ryder System, Dell Computer, and Aflac Insurance. He also served in the armed forces as part of the United States Special Operations Command. Stephen is a graduate of the University of Miami School of Law (J.D.), University of Maryland University College (M.S.M.), and Saint Leo University (B.A., summa cum laude). He is a licensed attorney and a member of the Virginia and District of Columbia Bars. He holds multiple professional certifications, including Certified Commercial Contract Manager (CCCM), Certified Purchasing Manager (C.P.M.), Certified Professional in Supply Management (CPSM), and Certified Technology Procurement Executive (CTPE). Stephen is the author of *The Contract Negotiation Handbook: An Indispensable Guide for Contract Professionals*, *The Vendor Management Office: Unleashing the Power of Strategic Sourcing*, and *Project Procurement Management: A Guide to Structured Procurements*. Stephen is also the moderator of a blog that focuses on supply management, procurement, contracting, and vendor management topics (www.vmo-blog.com).

Contents at a Glance

Table of Contents

Introduction

Dates, rates, and space. That's what most folks focus on when they negotiate with hotels. The fine print and legalese of a hotel contract isn't nearly as interesting—until it comes around to bite someone (usually *not* the hotel). Then the contract becomes all-important.

Over my career, I've negotiated contracts small and large, easy and complex, across all different types of goods and services. By far, the most consistently complex—and most likely to haunt me after the deal—are hotel contracts. Why? Hotel rooms are similar to a perishable commodity, like fruits or vegetables. Once a night has passed without a room having what hoteliers call a "head in a bed," that room has essentially become *rotten*. The hotel will never be able to recoup the lost revenue for that night for that room. Another reason that hotel contracts are somewhat unique is that the person or organization contracting with the hotel usually isn't paying for the rooms—it's the individual attendees. In those cases, since a hotel isn't contracting directly with the attendees and the attendees generally don't have any liability to the hotel in terms of showing up for their reservation, the hotel wants to make sure someone (you, the buyer who is representing the group of attendees) is legally and financially on the hook. With that in mind, it's no surprise that hoteliers bargain hard to maximize their revenue and ensure that the person or organization representing a group of attendees is contractually hand-cuffed to the hotel.

The purpose of this book is to help a person[1] representing a group, such as a meeting planner, to level the playing field and negotiate a fair and reasonable contract with the hotel where the group will be

---

[1] That person is referred to as the "group representative" throughout this book.

holding a meeting. Keep in mind that hotels sell their rooms and hotel services day in and day out—they're experts at selling and getting the best possible deal for themselves and their shareholders. A group representative probably doesn't buy hotel rooms as frequently as hotels sell them, so that puts a group representative at a negotiation disadvantage. While I don't advocate that a group representative overreach and try to squeeze every last penny of profit from a hotel, I do advocate a group representative being prepared and educated in their negotiations with hotels. And that's what this book is about—to help you (as the group representative) get a good deal for you and your group.

To achieve that goal, I'll take a hotel contract template that I use on a routine basis and I'll deconstruct it section-by-section and provision-by-provision in this book. For key provisions, I'll describe and explain any tips, tricks, and traps that you should be aware of. Since it's helpful in any negotiation to put yourself in the shoes of the other party you're negotiating with, where appropriate, I'll include what I think the position of a hotel might be.

The contract template that I'll be deconstructing and reviewing is what I call the "Master Hotel Services Agreement" or "MHSA." This book isn't an academic guide or treatise on hotel contracts—it's a practical, *how-to* guide and it assumes some basic understanding of the hospitality industry and contracting. I won't cover contract basics such as what creates a binding contract, but, even if you don't have any hospitality industry or contracting knowledge, you'll at least be in a better negotiation position by reading this book than if you were to try to go it alone. I'll begin immediately using hotel contracting lingo such as "room block," "room pick-up," and "peak nights." Whenever you see a term or phrase you don't immediately recognize or understand, refer to the *Glossary* at the end of this book or to *Appendix II ~ MHSA Defined Terms* which contains terms defined and used in the MHSA.

I've negotiated, either directly or through my staff, hundreds of hotel contracts representing hundreds of thousands of sleeping room nights—which translate into tens of millions of dollars in revenue for hotels. I've experienced gut-wrenching situations such as weather events shutting down the cities where my meeting was being held, unions threatening to strike just before my meetings, hotels unexpectedly undergoing construction during my meetings, and being faced with hundreds of thousands of dollars in attrition damages. And those situations don't include the dozens of hotel power outages, water outages, over-bookings, missing food and beverage, and other problems my staff or I have experienced. In other words, I've seen it all—I've seen the best and worst of hoteliers and hotels. This book offers my unvarnished opinions as they relate to negotiating and contracting with hotels, with some readers certain to take exception to part or all of what I've written in this book. Use what makes sense to you and reform what you need to so that it works for you.

As you read through this book, the lens that you need to read it through is one of "fair and reasonable." Despite some of the tough positions I occasionally recommend that you take in this book or some of the shots that I take at hotels in describing their positions, I suggest being fair and reasonable. You want to get a good deal for your group and meeting, you want a relationship based on commitment (as demonstrated by a solid, written contract), and you want the hotel to make a reasonable profit. And, ultimately, you want to get what you and your attendees paid for. All of that is best accomplished by being fair and reasonable—and tough. So, let's get started...

Convention Industry Council

You might be wondering if there is any standard hotel contract template that hoteliers and groups have agreed upon. The answer, unfortunately, is no. But at least one industry group did *try* to develop a standard hotel contract template. The Accepted Practices Exchange (APEX), an initiative of the Convention Industry Council, has the goal of developing and implementing industry-wide accepted practices to create and enhance efficiencies throughout the meetings, conventions, and exhibitions industry. Several working panels of volunteers were created to address key areas in the industry with one panel being the Contracts Panel. The objective of the Contracts Panel was to review all aspects of industry contracts and develop contract guidelines and, where appropriate, acceptable contract language guidelines. Additionally, the Contracts Panel was to develop an outline to format industry contracts. The Contracts Panel determined that, for legal and practical reasons, acceptable contract language should *not* be created. The Contracts Panel did issue a 2006 report entitled "APEX Contracts Accepted Practices" that's worth reading.

I attended one of the Contracts Panel's sessions in 2005 and the phrase "herding cats" immediately came to my mind. At that session, I quickly recognized why the Contracts Panel would never accomplish their initial objective. The Contracts Panel consisted of hoteliers, meeting planners, and attorneys, all influential and all at the top of their game in the hospitality industry. This was at a time when the hotel industry was booming and occupancy rates were going through the roof, giving tremendous negotiating leverage to hotels. There was no way, given the make-up of the Contracts Panel with all of its biased interests combined with the economic environment of the times, that anyone was going to come to an agreement on a standard contract template. So, in my opinion, the Contracts Panel did the only thing it could do. It punted. By issuing its 2006 report.

In the changed economic era that this book has been written in, which favors groups and not hotels, the Contracts Panel would still fail. Unfortunately, hotel business cycles and the varied interests of meeting planners, hotel management companies, hotel owners, and attorneys are all such that it makes better sense to view hotel contract negotiations from either the buy-side or the sell-side rather than taking an ill-fated *kumbaya* approach. It would be nice to get to the point of having a common hotel contract template that is readily agreed-to by all involved, but that's not the world we live in at present. That's not to say it's not worth attempting every now and then, as the Contracts Panel did, but, in the interim, you're obligated to represent the best interests of your employer, whether that be a group or a hotel.

Getting the Best Deal for Your Meeting

To ensure you get the best deal with a hotel for yourself, as a group representative, and for your attendees, it's important to understand what your negotiation leverage is, how to value and competitively bid your meeting, and how to negotiate room rates and other concessions.

Negotiation Leverage

It's worth having a short discussion of negotiation leverage first, since, if you don't have any, you can't expect that you're going to have much luck with getting the best deal for your meeting. There are many different factors affecting your negotiation leverage, and almost all have to do with timing, location, and the make-up of your meeting.

Let's dream a bit... It's January. The economy is booming. You decide that you'd like to have your roughly 100 attendee meeting in sunny San Diego. During the middle of the second week in March. Oh, by the way, you don't need much food and beverage for your meeting, but you do need a ballroom on a 24-hour space hold basis for each of the 3-days that your meeting will be held. Take a guess as to how much leverage you have. If you guessed something right around "absolutely zip," then you're close to being right. In that scenario, you've picked a bad time (booming economy) on top of a bad time (winter is peak season for hotels in warm climates) on top of a bad time (hotels don't like mid-week meetings because that's usually their busiest time) with bad timing (your meeting is only two months away) at a high-demand location (San Diego) with a relatively small group (100 attendees) that doesn't represent much spend (no food and beverage) with the need for a substantial concession (you want a lot of function space, i.e., the ballroom, but you have a small group). Considering all of the foregoing, don't be surprised if some hotels don't even want your business let alone even thinking about giving you a great deal.

Here's another scenario… Your attendees love going to Orlando. They want to go back to Orlando every year. They love staying at the same hotel in Orlando. The hotel knows all of that when you approach them to book another meeting. Guess how much leverage you have in this case. Like with the first scenario, if you guessed something right around "absolutely zip," you're close to being right. Just as with cars at car dealerships and houses with realtors, don't fall in love with a hotel—ever. If you think that a hotel is going to reward you for your repeat business, you're sadly mistaken. The opposite is true—in my experience, a repeat-business hotel comes to expect your business, becomes complacent, and becomes non-competitive. Sure, if you sign-up at one time with a hotel for a multi-year contract, you might have some leverage, but if you go back to a hotel again and again but you contract separately each time, don't be surprised if you find out that you're not getting such a great deal after all.

Be smart and be creative in trying to figure out how to impact the timing, location, and make-up of your meeting to bolster your leverage. Realistically, there might be some things that you *can't* change that affect leverage, such as the size of your group or the rough time period that the meeting needs to occur (sometimes, a group's bylaws mandate when a meeting must be held). Even if you can't change any of the attributes or requirements of your group, there are ways to bolster your leverage: plan as far in advance as possible, be flexible in potential meeting locations, and competitively bid your meeting. By issuing a competitive bid (meaning a "Request for Proposals" or "RFP") to multiple hotels in multiple locations significantly in advance of when your meeting is scheduled to be held, you'll be able to play hotels and locations off of each other to get the best deal. If you're in a rush to contract with a hotel because your meeting is next month and you're dead-set on having your meeting in a hotel on Capitol Hill in Washington, DC, expect high room rates, high food and beverage minimums, attrition damages, and zero favorable contract terms. Change it up a bit by sending a competitive bid a year or more in advance and be willing to consider areas around Capitol Hill—you'll get a heck of a bargain as well as a favorable contract.

If you're going to be booking meetings pretty routinely (e.g., you're a meeting planner), you need to culture relationships with the (good) hoteliers. Be wary though, the hospitality industry is entrancing and hoteliers will ply you with fancy fam (slang for "familiarity") trips to visit their hotels and invite you to other exciting events where the hoteliers pay for everything (be sure to check your employer's ethics policy for what you can and can't accept). It's easy to fall into the trap of thinking that you really are special and the hoteliers really do *love* you just because it's you. Don't be fooled. If hoteliers can influence you as a result of their relationship with you, all the better for them. In fact, in my experience, hoteliers take a dim view and look down on customers (behind their backs, of course) that go on every fam, ask for free rooms for personal trips, and demand special amenities in their rooms when attending a meeting they've booked. It's reasonable to go on a fam to a hotel where you're likely to book a meeting, but don't abuse your relationships with hoteliers with all of your special, personal needs.

As long as you keep the foregoing in mind, it's helpful to have healthy, respectful, and arm's length relationships with hoteliers. The hospitality industry is surprisingly small and tight-knit. Consequently, there is a pseudo-karma in the hospitality industry…if you gouge or rip a hotel, or do something else unreasonable or unfair to a hotelier, it will likely come back to haunt you. Similarly, treat hoteliers fairly and with respect, and those same hoteliers will save your hide in a time of need. I've come across some horrible hoteliers and, mostly, I've come across great hoteliers. I've had some hoteliers kick me when I was down with attendance issues, and, mostly, I've had hoteliers come to my rescue when I've really needed it.

How to Value Your Business

During the economic heyday of 2004 – 2007, when the hospitality industry was at a peak and hotels had an extreme amount of negotiation leverage, some hotel execs became power-drunk and ranted in the industry press that the business represented by group customers (which had sustained hotels during prior tough times) just wasn't good enough anymore. In a 2006 article contained in a widely-read trade publication, an industry relations executive for a prominent flag sent an unvarnished message to group customers: "...in the last two years, your baby got ugly...our hotel doesn't want your business because they've got six or seven other choices that are all better." Times have changed, and those same "ugly babies" of 2006 have since become the darlings of the hotel industry. In good economic times or bad, an important part of determining how much negotiation leverage you have (or don't have) is to understand the value of your business to hotels. That understanding is critical to have before approaching hotels for proposals. There are two key components of putting a value on your business: creating a group profile and developing a history for the meeting. Together, these documents will help in projecting the potential revenue that a group will generate—your group's value to a hotel—for a particular meeting.

Group Profile

A group profile, which is essentially a "fact sheet" for your group, helps hotels to understand your group and is an integral part of competitively bidding out your meeting. The more that a prospective hotel understands your group, the more precise the hotel can be when bidding on your business. A group profile typically contains the following:

- A brief description of your group (e.g., business, mission)
- The purpose / type of the meeting (e.g., board meeting, sales meeting)
- The location of the meeting (if at a different venue than the hotel, such as a convention center)
- The gender and age make-up of attendees (including guests or spouses)
- How many attendees typically occupy sleeping rooms (e.g., single or double occupancy)
- Any special needs of attendees (such as disabled individuals)
- Number of "fly-ins" versus other modes of transportation attendees will use to travel to the meeting

Group History

A group history describes how your group has performed in terms of room pick-up and spend for a prior meeting. It tells a hotel whether the room block, function space, and services you've requested from the hotel, as compared to the same meeting at prior hotels, is reasonable or not. If your history shows a significant increase in the room block year-over-year or you're asking for the same number of sleeping rooms for a room block that didn't pick-up in the past, the hotel will want to hear some rationale from you to justify the requested room block. Similarly, if you don't anticipate that the same level of room pick-up or spend performance that your history describes will apply for a future meeting for whatever reason (e.g., attendance is trending downward because of the economy), be sure to caveat the history when you provide it to the prospective hotel or when you include it as a part of an RFP.

Your group's history—almost all of which is data supplied from previous hotels—should include as much of the following information as possible. The primary reason for history is to demonstrate room pick-up as support for the requested room block, so the number and types of sleeping rooms is the most important part of history.

- Room block pattern
- Number and type of sleeping rooms requested per night (the adjusted, not contracted, room block)
- Number and type of sleeping rooms occupied per night (the room pick-up)
- Number of staff and speaker sleeping rooms occupied
- Number of sleeping room upgrades
- Room occupancy (single / double, etc.)
- Types of beds requested (e.g., King)
- Function space used
- Food and beverage spend (see caveat below)
- Audio-visual spend (see caveat below)
- Number of attendees valet parking or self-parking
- Attendee restaurant and room-service spend
- Attendee in-room Internet access spend
- Attendee resort and / or spa usage or spend
- Gift shop spend

Based on historical spend data, you can estimate the profit potential of your group. Generally, profit margins based on categories of business within the hotel industry are fairly consistent from hotel to hotel and from year to year. The most common categories of business used by groups at a hotel are listed below with corresponding, approximate profit margins:

- Sleeping rooms – 80%
- Function space (when charged) – 90%
- Food and beverage (non-alcoholic) – 30%
- Beverage (alcoholic) – 80%
- Audio-visual – 20+% (dependent upon the hotel's arrangement with the in-house audio-visual provider)

As a part of your history, a prospective hotel may ask for prior room rates paid at hotels where the meeting was held at in the past. Don't do it! It's a negotiation ploy and a ruse. I usually get the historical room rate question from either a really new hotel sales person or a not-so-great sales person. A hotel's asking for your historical room rate is over-reaching and should be irrelevant. A hotel will likely tell you that they would like to understand what "target room rate" your group is looking for because they want to make sure they're "in the ballpark" for your group. That's bogus. Clearly, you've done some amount of research in advance and you wouldn't be asking a Ritz-Carlton to propose on a meeting that has been held at La Quinta properties in the past. In reality, what the hotel really wants to know is if your group has paid a higher room rate in the past so that the hotel doesn't under-sell their sleeping rooms and so that the hotel can jack up their rates to what your group is used to paying. By providing a prospective hotel with prior room rates paid, you've just told that hotel what your group has been willing to pay and those prior room rates have now just become the floor for the prospective hotel. You will now get a proposal at or above those prior room rates. Exclude the prior room rates from your history and tell the prospective hotel to propose their room rates based on your group profile, group history, and the hotel's other considerations (such as season and how bad they want the business). There's no good reason that a prospective hotel should ever need to know your group's prior room rates. When a hotel asks for your group's history related to room rates, tell the hotel that what your group has paid in the past is irrelevant and that the hotel should instead focus on giving you a competitive proposal.

Similar to past room rates, a hotel may ask what your budget is for your meeting. In the negotiation world—even outside the hospitality industry—revealing budget is considered a leverage-killer. If a hotel asks the budget question, advise the hotel that you can't or won't reveal that information, but, if the hotel provides you with a competitive and aggressive proposal, you'll have the necessary budget to back up your meeting.

Another caveat is providing food and beverage spend or audio-visual spend. Whatever your past spend was, the prospective hotel will now know what you're willing to spend—and whatever you did spend will become your new food and beverage and audio-visual minimums. Instead of providing spend data, a better approach is to provide what food and beverage functions were held (with attendee counts) and audio-visual equipment used (e.g., 10 LCD projectors, 15 lav mics).

For meetings that have never been held before (you have a "new" meeting), you clearly don't have any history. If you have past performance for a similar meeting with the same group, that history will suffice. Another option is to estimate your performance. You've likely already projected at least the financial performance for the new meeting as a part of developing the meeting budget. Be conservative, however, in the estimations that you provide to the hotel to avoid any sort of attrition damages or damages associated with not meeting your minimums.

Bidding Out Your Meeting

Competitively bidding out your meeting to multiple hotels is the most efficient and effective way to get the best deal for your meeting. Beyond significant concessions in room rates, food and beverage pricing, and the like, a huge benefit of bidding out a meeting is that you can avoid many of the annoyances and headaches that I'll go on to describe in this book. If hotels know that they're competing for your business with other hotels, they'll be negotiating against themselves and you don't have to do any real negotiations yourself. If you include an MHSA as a part of your competitive bid and require prospective hotels to provide comments to the MHSA as a part of their proposals, as I do, you'll also get contract issues out of the way before you commit your business. Once you commit your business and try to negotiate contract provisions, you're no longer negotiating—you're begging. If I don't like the redlines to the MHSA that a hotel submits along with its proposal (such as mathematically-challenging, overly complex sliding-scale rental formulas for function space based on room pick-up), I point out my concerns to the prospective hotel and ask that the hotel reconsider its redlines—or I'll cut the hotel from further consideration. Mostly, the hotels get smart and then only redline MHSA provisions that they feel are really an issue for them.

Your competitive bid, in the form of an RFP, should accurately but succinctly describe your meeting specifications. An RFP need not be elaborate or complex, and can be as simple as attaching a document to an e-mail that you forward along to the intended recipients. Depending on the situation and my needs, I've sent RFPs to hotels directly, to CVBs to serve as a lead sheet point-of-contact, and to the national sales organizations at the flags. For a hotel to provide a comprehensive proposal, the following specifications should be included as a part of your RFP:

- Group profile
- History (if available)
- Preferred dates (in-house and official; indicate any flexibility by specifying alternate dates)
- Reservation procedure (including housing coordinator[2], if any)
- Function space requirements[3] (including storage, also specify materials handling needs)
- Space hold requirements
- Exhibition space requirements
- Food and beverage requirements
- Audio-visual requirements (specify if you will be using your own audio-visual provider)
- Electricity needs
- Special security needs
- Who is responsible for payment (e.g., attendees for sleeping rooms, group representative for the master account)
- Required concessions
- The MHSA (for the hotel to review and redline)

---

[2] If a housing coordinator will be used, the need for a commissionable room rate should be specified in the RFP.

[3] If possible, it's extremely helpful to have a detailed program of events as a part of the RFP that describes function space, food and beverage, and audio-visual needs on a per-function basis.

- RFP timetable (including when proposals are due)
- Proposal submission instructions

In addition to your specifications, you should also ask the hotel to provide information that is relevant to help you make your decision, such as:

- Taxes
- Fees such as resort fees, surcharges, mandatory gratuities, porterage and baggage, and parking
- Mandate or requirement, if any, to use in-house service providers (or any special fees for "patching-in")
- Function space lay-outs
- Food and beverage menus and pricing
- Audio-visual equipment and pricing

To properly and efficiently evaluate proposals that you receive, you may want to consider developing a simple spreadsheet that allows you to input pertinent proposal data and that provides for an apples-to-apples comparison. If warranted, you can create additional precision in your proposal evaluations by weighting items that are more important to you and your group than others before you begin scoring the proposals.

In a traditional competitive bidding process, the group representative receives proposals from hotels, evaluates the proposals, eliminates all but the best proposal, and then begins negotiations with the "finalist" hotel. At that point, the selected finalist hotel assumes, and probably correctly, that the other hotels have been eliminated and possibly notified of their non-selection. In other words, the hotel's competition has actually been eliminated by the group representative. If the hotel is shrewd, it'll drag out the negotiations a bit, seeking to create a length of time (and drawing nearer to the meeting) from the point of the finalist selection. If the group representative wants to negotiate further at that point, either on price or terms, with the finalist hotel, good luck! The finalist hotel most likely will suddenly become hard to deal with because now, after the other hotels have been eliminated, the finalist hotel is "the only game in town." The group representative then has a vested interest in bringing the deal to a close because the meeting is drawing closer (in fact, the group representative may have even already announced the hotel to attendees) and, if the hotel is opportunistic, the group representative will leave significant concessions on the table. That's why "negotiating" after selecting a single, finalist hotel is called "begging."

A better strategy is to create a "short-list" of hotels and select two or more finalist hotels to "pre-negotiate" with before making a contract award. Hotels should be made aware of the fact that there are other hotels still in the mix after the short-list cut and that the remaining hotels are being asked to provide "best and final offers" or "BAFOs." A "BAFO" is a negotiation tactic where vendors (here, hotels) in a competitive bid are asked to further refine their already-submitted proposals and to submit revised proposals in the form of a best and final offer. Here's how it works… Once you have all of the hotels' proposals evaluated and have eliminated the least desirable hotels, take the best of each proposal from the remaining hotels on your short-list and then determine what additional concessions you would like to see included in a BAFO (e.g., better room rate, reduced food and beverage / audio-visual price, other concessions, better contract terms and conditions). The end result is your benchmark to help guide (without violating your obligation of confidentiality) hotels to the desired proposal. At that point, send an e-mail to all of the hotels that haven't yet been eliminated asking for their BAFOs and providing general guidance on what you would like to see in the BAFOs (in terms of the additional concessions described above). After receiving the BAFOs back from the hotels, eliminate the less desirable hotels to get down to two remaining hotels. At that point, enter into contract negotiations with each finalist hotel. The one that agrees to all of your terms and conditions gets your meeting. Only when the deal is agreed-upon and the contract is ready for signature—and only then—the contract award and finalist hotel are announced. The BAFO tactic works because it implies to hotels that they have competition and that there may be a better deal than theirs on the table. Because a hotel is being "kept in the game" and hasn't (yet) been eliminated, that hotel feels that its offer is close and that the hotel will only have to make a few more concessions to get competitive and win the deal.

Negotiating Room Rates

Negotiating a great room rate for attendees is usually one of the top goals of a group representative. Negotiating discounts on pricing for food and beverage functions and audio-visual are clearly important as well, but room rates influence meeting attendance and can be a sore spot for attendees even though the room rate typically comes out of their employer's pockets. While following a competitive bidding process is the easiest and best way to negotiate room rates, there are cases, such as the need for a fast turn-around time, where going through that process isn't feasible. In those cases, and even if you have gone through a competitive bidding process and still don't like the proposed room rates, you'll have to square off face-to-face with the hotel to negotiate your best room rate. If you do, you better have done your homework first.

Generally, the room rate you're quoted is based upon the number of sleeping rooms needed, the arrival and departure pattern of your group, the type and size of the hotel, the amount of any function space needed, the value associated with any needed food and beverage, and the value associated with any needed audio-visual. Therefore, before you begin negotiations, review the group profile and history so you have a solid understanding of the value of your group's business.

Clearly, you need to know how the room rate proposed by a hotel compares against the room rate that same hotel has offered to other groups. It's best to have that information in advance of discussing room rates with a hotel—when the hotel pops their proposed room rate on you, it would be helpful for you at that point in time to know whether you were just offered a great room rate (and should accept it) or a not-so-great room rate (and should argue for a lower room rate).

Obviously a hotel won't tell you—directly—what room rates they offered to other groups. This means that you need to do your research. Absolutely the best resource for researching a hotel's room rates is the Internet. Be sure to check the hotel's website. If the hotel has an online reservation system, you can check the dates before, during, and after your future meeting to gauge the hotel's pricing and seasonality. Also check the major travel websites. Unfortunately, those websites will only reveal individual traveler room rates, but at least you'll have a high-water benchmark. But a hotel will tell you—indirectly—what room rates they offered to other groups. But you'll have to get that information from the groups themselves. The way to do that, which I use and which has yielded tremendous results in terms of room rate reductions, is to use an Internet search engine to find group rates offered by a hotel. A keyword search using terms such as the year, hotel name, "group rate," or "special rate" will likely result in various groups (such as trade associations) advertising the negotiated room rate to their attendees. Sometimes a

CVB website will list the group rates for citywides, so be sure to check the CVB website for the locations that you are targeting for your meeting. Where hotels have been particularly tough to deal with on room rate negotiations, I've compiled a list of all of the other group rates I found on the Internet for that hotel for the dates just before and just after my meeting (in some cases, the dates *over* my meeting if another group was in-house). When presented with that information, hotels have tried to formulate some sort of response to justify saving face but I have always gotten a lower room rate as a result.

One key factor in room rates that will clearly result in a higher room rate is when the dates for a meeting aren't flexible. Fixed meeting dates tell a hotel that the dates have been mandated (by someone) and the group representative has therefore immediately ceded negotiation leverage because he or she doesn't have the flexibility to change dates. The hotel can now quote any room rate it wants, and the group representative has no real option other than to accept the proposed room rate if the group representative wants that hotel. In contrast, if the meeting dates are flexible, a hotel may have an available block over a period that is low in demand and the hotel may be willing to offer a discounted room rate to book the business. In some cases, a shift in dates may not seem that dramatic to a group, but that shift makes a dramatic difference to a hotel. For example, moving meeting dates from a hotel's peak season to a shoulder season might mean only a few weeks difference but the effect on room rates may be significant. Even moving a meeting to different days within a week can have an impact on room rates. Consequently, it's helpful to understand what the peak and non-peak seasons and patterns are for hotels generally and then to apply that to the hotel you're interested in having your meeting at. While a hotel likely won't tell you what room rate they've offered to other groups, the hotel will likely tell you about their seasonality and patterns. Again, Internet research is extremely useful in determining hotel seasonality and hotel pattern preferences. Here are some obvious or "rule of thumb" examples:

- Hotels in winter destinations have higher occupancy in the winter than other periods (e.g., hotels in Orlando—to get away from the cold, hotels in Colorado—to enjoy winter sports)
- While December is a slow month for many hotels, New York City hotels have high occupancy because of holiday shoppers
- Washington, DC hotels have higher room rates on the days that the U.S. Congress is in-session
- Most hotels want group business over the weekend, when they have less demand—except for Las Vegas hotels, which see higher occupancy on weekends resulting from leisure travelers
- Mondays through Thursdays are peak arrival / departure days at hotels that cater to groups and individual business travelers
- Thursdays through Saturdays are peak arrival and departure days at hotels that cater to leisure travelers (such as resorts)

Another option to consider, if it's viable, is a multi-year contract—where you hold the same meeting at a hotel over multiple, but not necessarily contiguous, years. This type of arrangement has a number of possible benefits beyond a reduced room rate such as preferred dates, lower costs for other aspects of the meeting such as food and beverage, and / or additional concessions. However, multi-year contracts can work against you. In my opinion and experience, there are significant drawbacks—most of which stem from a lack of negotiation leverage—to multi-year contacts. I had a situation where I had just completed the last meeting in a multi-year contract with a hotel and wanted to enter into another multi-year contract with the same hotel. Instead of being aggressive in their proposal, the hotel expected the business, jacked up the room rates substantially over what had previously been barely market-competitive room rates, and got fussy over the contract terms that they had previously agreed-to. Another situation I experienced was when I was roughly halfway through a multi-year contract where the hotel was only willing to barely perform—the hotel had become complacent because they knew my group was locked-in for a couple of more years. So, while some individuals espouse multi-year contracts—and they can be a viable option—keep in mind that you may not end up with the overall result you expected.

It's worth pointing out in a discussion on room rates the typical division of attendee / group representative financial responsibilities: attendees (usually through their employers) pay the room rate for their sleeping rooms and a group representative pays for "meeting-wide" costs such as food and beverage, audio-visual, and material handling. That division of payment presents a potential dilemma. If a group representative negotiates a highly-discounted room rate, free in-room Internet, and a daily coupon for a free breakfast buffet, the hotel isn't going to be as flexible on food and beverage functions, audio-visual, and so on. On the other hand, if a group representative negotiates deep discounts on menu prices and audio-visual and gets better than the typical comp room ratio, the attendees aren't going to get such a great room rate. It's a whack-a-mole dilemma in that concessions that benefit an attendee may end up costing a group representative and vice versa. Because a group representative is the one who negotiates the hotel deal (and not the attendees) and is closer to the hospitality industry, he or she might load up a room rate to something passable in return for hotel concessions that lighten the financial responsibility of the group representative. I've heard ethical debates that cut both ways as well as arguments that supported a duty to disclose loaded room rates to attendees and arguments that supported not having such a duty. Despite all of that debate, it boils down to the fact that attendees (usually via their employers) almost universally fund the entire cost associated with a meeting regardless of who is "writing the check." For example, if a group representative gets the best possible room rate but doesn't do so well on audio-visual, the group representative has to cover his or her costs somehow—commonly through registration fees. So, it's frequently "six of one, a half dozen of the other" in that an attendee pays a lower room rate / higher registration fee or a higher room rate / lower registration fee. Keep in mind that attendees have a lower tolerance for registration fees that fluctuate year-to-year versus room rates that fluctuate—attendees "get" that room rates are likely to fluctuate over time and in different locations, but they don't have the same degree of understanding or tolerance when it comes to fluctuating registration fees.

Concessions You Should Always Ask For

The following is a list of typical concessions, not sorted in any particular order, that hotels routinely agree to provide on a "no-charge" or discounted basis. My philosophy is "you won't get what you don't ask for," so it's worth asking for any one or more of the following. Keep in mind, however, that the more concessions that are granted by a hotel, the less flexible a hotel may be on the room rate.

- Airport transfers
- Better comp room ratio
- Daily newspapers

- Discounted audio-visual rates
- Discounted menu prices for food and beverage functions
- Early check-in and late check-out times
- Elimination of resort fee
- Fitness center access
- Increased number of sleeping room upgrades
- In-room Internet access
- Function space Internet access
- Meal coupons (e.g., breakfast buffet) for attendees
- No receiving or handling charges
- One urn of coffee for every paid [insert number] urns
- Parking
- Shuttle service to local attractions
- Welcome amenities for VIP attendees

Master Agreement / Exhibit Structure

Before I delve into deconstructing and reviewing the MHSA, it's important to understand the structure of the MHSA. The MHSA is one overall agreement, but it contains two separate components: the master agreement component and the exhibit component. The master agreement contains all of the legal terms and conditions and what I call the magic "unless otherwise specified" language. This magic language, which I'll describe more in a subsequent paragraph, provides the flexibility for the master agreement to be used over and over with the same hotel. Think of the master agreement component as the "legalese." The other component, the exhibit, contains the "dates, rates, and space," and describes a specific meeting. The exhibit only lives (under the master agreement) for the life span of a meeting.

It's not uncommon for a group representative to hold a meeting at a hotel, and at some later point in time, hold another meeting at that same hotel. I've held meetings at the same hotel—either because I wanted to or because I *had* to because of the location—dozens of times over a period of years. The benefit of the master agreement / exhibit structure is that all of the legalese is negotiated once. Want to hold another meeting at the same hotel? No need to do anything with the master agreement and no need to re-hash all of the legal terms and conditions with the accompanying arguing, debating, and hand-wringing. The group representative simply needs to wrap up the dates, rates, and space with the hotel and write-up another exhibit for the new meeting.

If a group representative does use a hotel again—and didn't use a master agreement / exhibit structure the first time—the group representative will need to negotiate another contract. In my personal experience (I could be over-generalizing), the folks I've negotiated with on property tend to be young in the careers. Thus, I spend a fair amount of time educating them on hotel contract terms and conditions. These same folks tend to be upwardly mobile in the careers, so there seems to be a lot of turn-over at hotels: the person who I spent time educating and negotiating with likely won't be there the next time I hold another meeting at that hotel. Even if I'm negotiating with the same person, he or she may not be as agreeable on terms and conditions during a subsequent negotiation. If I don't deal with a hotel directly on a contract and deal instead with a hotel's attorney, for a number of reasons, I probably don't want to go through that same, usually arduous, process again. For all of these reasons—time, efficiency, and favorable terms and conditions—I prefer using a master agreement / exhibit structure which I can use repeatedly without much effort.

In order for the master agreement / exhibit structure to work well, the master agreement needs to be flexible. For example, the master agreement may contain a comp room ratio provision (described later in this book) that specifies one comp room for every thirty-five room nights consumed. If I bring a large meeting to a hotel, the hotel may be agreeable to a 1-to-35 comp room ratio. If I bring another, much smaller, meeting to that same hotel, the hotel may not be agreeable to anything better than a 1-to-50 comp room ratio. That's where the magic language I referenced earlier comes into play. Where certain deal points, such as a comp room ratio, may be subject to change based on the specifics of the associated meeting, the MHSA master agreement contains language that permits modification of the master agreement by the exhibit. The magic language in the MHSA typically is found in the form of "Unless otherwise specified in an Exhibit A…." This simple phrase gives me a tremendous amount of flexibility and alleviates me from having to write all sorts of amendments and addendums to the

MHSA as needs change and specific situations dictate. Here's the comp room ratio example with the magic language starting the provision off:

> 3.5   <u>Complimentary Rooms</u>. Unless otherwise specified in an <u>Exhibit A</u>, Hotel shall provide one (1) complimentary Guestroom (each a "Comp Room") per night for every thirty-five (35) Room Nights associated with the Meeting on a cumulative, and not daily, basis. For purposes of determining the number of Comp Rooms, each room in a suite will count as a separate Room Night. In the event Comp Rooms earned are not used, Hotel agrees to: (a) apply the corresponding value of the applicable single standard Room Rate against any amounts due to Hotel; or, (b) where such corresponding value cannot be consumed in the context of the applicable Meeting, Hotel shall remit to Customer such corresponding value.

Where I don't have a large enough meeting to warrant a 1-to-35 comp room ratio as provided for in the above provision, instead of amending the above language from the master agreement to something different, I can indicate to the hotel that the exhibit permits the comp room ratio to be modified by referring to the "Unless otherwise specified in an Exhibit A..." phrase. The 1-to-35 comp room ratio is only the default, and can be easily changed by specifying otherwise in the exhibit. When the hotel pushes back on the default comp room ratio contained in the master agreement, I usually respond that there could be a bigger meeting on the horizon, and we can just specify in the exhibit for the current meeting that the comp room ratio is 1-to-50. Usually the hotel buys into this, and, inevitably, forgets about the default comp room ratio by the time the next meeting (and exhibit) is being negotiated.

The MHSA master agreement is a perpetual contract, so it never terminates unless one of the parties terminates it, there's a breach, or some other event of default. That gives me the ability to use the MHSA to contract for a meeting and then, any time later, contract for another meeting without having to negotiate another contract.

The Master Hotel Services Agreement

I n this section, I break down and explain the MHSA provision-by-provision. The general format of this section is the explanation of the provision first with the actual provision from the MHSA immediately following the explanation. To better tie specific explanations to specific parts of a provision, a number (e.g., ❶) is used to link ❶explanation to ❶provision. Some provisions, such as those that are relatively innocuous or standard, won't have much or any commentary. The MHSA is contained in *Appendix I ~ Master Hotel Services Agreement* in its entirety and is filled-out in the context of a future, fictitious meeting for illustrative purposes. If there are defined terms used in the contract provisions (a capitalized word or phrase is likely a defined term) for which the meaning isn't immediately obvious, *Appendix II ~ MHSA Defined Terms* will describe what the defined term refers to.

Preamble, Recitals, and Words of Agreement

The first part of the MHSA—and, for that matter, any well drafted contract—contains the ❶ preamble, ❷ recitals, and ❸ words of agreement.

❶ The preamble contains basic information about the contract, such as the name of the agreement, the date that the agreement is to be effective, and the names and addresses of the parties. Some parties consider the preamble and recitals to be one and the same, and refer to both collectively as the "preamble." Hotels are frequently owned by other entities, so it's important for a group representative to be sure to contract with the appropriate entity. This is important should a group representative have a subsequent legal issue—if the group representative doesn't contract with the appropriate entity, he or she may have difficulty asserting any legal rights against an entity that the group representative has failed to name in the contract. A group representative must be sure to ask the hotel what the hotel's "real" name is and include that name in the preamble. Typically, hotels operate as a "d/b/a," which is short for "doing business as"—in other words, it's another entity "doing business as" the hotel. For that situation, here's an example of what might be included in the preamble: RJG Hotel Enterprises LLC d/b/a Old Northeast Hotel and Spa. The MHSA in this book contemplates that the hotel is its own entity and is not owned by another company.

❷ The recitals, sometimes referred to as the "preamble" or "whereas" clauses, aren't really terms and conditions of the contract (I'll explain why when I discuss the words of agreement). Instead, the recitals help to explain the purpose of the contract and the intent of the parties in a relatively brief format. Recitals are an easy way to gain an understanding of the contract before (and instead of) having to read all of the fine print. Some consider the recitals to be unnecessary legalese, but I'm a big fan of recitals. In addition to "telling the story" of the contract, I try to explain in the recitals why I depended and relied on the hotel in hosting my meeting and in providing top-notch services. If the hotel doesn't provide those top-notch services—as stated in the recitals—I might be damaged.

This dependence and reliance may be extremely helpful if a group representative is trying to show in a subsequent dispute that he or she relied on the hotel in meeting the needs of the group. That's exactly what I've done in the recitals below: that the hotel has experience and expertise in providing hospitality-related services (first whereas), that the meeting the hotel is going to be hosting for me is critical to my business operations (second whereas), that the hotel understands how important the meeting is to me (third whereas), that the hotel acknowledges that their lack of adequate performance might harm me economically and otherwise (fourth whereas), that I want the hotel to host the meeting (fifth whereas), and that the hotel wants to host the meeting (sixth whereas). It's obvious where I'm going with my story: if the hotel screws up, they were aware of the impact of their screw-up, and they had better make good.

A group representative should modify the recitals to meet his or her specific situation, but I recommend following the same logical, step-by-step format, culminating in the hotel acknowledging that they do in fact want to provide the services the group representative contracted with them for. If a hotel doesn't want a group representative to include any recitals, or the hotel significantly modifies them such that they're watered-down, the obvious question that should be raised is "why?" But, if the hotel is adamant about their deletion or changes, it may be appropriate to give up on the recitals as a concession. However, the group representative should ensure that any changes the hotel makes to the recitals doesn't put any potential liability or burden back on the group representative.

❸ The words of agreement are a formality, used to signify that the parties are expressly agreeing to all of the following terms and conditions, and that the parties have exchanged "consideration." Consideration is a necessary element of the three most basic elements of contract formation in the U.S. (offer, acceptance, consideration). Consideration is anything of value—it doesn't *have* to be money— promised to another when making a contract. In the context of the MHSA, it's the group representative or attendees paying the hotel for their hospitality-related services (such as providing sleeping rooms) and the hotel promising to provide such services. Everything before the words of agreement, such as the recitals, does *not* have contractual force, but everything after does.

❶MASTER HOTEL SERVICES AGREEMENT

This agreement ("Agreement") is entered into, to be effective as of August 16, 2010 ("Effective Date"), by and between **GUTH VENTURES LLC** ("Customer"), with its principal place of business located at 16141 Cobb Island Road, Newburg, MD 20664, and **OLD NORTHEAST HOTEL AND SPA** ("Hotel"), with its principal place of business located at 625 17th Avenue N.E., St. Petersburg, FL 33704.

❷RECITALS

WHEREAS, Hotel has experience and expertise in the business of providing certain hospitality-related services that may include accommodations, housing, function space, and food and beverage (such services and similar services shall be individually and collectively referenced herein as the "Services");

WHEREAS, Customer conducts various events, conventions, and meetings (each, a "Meeting," as further described in an Exhibit A attached or to be attached hereto) that are critical to the business operations of Customer and its members;

WHEREAS, Hotel acknowledges the importance to Customer of Hotel's Services in support of a Meeting;

WHEREAS, Hotel acknowledges that non-performance of the Services may result in loss of revenue to Customer, negative impact upon the credibility and good will of Customer, and other financial and non-financial harm to Customer;

WHEREAS, Customer desires to have Hotel provide Services to Customer; and,

WHEREAS, Hotel desires to supply Services to Customer on the terms and conditions contained herein.

❸NOW THEREFORE, in consideration of the mutual promises and covenants contained herein, and for other good and valuable consideration, Hotel and Customer hereby agree as follows:

Hotel Services

There's nothing particularly remarkable or contentious about the *Hotel Services* provision. The provision ❶ sets-up and describes the master agreement / exhibit structure. The second whereas clause in the recitals, which describes the purpose of an Exhibit A to the MHSA, also contributes to the set-up of the master agreement / exhibit structure. Each meeting under the MHSA becomes a different exhibit (Exhibit A), and each different exhibit is numbered accordingly (Exhibit A-1 for the first meeting, Exhibit A-2 for the next meeting, and so on). ❷ The <u>form</u> of an Exhibit A is attached to the master for reference purposes only to illustrate what the Exhibit A to the MHSA looks like. Therefore, the first time a group representative executes the MHSA with a hotel and conducts a meeting, the following documents will exist: the MHSA, Exhibit A (the form, for reference purposes only), and Exhibit A-1 (for the first meeting) to the MHSA. As I explained earlier, the next time the group representative holds a meeting at that same hotel, only another exhibit needs to be created and executed (Exhibit A-2 in this example)— there is no need to execute another MHSA.

In some cases, a hotel might provide a group representative with a document that contains all of the information that an Exhibit A to the MHSA would contain and, for whatever reason, it doesn't make sense to transfer all of that information in the format specified by the Exhibit A form that's attached to the MHSA. This part of the provision ❸ contemplates that possibility and allows for a document not in the Exhibit A format to be used in place of that format. However, a group representative should use the form of the Exhibit A as a checklist to ensure that the hotel's document covers everything that needs to be included. A group representative must also ensure that the preamble from the Exhibit A form is copied and pasted to the beginning of the hotel's document and the signature block from the Exhibit A form is copied and pasted to the end of the hotel's document. Without the preamble included at the beginning of the hotel's document, it won't be covered by the MHSA since it won't be legally integrated. Keep in mind that using the hotel's document isn't optimal and perhaps a little sloppy because there are defined terms in the MHSA that aren't likely the same terms as used in the hotel's document.

At this point, it makes sense to describe what a defined term is and the process of defining a term. Sometimes a word or a phrase is used repeatedly in a contract. When that word or phrase has special meaning or emphasis attached to it, it should be defined on its first use (or it can be included in a definitions section at the beginning of the contract) and then all subsequent references to that word or phrase should be capitalized. The provision here contains three good examples using defined terms. The first example is the word "Agreement." It's capitalized in this provision because it was defined elsewhere (in the preamble). Thus, whenever a group representative uses "Agreement," the contract reader knows that the group representative is referring to the agreement that they're reading and not some other agreement. Another example is the phrase "room rate." It doesn't require much explanation, but it's helpful to be clear that a reference to room rate in the MHSA means the room rate described in an Exhibit A (so, "room rate" is defined as "Room Rate" as well as its plural form, "Room Rates"). The final example is the phrase "official dates." This phrase ❸ requires some explanation and then the connection is made to an Exhibit A to the MHSA, defining "Official Dates" as those dates that the meeting will be held and those dates are described more specifically in the Exhibit A for that meeting. In terms of negotiating this provision, I've never had a hotel object to this provision or modify it in any really substantive way.

1.   <u>Hotel Services</u>. Hotel agrees to provide, in accordance with the terms of this Agreement, the Services for the Meeting on the Official and In-House Dates and at the room rate(s) ("Room Rate" or "Room Rates") and other fees, if any, ❶as set forth in an <u>Exhibit A</u> (sequentially numbered) in the ❷form of the <u>Exhibit A</u> attached hereto or in other scope of services exhibits or attachments containing substantially similar information and identified as an <u>Exhibit A</u>. ❸The dates that the actual Meeting will be held shall be known as the "Official Dates," as further described in an <u>Exhibit A</u>.

Service and Staffing Requirements

This provision requires that a hotel provide adequate (in both number and skills) staff to successfully conduct the meeting. As a general matter under professional services-types of contracts, when a contracting party begins dictating the number and skills of staff to be provided by a supplier, the supplier begins relinquishing control (and responsibility) to the contracting party. In that case, if something goes wrong with the performance of the services, the supplier can hold up their hands and say that they gave the contracting party what was requested—people instead of service. This provision successfully walks the fine line between requiring adequate staff to perform the service that was contracted for but not taking on control and responsibility from the supplier relating to the performance. This provision is innocuous and hotels rarely object to it.

    1.1   <u>Service and Staffing Requirements</u>. Hotel represents and warrants that it shall assign an adequate number of trained staff to perform its obligations under this Agreement and an <u>Exhibit A</u> in accordance with industry standards and Hotel facilities of similar size and quality as Hotel.

Health and Safety

Hotels have a duty to provide safe premises to their guests. This duty originates from jolly old England and back in the days of inns and innkeepers. In fact, many state laws relating to hotels and motels are commonly and quaintly referred to as "innkeeper laws." Obviously, for the health and safety of a group, the group representative doesn't want the group staying at some sort of death trap and the group representative is going to want to depend on something more (and more specific) than an innkeeper's general duty to provide safe premises.

This provision requires ❶ that the hotel comply with basically everything as it relates to the safety of a group's attendees, including the Hotel and Motel Fire Safety Act of 1990 (the "Act"). The Act, amended in 1996, imposes additional safety requirements upon hotels above and beyond those found in local building codes. The U.S. Congress, reacting to a number of hotel fires in the 1980s in which U.S. Federal Government employees perished, passed the Act which requires that 90% of all U.S. Federal Government travel room nights and 100% of all U.S. Federal Government meetings be at "fire safe" hotels. It might appear odd that Congress at the time seemed to be only worried about U.S. Federal Government employees and didn't include the public-at-large in the Act, but Congress didn't want to pass a law that required older hotels to bear the economic burden of complying with the Act. Instead—and I have to remark that the Congress at the time was smart about this—they influenced hotels to make the necessary safety changes by not allowing U.S. Federal Government employees to stay at hotels that didn't comply with the Act. To demonstrate compliance with the Act, a hotel must apply to be on the Hotel-Motel National Master List (currently administered by the U.S. Department of Homeland Security). Hotels that don't comply with the requirements of the Act, or comply but do not appear on the Hotel-Motel National Master List, risk losing U.S. Federal Government business, including having U.S. Federal Government employees on official business as guests. Be aware that there are exceptions relating to the Act, so a hotel may technically be in compliance, but not necessarily be safe; for example, hotels that are three stories or lower in height are exempt from the fire sprinkler system requirement.

The provision also requires, ❷should a group representative want to review them, the hotel to provide the group representative with all of the hotel's safety procedures and policies. Additionally, the provision requires ❸ that the hotel have at least one person trained in cardio pulmonary resuscitation available at all times and that the hotel have an automated external defibrillator on premises.

I've never had a hotel take issue with this provision. If a hotel balks at this provision, the group representative needs to delve into why the hotel has an issue with it—lives are at stake.

1.2 Health and Safety. Hotel represents and warrants that, at all times during the In-House Dates, ❶Hotel shall comply with all local, state, and United States Federal fire and life safety laws, regulations, codes, and ordinances including but not limited to the requirements of the Hotel and Motel Fire Safety Act of 1990, requiring, among other things, hard-wired smoke detectors in each guestroom and an automatic sprinkler system. Hotel further represents and warrants that it maintains procedures and policies concerning fire safety and other life safety issues and ❷Hotel shall make all such procedures and policies available to Customer upon request. Failure of Customer to request a copy of such policies and procedures shall not relieve or alleviate Hotel's responsibility to comply with the terms of this provision. Hotel further represents that ❸Hotel shall have: (a) at least one (1) person trained in cardio pulmonary resuscitation on premises at all times; and, (b) an automated external defibrillator on premises.

Security

Another general duty that hotels have is to exercise reasonable care for the security of their guests. That duty includes the hotel undertaking adequate security measures such as dead-bolt locks, peep holes, and now, in the electronic age, monitoring cameras. The duty for a hotel to provide adequate safety is codified in innkeeper laws—which are state laws and can vary significantly from state to state. Hotels can obviously foresee some, but not all, security issues and it's reasonable for a hotel to want to limit its liability in that regard. Many states have placed limits on a hotel's liability as long as the hotel follows certain measures (such as providing a safe in a sleeping room). Sometimes hotels try to get even more protection from liability than an innkeeper law provides by posting a notice in sleeping rooms (part of what's on the notice stuck on the back of the sleeping room door) that further limits or entirely disclaims a hotel's liability.

The *Security* provision does two things. First, it requires ❶ that a hotel provide adequate security for both sleeping rooms *and* function space. Second, it requires ❷ a hotel to advise a group representative if there has been any recent criminal activity at the hotel. The purpose of the advisement is to raise a group representative's awareness. If there has been a rash of thefts at a hotel, a group representative will want to know from the hotel why and what the hotel is doing about it. Considering the crime spree, the group representative might also want to check the innkeeper laws in the state where the hotel is located and will want to check with the hotel to determine what their limits of liability are relating to the loss of a guest's personal property. Finally, if it turns out that there was a crime spree which the hotel failed to notify the group representative of and one or more of the group's attendees experiences a theft, the group representative would have a strong argument that the hotel should be completely responsible since they breached this provision.

1.3   Security. Hotel represents and warrants that it ❶provides adequate security (the same or better than hotel properties of similar size and quality) for Attendees by ensuring that, among other things, corridors, parking lots, recreational and public areas are adequately monitored. Hotel also agrees to ❶provide adequate security and secured areas for setups in Function Spaces, such as locked-facilities or security guards. ❷Hotel agrees to promptly notify Customer of any criminal incident of personal injury (including death) or theft of personal property valued at over Five Hundred Dollars ($500.00) involving a Hotel guest or employee that occurs within six (6) months of the start of the In-House Dates.

Hotels occasionally take issue with this provision with the typical (and acceptable) change being as follows.

1.3   Security. Hotel represents and warrants that it provides adequate security (the same or better than Hotel properties of similar size and quality) for Attendees by ensuring that, among other things, corridors, parking lots, recreational and public areas are adequately monitored. Hotel also agrees to provide adequate security and secured areas for setups in Function Spaces, such as locked-facilities or security guards. ~~Hotel agrees to promptly notify Customer of any criminal incident of personal injury (including death) or theft of personal property valued at over Five Hundred Dollars ($500.00) involving a Hotel guest or employee that occurs within six (6) months of the start of the In-House Dates.~~ Where Hotel experiences an unusual number of criminal incidents within six (6) months of the start date of the In-

House Dates, Hotel agrees to take appropriate measures to mitigate further occurrences of such criminal incidents.

Attendees

This provision seems relatively straightforward, but it's actually one of the more important provisions in the MHSA because it has an effect on whether or not other provisions (e.g., attrition) are triggered. The primary issue that this provision is intended to address is what is commonly called "booking around the block." Booking around the block occurs when an individual intended to be a part of the group (i.e., a part of the room block) books a reservation at a hotel using a different means than the one prescribed by the group representative's procedure with the hotel. Booking around the block can be intentional; for example, an attendee finds a lower rate online than the room rate negotiated for the group (the issue of a hotel offering a lower room rate is discussed as a part of the *Lowest Room Rate; Published or Confirmed* provision). It can also be unintentional; for example, an attendee forgets to use the "group rate code" when booking a sleeping room.

With this provision, everyone associated with a meeting, regardless of how they booked a sleeping room at the hotel, will be considered an attendee for purposes of the MHSA.

Hotels understand the issue of booking around the block and this provision isn't contemplating anything other than the definition of attendee for purposes of other provisions contained in the MHSA. Hotels sometimes have questions about this provision but rarely make any changes and almost never object to it. If the hotel that the group representative is dealing with makes any substantive changes to this provision, the group representative should ask the hotel why and then push back—hard. There's no reason why any guest associated with a meeting shouldn't be included as an attendee for purposes of the MHSA, regardless of how a reservation was made.

> 1.4   <u>Attendees</u>. For the purpose of this Agreement, the term "Attendee" means any individual, group or entity associated with a Meeting, including Customer and its directors, employees, members, representatives, agents, speakers, exhibitors, members, delegates, guests, invitees, contractors, and subcontractors with reservations at Hotel, regardless of how the guestroom reservations ("Guestroom Reservations") were made or accepted by Hotel, including, without limitation, Guestroom Reservations accepted through Customer's designated Housing Coordinator, if described in an <u>Exhibit A</u>, Hotel's reservation system, any Web sites and e-commerce sites on the Internet / World Wide Web, travel agents and corporate travel departments, or any other reservation portals.

Room Block

This section mostly focuses on how adjustments to the room block are made. The room block represents the most significant source of revenue for a hotel—industry averages peg the profit margins for sleeping rooms at an impressive 70% - 80%. Not surprisingly, hotels get touchy when a group representative tries to adjust the room block that was originally contracted. On the other hand, estimating the number of sleeping rooms needed as compared against the human behavior of individual attendees (and their corresponding circumstances) isn't an exact science. Thus, it's only reasonable that a group representative have some flexibility in adjusting the contracted room block.

Adjustment of Room Block

The *Adjustment of Room Block* provision is the contractual mechanism that permits a group representative to adjust the contracted room block. One reason that a group representative would want the contractual right to adjust the room block is that attendance was (unintentionally) over-estimated when the hotel contract was first executed; therefore, the group representative will want to reduce the room block so that he or she will not liable to the hotel in any way for the sleeping rooms that go unfilled, and, because the room block is being reduced, the group representative will want the ❺ hotel to have as much advance notice as possible to resell unneeded sleeping rooms. As I explained earlier, estimating attendance is not an exact science and a group representative shouldn't be penalized for not being able to do something that no one else in the world can do. Without being able to reasonably adjust the contracted room block, a group representative could be left "holding the bag."

The provision first ❶ sets up some defined terms and makes clear that the room block is specified in an Exhibit A to the MHSA. The provision then ❷ indicates that, if the Exhibit A has review dates, the hotel and the group representative will review the room block on the review dates. Sometimes meetings are contracted so far in advance that more than one review date is warranted. If a group representative is contracting for a meeting to occur within the next six months, it's very likely that only one review date is necessary. Keep in mind that the more review dates a group representative seeks to include in an Exhibit A to the MHSA (which means more flexibility for the group representative) the more pushback from the hotel (because of the accompanying room block revenue uncertainty).

Unless the Exhibit A to the MHSA indicates otherwise, ❸ a group representative can adjust the room block on the review date(s) without any sort of liability. In practice, this means that a group representative needs to stay on top of events impacting the meeting and respond accordingly. For example, if a meeting requires advance registration and the registration numbers aren't hitting targets (and the group representative has tried other actions to improve registration such as better promoting the meeting), the group representative will likely want to reduce the room block on a review date. Frequently, hotels will want to limit a review of the room block to one review date and will want to specify that the adjustment cannot be greater than a specified percentage (usually 10% to 20%). I usually argue to allow the Exhibit A to the MHSA to specify the number of review dates since I don't want to change the MHSA itself (because doing so restricts me in the future), and, if the situation is appropriate, I will agree to only one review date in the Exhibit A to the MHSA for the meeting currently under discussion (which affects only that meeting and not future meetings versus if I had modified the MHSA). I typically agree to a 20% limit on the room block adjustment for a review date. Sometimes hotels will object to my being able to unilaterally adjust the room block on a review date and will replace the existing language to make the change mutual. Here's an example: "Customer and Hotel shall discuss and mutually agree upon any adjustments to the Room Block. At this time, and upon mutual agreement, the Room Block may be adjusted." That language proposed by the hotel is absolutely unacceptable because it's very unlikely that the hotel is going to agree to the adjustment. Instead, the group representative will get into a long protracted debate about what he or she did / is doing to get better attendance and so on and so on. Even after a group representative jumps through all of those hoops, the hotel may still not agree to adjust the room block.

In addition to being able to adjust the room block on the review dates (specified in an Exhibit A to the MHSA) without liability, ❹ the provision goes on to permit the group representative to adjust the room block at any time review dates *aren't* specified in an Exhibit A to the

MHSA. That's an important and beneficial nuance that results from the master agreement / exhibit structure. If this language stays in the MHSA, here's the practical effect: a group representative specifies review dates for the first meeting in Exhibit A-1, then has a subsequent meeting at the same hotel (now, an Exhibit A-2) and leaves out the review dates in the Exhibit A-2, the group representative now has extreme flexibility. If the group representative needed to or wanted to, he or she could reduce the room block down to one sleeping room without liability and still be in compliance with the contract with the hotel—although doing so wouldn't be very professional nor would it be very smart because the hotel would ensure that it never happened again. Hotels occasionally catch-on to this nuance and object to it, and I don't push back when hotels do object.

Sometimes hotels object to the language that indicates ❺ attempts are being made by a group representative to give a hotel as much notice in advance as possible to resell sleeping rooms that the group doesn't need. A hotel's reason for not liking the language is that it implies the hotel must take reasonable measures to resell the sleeping rooms. Whether a hotel likes it or not, the hotel does have a duty to mitigate damages under a contract. If push comes to shove, I'll agree to strike the language since a hotel does have an implied duty to mitigate damages (even if the contract doesn't expressly state the duty) and because that same implied duty is expressly described in the *Obligation of Hotel to Mitigate Damages* provision.

So far, I've explained room block adjustments in terms of reducing the contracted room block. What happens if a meeting exceeds all expectations and the group representative has more attendees than the contracted room block provided for? That's a good situation to have, but the group representative needs more sleeping rooms. That's what the next sentence in this provision addresses. ❻ When a group representative does need more sleeping rooms, he or she will be permitted to adjust the room block *upward* at the contracted room rate provided that the hotel has availability and agrees to allow the group representative to add more rooms. Because the hotel must have the availability and must agree to add more sleeping rooms to the room block, hotels rarely object to this language.

After contracting with the hotel, a group representative will want to be sure that the room block is protected and the hotel won't try to chip away at it if a better piece of business for the hotel comes along. One might think this wouldn't happen frequently, but it has happened to me enough that I had to include this language in the MHSA to protect my room block. I've had a number of hotels come to me over the years, tell me that they have another group that would like to be on property at the same time as my group, and then try to strong-arm me to give up part of room block to accommodate the other group. When I've said no to these requests, the hotel typically quizzes me about the accuracy of my room block, how I expect it to pick-up, and so on in a harassing effort to get me to change my mind. I've never had a hotel actually yank sleeping rooms from me, but I'd much rather have a contract provision to fall back on. Simply, the language ❼ prohibits a hotel from reducing the room block before the reservation cut-off date without getting express permission from the group representative. After the reservation cut-off date, if a group representative has unreserved sleeping rooms in the room block, the hotel isn't precluded from reselling those sleeping rooms. In fact, the group representative really, really wants the hotel taking back some of the sleeping rooms after the reservation cut-off date (to avoid possible attrition). Hotels rarely object to this language, but, if they do, a group representative should question the hotel's rationale. Does the hotel actually plan on taking some sleeping rooms from the group? Why would the hotel want that kind of flexibility?

2.   Room Block. In consideration of Customer selecting Hotel to provide the Services and host the Meeting, ❶Hotel agrees to hold the room block ("Room Block") for the type of accommodations (each a "Guestroom") as specified in an Exhibit A.

    2.1   Adjustment of Room Block. ❷Hotel and Customer shall review the Room Block periodically, if so specified in an Exhibit A, on the review dates ("Review Dates") indicated therein. Unless otherwise provided in an Exhibit A, ❸Customer shall have the right to adjust the Room Block, if necessary, without liability on the Review Dates ❹or at anytime where Review Dates are not so indicated. ❺Such adjustments, if any, shall be provided by Customer to allow Hotel to receive Room Block estimations with reasonable advance notice, when possible, in order for Hotel to resell rooms unused by Customer. ❻Based upon availability and subject to Hotel's approval, Customer may increase the Room Block at the Room Rate specified in the applicable Exhibit A. ❼In no case shall Hotel unilaterally reduce the Room Block prior to the reservation cut-off date ("Reservation Cut-Off Date") set forth in an Exhibit A, if any, without the prior written consent of Customer.

The following revisions reflect common changes made by hotels to this provision, which are restricting but reasonable (subject to whether a certain amount of slippage of the actualized room block is permitted or not). Any more changes than the following and the provision becomes unfavorable and restrictive.

    2.1   Adjustment of Room Block. Hotel and Customer shall review the Room Block periodically, if so specified in an Exhibit A, on the review dates ("Review Dates") indicated therein. Unless otherwise provided in an Exhibit A,

Customer shall have the right to adjust the Room Block, if necessary, <u>by no greater than twenty-percent (20%)</u>~~without liability~~ on the Review Dat~~es or at anytime where Review Dates are not so indicated. Such adjustments, if any, shall be provided by Customer to allow Hotel to receive Room Block estimations with reasonable advance notice, when possible, in order for Hotel to resell rooms unused by Customer.~~ Based upon availability and subject to Hotel's approval, Customer may increase the Room Block at the Room Rate specified in the applicable <u>Exhibit A</u>. In no case shall Hotel unilaterally reduce the Room Block prior to the reservation cut-off date ("Reservation Cut-Off Date") set forth in an <u>Exhibit A</u>, if any, without the prior written consent of Customer.

Check-In Time / Check-Out Time

The *Check-in Time / Check-Out Time* provision is relatively straightforward but there are a couple of items that a hotel may occasionally object to. First, a hotel may object to an ❶ attendee not being required to pay a cancellation or other fee based on his or her departing early. The counter to the hotel's objection may change subject to whether or not the MHSA or Exhibit A to the MHSA contains an attrition damages provision. The first counter is to ask what the hotel charges transient travelers for early departures. The answer is almost always nothing, and, therefore, that policy should apply to the group as well. If the group is subject to an attrition damages provision, the second counter is that the group representative will be on the hook for possibly paying attrition damages and the hotel would be double-dipping if they get both early departure fees and then get to charge attrition damages on top of that for the group not picking-up the room block.

Second, a hotel may object to ❷ deposits and cancellation fees being refunded to an attendee for whom a sleeping room was booked but who cannot attend the meeting because of an emergency. The counter to the hotel is that the cancellation involves an emergency and not some random excuse for cancellation—and that the language specifies that the hotel is the sole decision-maker as to whether a cancellation was the result of an emergency or not. The other counter is similar to the double-dipping attrition damages argument described above.

2.2 <u>Check-In Time / Check-Out Time</u>. Hotel guarantees that Attendees' Check-In Time shall be 3:00 P.M. Hotel local time and Check-Out Time shall be Noon Hotel local time, unless such times are otherwise specified in an <u>Exhibit A</u>. For Attendees who arrive prior to Check-In Time, Hotel will assign rooms, as they become available. Hotel will use its best efforts to provide early check-in for Attendees. Hotel will accommodate late check-out on a complimentary basis, up to four (4) hours for Attendees, subject to space availability.

2.2.1 <u>Early Check-Out</u>. Where an Attendee elects to depart Hotel earlier than the Attendee's original check-out date, ❶ Hotel agrees that Attendee shall not be required to pay any additional fee for such early check-out.

2.2.2 ❷ Cancellation fees shall be waived and all deposits will be refunded immediately to no-show Attendees who cancel because of an emergency. Such emergency cancellation requests will be reviewed by Hotel and a determination will be made by Hotel on a case by case basis.

Room Rates

The *Room Rates* section is a catch-all of provisions for everything related to the dollars associated with a sleeping room. A hotel will review all of the provisions in this section very closely, and, depending on the provision, may bargain hard. Needless to say, from an attendee perspective, this is the most important provision.

When a group representative negotiates room rates, there are many factors that determine what the room rate will be. For example, as discussed in the *Getting the Best Deal for Your Meeting* section, the season and the day of the week will affect the room rate. The make-up of a group and the business it represents is clearly a major factor in determining room rate. If a group representative is booking a significant amount of a hotel's sleeping room inventory, consuming a good amount of food and beverage, and the attendees love to get spa treatments and love to eat at hotel restaurants, the group representative will likely do better on the room rate. If the group representative is planning to have a meeting for a small church group in Las Vegas, the prospective hotels aren't likely to think that the attendees will be throwing back hard liquor at the R-rated show in the hotel after a long night of losing fistfuls of cash in the hotel's casino. In that case, the group representative will likely end up paying a higher room rate than the big group of hard-partying lawyers that are headed to Sin City for their annual convention. A group representative needs to "sell" the group's business to a prospective hotel in the best possible light to get the best possible room rate.

The lead-in provision of this section, the *Room Rates* provision, simply points out that the room rates are described in an Exhibit A to the MHSA. There are some nuances that are worth pointing out and that may or may not be contentious for a hotel. First, the provision stipulates that the ❶ room rate is available to attendees 3-days before and after the in-house dates for the meeting. The rationale is that, in attractive locations, many attendees combine the meeting with some vacation days—usually arriving a few days before the meeting or leaving a few days after the meeting. This is also beneficial for a hotel in that the attendee is likely to stay over a weekend, which is typically a period of low occupancy for most hotels. Every now and then, a hotel might strike this language out. If the hotel is located in an undesirable location, such as Columbus, Georgia, then I'll likely agree to the deletion. If it's an attractive location, such as Chattanooga, Tennessee, I'll probably argue a bit to keep the language in, but likely cave if I can use it as a bargaining chip for something else in the MHSA that I think is more important.

The other nuance in the provision is a bit out-dated in that hotels don't seem so intent on charging an additional fee or rate for children as they once were, but I still include language specifying that the ❷ hotel won't charge such a fee or rate. Hotels rarely object to this language, and, in the rare instances they do, I usually bargain the fee or rate away quality.

> 3.1 <u>Room Rates</u>. Room Rates shall be described in an <u>Exhibit</u> <u>A</u> for the Room Block. The ❶ Room Rate shall be offered and available to all Attendees for the three (3) days prior to and three (3) days after the In-House Dates. There will be ❷ no additional charge for persons under the age of twenty-one (21) staying in the same room with a parent, relative, or guardian Attendee.

Sometimes a group representative will enter into a multi-year contract with a hotel where the group desires to rotate back to a certain hotel for a particular meeting over some span of time. This is an opportunity for a group representative to maximize the value of its business and to get a great room rate for the upcoming meeting and for the meetings scheduled in the out-years. However, the desire (or mandate) of a group to be at a particular hotel over multiple years can sometimes work against a group representative. The hotel likely has figured out that the group wants (needs) to be at the hotel and the hotel uses that knowledge as negotiation leverage. Instead of offering a discounted room rate in return for the future blocks of business resulting from a multi-year contract, the hotel proposes not setting the future room rate and, instead, tying the current room rate to some index or to a pre-determined annual percentage increase. One argument that I heard from a hotel when it refused to set a future discounted room rate was "the owners will not accept contracts with pre-determined room rates for anything greater than three years in the future." That's absurd and I'm surprised the hotel's sales person could keep a straight face when saying that, but I didn't have any real leverage to combat that absurdity and had to accept the room rate-to-index structure, which in that case was tied to inflation but no less than a 3% annualized room rate increase. Needless to say, I did everything in my power to ensure that my group never stays at that hotel again once the multi-year contract was over and I'll certainly never book any other meeting at that hotel.

Commissionable Room Rates

Similar to other industries such as insurance and real estate, the hotel industry has the concept of brokers. These brokers, commonly referred to as "intermediaries" or "ten percenters," represent groups to hotels and help groups that may have unsophisticated negotiators to get better overall deals from hotels. The rationale in using an intermediary is that they have buying clout with hotels—more clout than a small group would have and more negotiation experience. If a deal is done between a group and a hotel, the intermediary is paid a percentage of the business as a commission (usually based on room revenue) by the hotel (and not by the group). Some more prominent intermediaries are ConferenceDirect, Experient, and HelmsBriscoe.

It can be argued both ways whether or not a group *really* ends up paying for the services of an intermediary. Some argue that the group pays for the commission because the commission is just added to the room rate by the hotel. Others argue that intermediaries will steer a group to hotels—whether a right fit for the group or not—that the intermediaries have a "special" relationship with (meaning a higher commission). If a group representative is considering the use of an intermediary, he or she should do significant research first to determine whether the use of an intermediary is really going to provide value to the group for the commissions received (which can be enormous) and whether using an intermediary makes sense or not.

I've carefully considered using intermediaries in the past and have researched them quite thoroughly. As a result of my consideration and research, it doesn't make sense for me to use them. In my opinion, I can negotiate as good of a room rate as an intermediary can (or better) by competitively bidding my meeting to multiple hotels in multiple locations. Also, the intermediaries don't want to use my MHSA with hotels—they want to use their watered-down contract template because it's faster and easier—for them. Not using my MHSA translates into me signing up for less than advantageous terms and conditions, and, almost always, means that I'm signing up for attrition damages (more on that later). However, just because I don't use an intermediary now doesn't mean that I may not want to use one in the future. Consequently, that's why the *Commissionable Room Rate* provision is included in the MHSA. Further, since I already went through the trouble of putting an MHSA in place with a hotel, I don't have to worry about using an intermediary's watered-down contract template and I'm therefore more inclined to use an intermediary provided that I see a dramatic benefit in terms of a discounted room rate.

The provision is standard fare as far as intermediaries go. Even so, I've occasionally had a hotel object to it. Keep in mind that there is often a love-hate relationship between intermediaries and hotels—hotels would rather do business directly with a group representative and not have to pay a commission. A group representative may come across a hotel that refuses to provide commissionable room rates and won't consider the use of an intermediary, and the group representative may have to give on this provision. As the provision is written, it provides flexibility in that, if a group representative does decide to use an intermediary, it can be specified in the Exhibit A to the MHSA. If not, this provision isn't triggered and doesn't apply.

> 3.1.1 <u>Commissionable Room Rates</u>. If so specified by Customer, where third-party intermediary ("Intermediary") is designated to act on behalf of Customer in booking a Meeting with Hotel, and unless an <u>Exhibit A</u> expressly states to the contrary, Hotel agrees that: (a) Hotel shall pay a ten percent (10%) commission to such Intermediary on the actualized room revenue; (b) such Intermediary shall be paid such commission within thirty (30) days following the In-House Dates; and, (c) the commission due to such Intermediary is not transferable to another party or agency.

Rebated Room Rates

"Rebated" room rates are a derivation of commissionable room rates and are a bit of an oddball. In some cases, a hotel will be willing to offer a commission on a room rate but will adamantly refuse to lower their room rate by the amount of the commission if the commission isn't needed. As an example, a hotel may specify that its room rate is "$100, 10% commissionable," but, when a group representative asks the hotel to lower the rate to $90 because he or she doesn't want the commission, the hotel refuses to do so. That's the oddball part—why won't the hotel further lower the room rate by the amount of the commission that the group representative doesn't want? I've never gotten a straight answer from a hotelier as to why, but here's what I've been able to surmise... Apparently, the revenue from a room rate is captured within a hotel's *sales* budget. Commissions, on the other hand, are paid from a hotel's *marketing* budget. Since the sales budget determines compensation for a hotel sales person, and the marketing budget doesn't, a hotel sales person will refuse to lower the room rate (which would cut into the sales person's compensation) but still be willing to offer a commission (which doesn't affect compensation because it's coming out of a different budget). I'm not sure if that's really accurate, but it's my best educated guess. By the way, my guess as to the behavior of hotels in regard to commissionable room rates counters the argument that using intermediaries actually increases room rates for groups.

What does a group representative do in this circumstance? The group representative isn't using an intermediary, so he or she doesn't need the commission. The hotel refuses to lower the room rate by the amount of the commission. But the hotel is still willing to pay a commission. Therefore, there's money (in the amount of the commission) laying on some table somewhere. Here's a possible solution: the group representative should ask for the commission in the form of a rebate paid to the group representative. Some hotels readily give up commissions in the form of a rebate versus lowering the room rate. The *Rebated Room Rate* provision accounts for this oddball situation.

Similar to the *Commissionable Room Rate* provision, this provision is standard fare and doesn't apply unless triggered by an Exhibit A to the MHSA. I've had hotels object to this language because they don't, as a practice, rebate commissionable room rates to a group representative—which is fine. In this provision, the rebate is first used to ❶ pay any amounts due to hotel, and, ❷ if any amount remains unused, to be paid to the group representative. Be sure to read my discussion of "duty to disclose" following the provision below.

> 3.1.2 <u>Rebated Room Rates</u>. If so specified by Customer, and unless an <u>Exhibit A</u> expressly states to the contrary, Hotel agrees that where no Intermediary is designated to act on behalf of Customer, Hotel shall provide a ten-percent (10%) rebate to Customer based on the actualized room revenue. Such rebate shall be: (a) ❶applied against any amounts due to Hotel from Customer; or, (b) ❷where such rebate cannot be consumed in the context of the applicable Meeting, Hotel shall remit a rebate to Customer for such corresponding value. Such rebate shall be due to Customer no more than thirty (30) days following the In-House Dates.

There's another practice of "rebates" that is worth noting here but that the foregoing provision doesn't cover (nor the MHSA covers)— that's the practice of a group representative asking a hotel to add a specified amount as a rebate (usually in dollars versus a percentage like commission) to the room rate. The attendees then pay the room rate which includes the rebate and the hotel pays the rebate to the group representative. A legitimate example for using such a rebate would be to add $5 to the room rate so that the group representative can use that amount to pay for shuttle service for attendees. A not so legitimate purpose would be for a group representative to put the rebated amount to their bottom line. A question arises as to whether there is a duty to disclose a room rate rebate to attendees. In my personal opinion, there is no duty to disclose the rebate if it is being used to solely and directly benefit the attendee. As a further basis for my position that there is no duty to disclose, the attendees are paying the same room rate—the hotel wasn't willing to lower the room rate anymore but it was willing to provide me with a rebate as a concession. On the other hand, if the rebate is going to the bottom line of a group representative or a group representative asked for a rebate when in fact he or she could have gotten a lower room rate instead, then, in my personal opinion, the rebate should be disclosed (in advance) to attendees.

Taxes

There is nothing particularly exciting or controversial in this provision. It merely requires the hotel to be detailed in providing information relating to any mandatory taxes or fees imposed by state and local ordinances. Hotels rarely make changes to this provision, and, when they do, it's to clarify a certain mandatory tax or occupancy fee.

> 3.2   <u>Taxes</u>. If Room Rates are subject to state and local sales tax or an occupancy fee, all such taxes and/or fees shall be stated in an <u>Exhibit A</u>. Customer shall not pay any taxes on gratuities unless such tax on gratuity is set forth in an <u>Exhibit A</u> and in all cases only to the extent required by law.

Lowest Room Rate; Published or Confirmed

Imagine this… A group representative bargained hard on room rates with the hotel that's hosting the meeting. The group representative went back and forth a few times with the hotel and finally—and firmly—the hotel responded, "We're giving you an incredible room rate, and we're not going to lower it a penny more! Take it or leave it." The group representative smiles and feels proud that he got the best deal possible for his attendees. He responds to the hotel, "You've got a deal." At the meeting, an attendee approaches the group representative and says, "The Left-Handed Paint Ball Players Association is having a meeting here, too. In fact, I met one of the paint ball players, One-Eyed Carrie, at the bar last night. We got to talking and she said she was only paying $99 per night. Why the heck are we paying $129 per night?!" The group representative gulps, wishing he was back in his hotel room under the covers, and prepares to stammer out some lame response...

The group representative can avoid this type of dilemma through the *Lowest Room Rate; Published or Confirmed* provision. The general purpose of this type of provision—also called a "most favored group" provision—is to ensure that a group representative is getting the best room rate for the time period that the group will be at a hotel. The provision as written below, subject to certain conditions, will ensure that at least the hotel doesn't launch a major marketing campaign announcing lower room rates to the entire world than what the group representative negotiated and, if the hotel does broadcast a lower room rate, the hotel may have to make good on the room rate. Keep in mind that, while a group representative is trying to avoid the dilemma discussed above, a hotel has the dilemma of maximizing revenue for its owners. What that means is that hotels will look closely at this provision, discussions over this provision can become extremely contentious, and, frequently, there will be redlines made to this provision by a hotel even though I've tried to make it as fair as possible.

The provision contemplates that the group must book a reasonable number of rooms for the provision to even apply. In my scenario above, if the group was extremely small and the Left-Handed Paint Ball Players Association took up the bulk of the rooms in the hotel, it's only reasonable that paint ball players' room rate would be lower. In this provision, the group must ❶ book at least 25% of the hotel's net inventory (based on the peak night indicated in the Exhibit A to the MHSA) for the lowest room rate guarantee to apply. This percentage is frequently redlined by a hotel to be higher. I purposefully set the percentage low at 25%, so it's no surprise when hotels want to change it. I'll typically allow it to be changed anywhere up to and including 50% before I start getting fussy. Anything beyond 50% is where I start harshly questioning why the hotel can't guarantee me the best room rate when I've filled up over half their hotel. In those cases, mostly, hotels back the percentage down to 50%.

Once the provision is triggered, the ❷ hotel agrees to not advertise or offer a lower rate during the in-house dates of the meeting and 30-days before and after. Hotels frequently object to and strike the 30-days before and after language arguing that it doesn't really matter what the room rates are before or after the meeting. A group representative might find the hotel's position reasonable, but it raises the question (for the group representative to ask the hotel) why. It would be odd, but possibly explainable, if a hotel's room rates in the 30-days before and after the meeting were dramatically lower. There is a nuance to this part of the provision that's worth noting: "advertise or offer." A group representative definitely doesn't want a lower room rate to be blasted across the Internet, but the group representative also doesn't want—especially considering that he or she booked a significant part of the hotel's sleeping room inventory—the hotel to quietly negotiate better deals with other groups. Hotels usually readily agree to the "advertise" part but occasionally object to the "offer" part. I don't care what hoteliers say or how they rationalize it; it's just not fair or reasonable for a hotel to offer another group a lower room rate if I've given the hotel a big piece of business. In other words, a group representative needs to bargain hard to keep the "advertise or offer" language in and strongly object when the hotel wants to eliminate the "or offer" part. The "advertise or offer" language will *nearly* eliminate that happy hour conversation I described earlier (*nearly*, meaning that there are still some

❺ legitimate exceptions where the hotel will have contracted a lower room rate for certain categories of other guests—and that's reasonable).

❸ If the hotel does, oops, advertise or offer a lower room rate (and it has happened to me more than once), the room rate in the Exhibit A to the MHSA is automatically reduced to the lower room rate. That's great, but the problem with that is timing. That language assumes that the group representative found out about the lower room rate before or during the meeting. What happens if the group representative finds out *after* the meeting? That's where the next part ❹ of the provision comes into play. If, after the meeting, it turns out that the attendees didn't receive the lowest room rate, then the hotel has to remit the difference between the lower room rate and the rate that the attendees paid. The problem is that the group representative now has an administrative dilemma in terms of trying to figure out which attendees did actually attend, how long they stayed, etc. to determine what the refund should be. If the hotel can figure it out and it's not an administrative burden on the group representative, then the refund should go to the attendees. But, if the hotel can't figure it out and / or the group representative is administratively burdened by trying to match refund to attendee, he or she shouldn't just leave the money on the table. In that case, the group representative should take the refund. Now there's obviously some ethical issues (at least in my mind) involved with the group representative (and not the attendees) receiving the refund (because it's technically their money), but that's for the group representative to figure out. In my mind, if I'm forced to take the refund because it's next to impossible or too expensive for me to get it back to the attendees, I think it's perfectly ethical for me to retain the refund if I plow it back into the next meeting that I hold—such as through upgraded food and beverage.

3.3   <u>Lowest Room Rate; Published or Confirmed</u>. Where Customer has ❶booked more than twenty-five percent (25%) of Hotel's net inventory ("Net Inventory," as further defined herein) on the peak night described in an <u>Exhibit A</u>, ❷Hotel agrees not to advertise or offer any lower group, leisure, or promotional room rate lower than the Room Rate via any booking media, including but not limited to the Internet / World Wide Web, toll-free numbers, consolidators, or otherwise during the In-House dates and the thirty (30) calendar day periods before and after such In-House Dates. ❸In the event that Hotel offers lower room rates to any party during the In-House Dates or the thirty (30) calendar day period preceding a Meeting the Room Rate shall automatically adjust to such lower room rate; in such event, an <u>Exhibit A</u> is deemed to have been revised and amended to reflect such lower room rate. ❹In the event that Attendees have not received the lowest published or confirmed room rates, Hotel agrees that Customer shall be due the total of the difference between such lower room rates and the Room Rates for all room nights ("Room Nights") during the In-House Dates, and Hotel shall, at the sole election of Customer remit payment of such amount due to the Attendees or Customer, as the case may be, within fourteen (14) calendar days following the Meeting. ❺The foregoing provision does not apply to qualified discounts such as government, corporate, or crew rates previously negotiated with Hotel.

Here's what an acceptable version of the provision might look like after a tough (but fair) negotiation has taken place.

3.3   <u>Lowest Room Rate; Published or Confirmed</u>. Where Customer has booked more than fifty percent (50%) of Hotel's net inventory ("Net Inventory," as further defined herein) in an <u>Exhibit A</u>, Hotel agrees not to advertise or offer any lower group, leisure, or promotional room rate lower than the Room Rate via any booking media, including but not limited to the Internet / World Wide Web, toll-free numbers, consolidators, or otherwise during the In-House dates. In the event that Hotel advertises or offers lower room rates to any party during the In-House Dates, the Room Rate shall automatically adjust to such lower room rate; in such event, an <u>Exhibit A</u> is deemed to have been revised and amended to reflect such lower room rate. The foregoing provision does not apply to qualified discounts such as government, corporate, or crew rates previously negotiated with Hotel.

Despite a group representative getting the best possible "lowest room rate" language in the MHSA, inevitably, one day, an attendee will complain about the room rate for a meeting the group representative booked: *The hotel had a lower room rate 6-months ago. The room rate seems high for this area. Other hotels are cheaper.* Well, all of the foregoing might be true. And there may be many different reasons why and the group representative needs to be prepared to answer why: *It's "high" season for the hotel now. Being connected to the convention center, this hotel is in a prime location. This hotel is a full service hotel and the other hotels are limited service hotels.* But it may also be a problem that a group representative "intentionally" created by artificially inflating the room rate—and that might be appropriate. The issue is what I stated at the beginning of this book: attendees pay the room rate (via their employers) and the group representative pays for everything else associated with the meeting such as food and beverage, audio-visual, talent, etc. In some cases, a group representative will decide to shift some of the cost of the meeting to the attendee by tacking costs on to the room rate. For example, a group representative may be using a housing coordinator and that fee is tacked on to the room rate. A group representative might have asked for a discount or reduced rate on food and beverage with some of the discount or reduced rate being tacked on to the room rate. A group representative might have asked for complimentary function space beyond what's typical and the reality is that the "complimentary" function space resulted in a higher room rate than the hotel would have given the group representative otherwise. A group representative may have asked the hotel to tack on an extra $5 to the room rate to be paid to the master account to fund, e.g., shuttle service or possible attrition damages. Those are all legitimate business decisions, but affect the room rate. The group representative can ask for a rock bottom room rate, but the group representative will pay for everything else, maybe even function space, out of pocket since the hotel wasn't compensated through the room rate.

Staff Rooms

Like many other organizations that conduct a meeting, a group representative will likely have some staff (contracted or otherwise) on-site at the hotel to help conduct the meeting. For example, a group representative may have speakers coming to the meeting who live elsewhere and who will need a sleeping room at the hotel. A group representative may also have his or her own staff, such as meeting planners, who need sleeping rooms. For those staff, it's common in the hotel industry for a hotel to provide a group representative with a certain number of sleeping rooms on either a no-charge or discounted basis.

This provision specifies that the hotel will provide ❶ the number of staff sleeping rooms specified in an Exhibit A to the MHSA on a complimentary basis or some other discounted basis that is described in the Exhibit A to the MHSA. The group representative has the ❷ responsibility to make sure that he or she provides a list of what staff will be staying at the hotel. For important reasons that I'll describe later relating to room pick-up and attrition, the ❸ staff rooms are counted as a part of the Room Pick-Up.

If a group representative asks for too many staff rooms, he or she shouldn't be surprised if the hotel slashes what the group representative is asking for. Similarly, a group representative shouldn't be surprised, in the context of high occupancy (either due to the hotel's location, the season, the night, or whatever constitutes high occupancy), that a hotel slashes what the group representative is asking for, only offers a discount instead of complimentary sleeping rooms for staff, or outright refuses to offer sleeping rooms for staff on either a complimentary *or* a discounted basis.

Hotels sometimes strike this provision in the context of the next provision I discuss, *Complimentary Rooms*. If a hotel points out that they're offering a group representative comp rooms as a part of the *Complimentary Rooms* provision and therefore they want to completely strike the *Staff Rooms* provision because it's duplicative of the *Complimentary Rooms*, it may be reasonable assuming the agreed-upon comp room ratio. As long as a group representative keeps the *Complimentary Rooms* provision in the MHSA as-is, he or she will likely be fine with giving up on the *Staff Rooms* provision.

With that stated, here's my rationale for including both the *Staff Rooms* and *Complimentary Rooms* provisions in an MHSA with a hotel, even though my rationale might sound a little weak. I look at staff rooms as the sleeping rooms that I need to facilitate and conduct my meeting. Conversely, I look at comp rooms as sort of a volume discount / benefit for me giving my business to a particular hotel. In other words, the more business (meaning, paid sleeping rooms) that I give a hotel, the more benefit (in the form of free sleeping rooms) I should receive.

3.4 Staff Rooms. ❶Hotel will provide the number of staff (inclusive of contracted staff of Customer such as speakers) rooms (each a "Staff Room") indicated in an Exhibit A on a complimentary, no-charge basis (unless otherwise specified to the contrary in such Exhibit A). ❷Customer shall provide

Hotel with a list of staff members staying at Hotel on or before the Reservation Cut-Off Date. ❸ Staff Rooms shall be included as part of the Room Pick-Up.

Complimentary Rooms

It's common practice for hotels to offer "comp rooms" to groups as a concession. Sleeping rooms are "comped" by a hotel to a group representative based on the number of sleeping rooms used by a group. Comp rooms can then be used by the group for their unique needs, such as for VIP attendees or staff (now it should be clear where I might be "double dipping" in terms of the *Staff Rooms* provision). A ratio of 1-to-50 (meaning 1 comp room night for every 50 room nights used by the group) was a historical standard. However, the ratio, called the "comp room ratio" is subject to the size of the room block. If a group representative books only a few sleeping rooms, he or she shouldn't expect any comp rooms, but if a group representative books 500 room nights over a couple of days, he or she should bargain for better than a 1-to-50 comp room ratio.

Typically, the comp room calculation is based on the *total* room nights picked-up (meaning actually used and not just contracted). For example, if a contract states a 1-to-50 comp room ratio and a room block of 1,000 total room nights, the group representative has an expectation to receive 20 comp room nights. Continuing with the example, if the group ends up only picking-up 850 total room nights, the group representative would only be entitled to 17 comp room nights. This type of comp room calculation is called the "cumulative" method. There's another, nuanced, way of calculating comp rooms that hotels like to use to chip away at the comp room concession. This type of comp room calculation is called the "per-night" method. Under this method, instead of calculating the comp room ratio using the total room nights used by the group over the entire room block, the comp rooms are calculated using the sleeping rooms used by the group *each night*. The best way to illustrate the difference is to use an example, as follows.

	M	T	W	Totals
Room Block	50	100	50	200
Pick-Up	34	75	30	139
Comp Room calculation (using 1/35 ratio)				
Using *cumulative* method				5
Using *per-night* method	0	2	0	2

By using the per-night method, it's clear that I would have lost out on three comp room nights that I would have otherwise been entitled to using the cumulative method. The reason is that on the first night, using the per-night method, I didn't even meet the 1-to-35 comp room ratio because I was one room night shy of 35—I don't get *any* comp rooms. The same thing happens to me on the last night in the example. That's why it's always better to use the cumulative method of calculating comp rooms.

In this provision, I like to start out at a ❶ 1-to-35 comp room ratio. When first negotiating the MHSA with a hotel this may or may not be an issue for the hotel. If I'm booking 1,500 room nights at a large hotel, I'm pretty certain to get a 1-to-35 comp room ratio. Anything less than a substantial number of room nights and a hotel might balk at the 1-to-35 comp room ratio. When a hotel does balk at the 1-to-35 comp room ratio on the basis that my first meeting with the hotel will be a relatively small room block, I explain the magic "Unless otherwise specified in an Exhibit A..." language—meaning that, for the first meeting I'll put a more reasonable comp room ratio in the Exhibit A to the MHSA (which overrides the comp room ratio default in the MHSA). Frequently, hotels will buy-off on this and I'll get to keep my 1-to-35 comp room ratio as a default. So, if I book another small meeting at the same hotel, and the hotel doesn't include a lower comp room ratio than the default that's in the MHSA, I'll get the 1-to-35 comp room ratio by default.

In addition to an aggressive comp room ratio, I ensure that the method of calculating comp rooms is clearly based on ❷ cumulative pick-up. I do get a little nit-picky in that ❸ I count each room in a suite as a separate sleeping room for purposes of calculating the comp rooms. Hotels occasionally strike this sentence and I usually don't make a fuss of it.

Another key point of this provision is how comp rooms are applied. If I can't use all of the comp rooms I've earned by filling them with attendees, then ❹ I want to be able to use the value of those unused comp rooms against any amount I might end up owing the hotel (such as for food and beverage) or, if there is no amount due, I want the hotel to cut me a check for the value of the unused comp rooms. Hotels rarely object to allowing the value of unused comp rooms to be applied against any amounts owing to the hotel, but occasionally object to cutting a check. However, despite a hotel taking exception with cutting a check, I frequently am able to keep the option in the MHSA.

This provision is worth bargaining hard over. To recap, as described above, a hotel will likely object to any comp room ratio that is lower than 1-to-50, will rarely want the calculation method to be on a per-night basis, will occasionally object to the method of counting separate rooms in a suite as sleeping rooms, will rarely object to applying the value of unused comp rooms against amounts owing to the hotel, and will occasionally object to cutting a check for the value of unused comp rooms.

3.5   Complimentary Rooms. Unless otherwise specified in an Exhibit A, Hotel shall provide ❶one (1) complimentary Guestroom (each a "Comp Room") per night for every thirty-five (35) Room Nights associated with the Meeting ❷on a cumulative, and not daily, basis. For purposes of determining the number of Comp Rooms, ❸each room in a suite will count as a separate Room Night. ❹In the event Comp Rooms earned are not used, Hotel agrees to: (a) apply the corresponding value of the applicable single standard Room Rate against any amounts due to Hotel; or, (b) where such corresponding value cannot be consumed in the context of the applicable Meeting, Hotel shall remit to Customer such corresponding value.

Guestroom Upgrades and VIP Suites

Depending upon the group, it's very possible that the group representative will have a need for suites for VIPs or hospitality purposes. The following two provisions are geared to help a group representative to obtain suites on either a complimentary basis or a reduced room rate basis. Occasionally, a hotel has objected to my including both provisions and asked me to pick one or the other (I usually go with the reduced room rate option because I can frequently—regardless of what the contract says—cajole a hotel into allowing me to convert comp rooms into suites but I can't always bargain for a reduced room rate for suites).

The first provision allows a group representative to ❶ convert some of the comp rooms to suites. Hotels frequently agree to this provision, but will modify the language to cap how many complimentary suites a group representative can obtain by modifying the language accordingly. A hotel may also require more than two comp rooms be used to convert to a suite. Either or both of those changes are likely reasonable considering that the way the language is written, the group representative could convert all of the comp rooms into suites on a 2-to-1 basis.

The second provision allows a group representative to book ❷ suites at the same room rate as for single room sleeping rooms. It's likely that a hotel will modify the language to cap the number of suites that can be booked at the reduced room rate, which is reasonable.

3.6 <u>Guestroom Upgrades</u>. At the request of Customer, ❶Hotel shall upgrade no less than two (2) Comp Rooms to suite (parlor and sleeping room) Guestrooms.

3.7 <u>VIP Suites</u>. In addition to any complimentary Suite upgrades, unless otherwise specified in an <u>Exhibit A</u>, ❷Hotel agrees to provide to Customer a minimum of four (4) suites (parlor and sleeping room) at the single Room Rate for a standard Guestroom.

Complimentary Planning Rooms

For large meetings, it's common for a group representative and contractors that may be assisting in conducting the group's meeting (such as a decorator) to visit the hotel where the meeting has been booked well in advance of the meeting. The *Complimentary Planning Rooms* provision provides accommodations in such a case on a complimentary basis provided that the hotel has space available. Additional sleeping rooms beyond those specified in the provision are at a reduced room rate and any necessary function space is complimentary. It's extremely common for a hotel to agree to this type of provision, so it won't be much of an issue for a hotel unless the group representative has a small event. Some hotels will object to complimentary function space (and ask that they be reimbursed) and other hotels will want to scope the function space to something reasonable.

> 3.8 <u>Complimentary Planning Rooms</u>. In addition to Comp Rooms, Staff Rooms, and complimentary upgrades, unless otherwise specified in an <u>Exhibit A</u>, Hotel agrees to furnish, on a space available basis, a minimum of two (2) complimentary guestrooms for a period of two (2) Room Nights for Meeting planning visits to Hotel. Additional Guestrooms beyond the two (2) complimentary planning Guestrooms Customer may require for meeting planning attendees will be charged at the applicable Room Rate and any required Function Space will be complimentary.

Reservation Procedures

While other services that a hotel may be providing for a meeting are important, one of the most critical elements of a contract with a hotel is sleeping room reservations. A reservation is a pretty solid indication to a group representative that the corresponding attendee will attend the meeting and it's also a pretty solid indication to the hotel that it'll have a "head in a bed." Therefore, while a group representative and a hotel might bicker over other items in the MHSA, when it comes right down to it, it's all about the room block and reservations.

This section of the MHSA describes reservation procedures, but doesn't cover the actual mechanics by which reservations are made. Instead, the mechanics of booking reservations (which are meeting and hotel specific) are described in the *Reservation Procedures* section of an Exhibit A to the MHSA. The purpose of this section and the following provisions are to describe certain parameters relating to the booking of reservations.

The all-important outcome—generated from whatever reservation method is used—is called a "rooming list" or "room list." The room list, in its final form, is used to determine which attendees are booked at a hotel.

Acceptance of Reservations after Reservation Cut-Off Date

The period leading up to a meeting is critical in the context of determining who has made reservations with a hotel under the MHSA and who will be attending the meeting. At some pre-determined date, typically called a "reservation cut-off date," the hotel will no longer be required to hold any unreserved sleeping rooms that were originally a part of the room block. A hotel wants attendees to make reservations as far in advance as possible so that the hotel knows that the sleeping rooms will be occupied. The human nature of attendees is to do the opposite, and wait until the last possible minute to make reservations. The hotel industry came up with the concept of the reservation cut-off date as a "stick" (versus carrot) approach to drive human behavior to make reservations sooner than later. The "stick" is that, if attendees don't make their reservations by the reservation cut-off date, the hotel will take the adverse actions of releasing the unreserved sleeping rooms for sale to other groups and to the public, only accepting attendee reservations on a "space available" basis, and no longer accepting attendee reservations at the negotiated room rate. Hotels obviously want the reservation cut-off date to be as far in advance as they can get a group representative to capitulate to in an effort to get sleeping room reservations as early as possible and to get the "stick" into place as soon as possible. Resort hotels are notorious for wanting an early reservation cut-off date because

The Master Hotel Services Agreement

it's theoretically more difficult for them to resell sleeping rooms because they don't proportionally have as many transient travelers as do non-resort hotels. That's their argument, anyways. The other reason a hotel would want an early reservation cut-off date is that it potentially locks a group representative into possible attrition damages (if the group representative has agreed to them) and doesn't give the group representative much wiggle room time-wise to try and drum up more attendees. The hotel's desire for an early reservation cut-off date is in direct conflict with the group representative's position. The group representative wants the latest reservation cut-off date as possible because he or she wants the opportunity to get as many attendees counted in the room pick-up as possible and to include that segment of busy attendees who just don't have time to get around to making reservations until just before a meeting.

The industry norm for a reservation cut-off date has historically been 30-days before a meeting, so a hotel may object to the ❶ 21-days specified in the following provision. A group representative should stand fast, since the 30-day norm originates from back before the Internet and when hotels needed more time to wrangle up business to sell the sleeping rooms left unfilled in a room block. Now, 21-days is becoming more common as a result of hotels being able to use third-party travel websites to advertise their sleeping rooms and because more people are making hotel reservations electronically.

As previously indicated, one reason that hotels like early reservation cut-off dates is because that's the date a group's specially negotiated room rate expires. So, if a group representative has attendees reserve rooms late, they would be subject to paying a higher room rate. The language in the following provision requires that, ❷ even after the reservation cut-off date, the hotel must offer the negotiated room rate to

73

late-reserving attendees. A hotel is likely to object to this, but the counter is that the reservations must only be accepted on a *space available* basis. So, if the hotel doesn't have the sleeping rooms, then it doesn't have to provide a sleeping room at the negotiated room rate. But, if the hotel does have sleeping rooms available, why wouldn't it want to sell them to attendees at the negotiated room rate? Isn't the reason that a hotel wants an early reservation cut-off date in the first place is to be able to try and quickly sell sleeping rooms to fill them? Well, the hotel knows that late-reserving attendees need to be at the hotel and the hotel now has the leverage to hold them hostage to the higher room rate. I've personally experienced situations in my past where a hotel had plenty of sleeping rooms available after the reservation cut-off date, but the hotel wanted an exorbitant room rate from my late-reserving attendees which (after I checked) was higher than what people could reserve sleeping rooms for on the Internet during the same dates from the same hotel. Consequently, I added the last sentence ❷ to the following provision to prevent a hotel from gouging my late-reserving attendees.

> 4.1 <u>Acceptance of Reservations after Reservation Cut-Off Date</u>. Hotel shall hold the Room Block until 11:59 P.M. Hotel local time on the Reservation Cut-Off Date, such date being ❶twenty-one (21) calendar days prior to the In-House Dates, or as otherwise specified in an <u>Exhibit A</u> if longer or shorter than twenty-one (21) calendar days. ❷After the Reservation Cut-Off Date, Hotel agrees to accept Guestroom Reservations on a space available basis at the Room Rate.

Substitution of Attendees

This provision addresses a vestige problem that is largely not an issue any longer, but, just in case, a group representative should include it as a part of the contract with a hotel. In the past, hotels contractually discouraged groups from substituting attendees for those who had cancelled a room reservation. Part of the reasoning for prohibiting substitutions pre-dates the Internet, when making substitutions were administratively burdensome for hotels. The primary reason was that hotels wanted to control room blocks, particularly after the reservation cut-off date. If an attendee in the group cancelled, it was the hotel's right to resell that sleeping room and, if the group representative had a late-reserving attendee in the group who wanted a sleeping room, that attendee might just have to pay a higher rate to get the sleeping room because it wasn't part of the room block. Hotels have backed off of this position significantly, and I've never had a hotel disagree with the substance of this provision.

4.2   <u>Substitution of Attendees</u>. Hotel agrees to allow Customer, at the sole discretion of Customer, Attendee, or the Housing Coordinator to simultaneously substitute Attendees at the Room Rate for Guestrooms canceled by Attendees with confirmed reservations both before and after the Reservation Cut-Off Date through to the first day of the Meeting.

Housing Coordinator

In the group context, there are a number of different methods to handle how reservations are booked: use the hotel, use a third-party such as a CVB or what is called a "housing coordinator," or a group representative can do it himself or herself. The method chosen for a particular meeting is described in an Exhibit A to the MHSA, but, if a group representative chooses to use the housing coordinator method, there's some contractual language that needs to be included in the master agreement component of the MHSA. Since the housing coordinator, a third party, isn't a party to the contract, it's necessary to describe the contractual terms of who the housing coordinator is and how the housing coordinator gets paid. Mostly, housing coordinators are paid (by the hotel) a percentage of the room rate associated with a meeting. For that fee—and I'm oversimplifying—a housing coordinator will provide an Internet-based interface for the attendees to reserve sleeping rooms, will process credit card transactions, will manage the rooming list, and will work with the hotel to ensure that the hotel has the most current rooming list. This provision is relatively straightforward—the hotel pays the housing coordinator the amount specified in the corresponding Exhibit A to the MHSA—and hotels rarely take exception to the language, but hotels occasionally have a question about the ❶ last sentence in the provision. In most cases, a hotel will absorb the housing coordinator's fee without raising the room rate. There have been a number of occasions where I negotiated a room rate with a hotel and then later decided to use a housing coordinator. When going back to amend the corresponding Exhibit A to the MHSA to designate the housing coordinator, the hotel declined (as a concession) to increase the room rate by a corresponding amount. The primary reason for this, other than the hotel being a good business partner, relates to my discussion of the *Commissionable Room Rates* provision where the cost of an intermediary (like a housing coordinator) is funded out of a budget other than the hotel's sales budget. However, there have been a very few cases where a hotel has increased the room rate to account for the housing coordinator's fee. In those cases, if I later decide to not use the housing coordinator, I want to make sure the room rate is reduced accordingly—which is the purpose of the last sentence. Some hotels will object to this sentence on the basis that they don't, as a matter of practice, increase room rates for a housing coordinator. If that's the case, then the last sentence can be deleted.

4.3 <u>Housing Coordinator</u>. Where designated in an <u>Exhibit A</u>, Customer's housing coordinator ("Housing Coordinator") will manage Guestroom Reservations and Hotel shall pay the Housing Coordinator the fee designated in the relevant <u>Exhibit A</u>. Hotel will work directly with the Housing Coordinator, Meeting Manager and staff on all matters relating to Hotel's provision of Guestrooms for the Meeting. Except as specifically expressed in an <u>Exhibit A</u>, the Housing Coordinator shall have no authority to bind Customer. ❶ In the event that Customer initially designates a Housing Coordinator in an <u>Exhibit A</u> and subsequently elects not to use such Housing Coordinator, then the Room Rate shall adjust down to the extent of Housing Coordinator fees not payable by Hotel.

Over-booking by Hotel

While it makes logical sense for this provision to appear at this point in the MHSA, it's probably beneficial for the reader to first review my discussion of the *Attrition* provision for a detailed discussion of the dreaded "A" word. The reason being is that this *Over-booking by Hotel* provision is essentially a "reverse attrition damages" provision. Consequently, this provision can be quite contentious.

Hotels, particularly during an economic era of high travel and hotel demand, are stubborn about holding groups to their room blocks with little or no margin for error. This stubbornness shows up in the form of overreaching attrition damages provisions for groups. At the same time (and like the airlines), a hotel doesn't want to be held *too* accountable for their over-booking. In a nutshell, if a hotel insists on charging a group damages for attrition then it's equitable that a hotel be responsible for over-booking. The reason for the damages stem from the costs that the group will likely incur as a result of the over-booking, such as communications to make the attendees aware of the issue and the group representative's time dealing with irate attendees.

Under this provision, if a hotel over-books but is still ❶ able to provide at least 90% of the sleeping rooms specified in an Exhibit A to the MHSA, the hotel is responsible for (a) paying damages of 30% of the average room rate for all of the sleeping rooms that the hotel could not provide, (b) all over-booked sleeping rooms are counted toward the room pick-up (e.g., for the purpose of comp room calculations) and, (c) relief from attrition damages that may result from attendees cancelling their reservations when they hear about the over-booking situation and that, for example, their friends were the ones that were over-booked and won't be staying at the hotel. If the hotel ❷ can't provide at least 90% of the sleeping rooms specified in an Exhibit A to the MHSA, then the hotel is deemed to be terminating the Exhibit A to the MHSA for convenience, at which point all of the obligations associated with that type of termination are triggered (see the later discussion of the *Termination for Convenience* provision).

I've had many hotels object to this provision. The main reason that I include the provision in the MHSA is to demonstrate that, if the hotel asks for an attrition damages provision, what's fair for them should be fair for me. Ultimately, after I've made my point to the hotel, I'll agree to delete the provision because I'm somewhat protected by the *Dishonored Reservations* provision and I can always fall back on the hotel's over-booking as a material breach of the MHSA.

4.4 <u>Over-booking by Hotel</u>. ❶In the event Hotel over-books prior to the Reservation Cut-Off Date and where Hotel has provided at least ninety percent (90%) of the Room Block: (a) within fourteen (14) calendar days of the occurrence of the over-booking, Hotel shall pay to Customer as liquidated damages, and not as a penalty, an amount equal to thirty percent (30%) of the average Room Rate for each Guestroom Reservation that Hotel is unable to accept prior to the Reservation Cut-off Date; and, (b) Hotel will include the displaced Room Nights caused by over-booking in the Room Pick-Up report; and, (c) Customer will not be liable for damages, if any, for any resulting reduction or shortfall in the Room Pick-Up. ❷In the event that Hotel over-books prior to the Reservation Cut-off Date and where Hotel is unable to provide at least ninety percent (90%) of the Room Block, for the purposes of this Agreement, such over-booking shall be deemed to be a termination for convenience by Hotel of an Exhibit A.

Room Pick-Up

The *Room Pick-Up* section of the MHSA contains two provisions which measure the group's fulfillment of its room block and how many sleeping rooms the hotel had in inventory. These provisions serve other purposes (e.g., the *Net Inventory* provision in this section is used as a part of the *Lowest Room Rate; Published or Confirmed* provision), but their real importance comes into play if the MHSA or Exhibit A to the MHSA contains an attrition provision that subjects a group representative to damages. If a group representative is subject to an attrition provision, then he or she needs to vigorously guard against any substantive changes made by a hotel to the following provisions.

Room Pick-Up Calculation

This provision describes the method of calculating room pick-up, and, financially, it's critically important in the face of possible attrition damages. Simply, a group representative wants as many sleeping rooms as possible to "count" as a part of the room pick-up. It's imperative that a group representative clearly understand the provision and be able to argue—if the group representative needs to—why a hotel should not make any changes to the language.

Just to be clear, the provision points out that ❶ the period for calculation is the in-house dates (not the typically shorter official dates) for the meeting and ❷ it doesn't matter when the sleeping rooms were booked. The remainder of the provision ❸ describes "what counts" for purposes of calculating sleeping rooms and room nights.

(a) is obvious and includes sleeping rooms used by any attendee (as defined by the *Attendees* provision).

(b) may seem to conflict with the *Check-In Time / Check-Out Time* provision because that earlier provision precludes early departure fees and limits cancellation fees. It's "just in case." If a group representative ends up having to give on the *Check-In Time / Check-Out Time* provision during a negotiation, and early departing attendees are subject to a departure fee, the group representative at least won't have to remember to update this provision. So how does an early departure fee translate into a sleeping room that should be counted as a part of the room pick-up? The answer is that the hotel has received at least some compensation for an attendee departing early, and, if the group representative is subject to attrition damages and ends up paying them, the hotel would be double-dipping if it got the early departure fee <u>and</u> attrition damages for the vacated sleeping room. It's not reasonable for the hotel to be paid twice. The same goes for cancellation fees. If an attendee canceled his or her reservation and had to pay a cancellation fee, the hotel has already been compensated for its "loss." Hotels rarely object to (b).

(c) and (f) count displaced sleeping rooms because the attendees would have filled the sleeping room if the hotel hadn't over-booked. The difference with (f) versus (c) is that (c) contemplates over-booking that a hotel made a group representative aware of in advance (and the hotel cut the room block) and (f) contemplates attendees who were advised on an individual basis that they couldn't be accommodated (e.g., an attendee showed up at the hotel only to be told that the hotel didn't have any sleeping rooms left and that the attendee would be "walked" according to the *Dishonored Reservations* provision). Hotels rarely, if ever, object to (c) or (f).

(d) and (e) includes comp rooms and staff rooms because, even if the group representative filled them at no room rate or a reduced room rate, they were included as a concession under the MHSA and because whoever were in those sleeping rooms likely benefited the hotel through expenditures at hotel restaurants and the like. Hotels rarely object to (d) and occasionally object to (e).

Finally, ❹ each "room within a room," such as rooms within a suite, gets counted as a sleeping room for purposes of room pick-up. The rationale is that the group representative or an attendee is likely paying substantially more for a sleeping room that has multiple rooms and that, due to this higher room rate, there should be more "credit" to the room pick-up. Hotels occasionally object to this.

5.1 <u>Room Pick-Up Calculation</u>. All of the following shall be counted, calculated in terms of Room Nights ❶over the In-House Dates, in the Room Block pick-up (the "Room Pick-Up"), ❷whether such Guestrooms were reserved before or after the Reservation Cut-Off Date: ❸(a) Guestrooms used by Attendees; (b) Guestrooms canceled by Attendees, where the Attendee has paid an "early departure" or other such fee for the cancellation; (c) displaced Guestrooms resulting from Hotel's over-booking; (d) Comp Rooms; (e) Staff Rooms; and, (f) Dishonored Reservations. ❹Where a Guestroom consists of more than one room, each room shall be counted as a separate Guestroom for the purposes of the Room Pick-Up calculation (for example, a Guestroom consisting of a sleeping room and a parlor shall be counted as two (2) Guestrooms).

Net Inventory

This provision is used by the *Lowest Room Rate; Published or Confirmed* provision), but the real reason it's in the MHSA is if a group representative gets stuck having to agree to an attrition damages provision. In typical attrition damages provisions, a hotel's actual inventory becomes an important factor when a group representative is faced with possible attrition damages. For example, some attrition provisions contain "last room sold" language, which means that attrition damages are reduced by the amount of sleeping rooms that a hotel resells. In other words, under "last room sold" language, if the room pick-up was such that a group representative owed attrition damages associated with, for example, 25 room nights for a particular night, it wouldn't be reasonable or fair for the group representative to have to pay for those 25 room nights if the hotel had only 10 sleeping rooms that went unsold that same night. In that case, the hotel obviously resold at least some of the sleeping rooms that had been assigned to the group representative to another paying customer. The hotel's charging of the group representative for attrition damages on top of the revenue the hotel received for those resold sleeping rooms would be double-dipping—the group representative should only owe attrition damages for 10 room nights, not 25. Thus, "last room sold" language might help get a group representative out of hot water (or at least the water will only be warm) if faced with attrition damages. So, how does a group representative know that some of the group's sleeping rooms were sold, or, looking at it from the other perspective, how many sleeping rooms the hotel had vacant on a particular night? First, the group representative needs access to the hotel's occupancy reports (as permitted by the *Customer Audit Rights* provision) for review purposes. Second, the group representative needs to know how many sleeping rooms are in inventory at the hotel. Then the math is simple... (A) Hotel's sleeping room inventory – (B) occupancy = (C) number of sleeping rooms available for sale. If the number of room nights that the group representative owes attrition damages for is greater than (C), then the group representative only pays for attrition damages associated with the difference. But here's a twist or two... What happens if the hotel's occupancy report counts sleeping rooms that someone else paid attrition damages for as unsold sleeping rooms? What happens if the hotel has sleeping rooms in its inventory that are undergoing renovations? It's not reasonable for a hotel to count sleeping rooms that it received (from someone other than the group representative) attrition damages for as "unsold" sleeping rooms and it's not reasonable for a hotel to say that it had X sleeping rooms in its inventory when it really only had Y. That's why it's important to use net numbers for both occupancy and room availability and that's what the *Net Inventory* provision is for.

The following table illustrates, as an example, the difference in an attrition situation where there is and isn't a *Net Inventory* provision under an attrition provision that includes "last room sold." The example is a little flawed in that it considers attrition on a per-night basis (a group representative should try to get attrition damages to be based on cumulative room nights), but it gets the point across. In the example, the group representative booked a certain number of rooms for Monday, Tuesday, and Wednesday (50, 100, 50). Unfortunately, the group's pick-up for those nights wasn't so hot (34, 75, 30). This leaves a gap (slippage) between the contracted room block and the pick-up for each of the room nights (gap of 16, 25, 20). Assuming a typical 80% attrition provision that permits 20% slippage, attrition damages must be paid on the difference, if any, between the room nights not used and the permitted slippage (6, 5, 10). Without a *Net Inventory* provision and after calculating occupancy at the hotel (90, 90, 95), the unsold room nights for each night are greater than the room nights subject to attrition. Thus, the hotel clearly didn't resell any of the group's sleeping rooms and the group representative owes attrition damages for 21 room nights (6 + 5 + 10).

With a *Net Inventory* provision, the sleeping rooms that the hotel was renovating (5, 5, 5) are removed from the gross hotel sleeping room inventory (105, 105, 105) to calculate net inventory (100, 100, 100). Further, there were some sleeping rooms that were vacant but that another group had paid attrition damages for (10, 5, 0). Those sleeping rooms are considered "occupied" for purposes of the *Net Inventory* provision and are then added to actual occupancy (90, 90, 95) to come up with the total occupancy. That means that the hotel was fully occupied on Monday (0 unsold room nights), and had only 5 unsold sleeping rooms on Tuesday and Wednesday. Thus, the hotel sold all of the group's 6 sleeping rooms that were subject to attrition on Monday, didn't sell any of the group's 5 sleeping rooms on Tuesday, and sold 5 of the 10 group's sleeping rooms that were subject to attrition on Wednesday. Now, the group representative only owes attrition damages for 10 room nights (0 + 5 +5) versus 21 room nights.

	M	T	W
Room Block	50	100	50
Pick-Up	34	75	30
Attrition Damages			
Room Nights Not Used	16	25	20
Permitted Slippage (20%)	10	20	10
Room Nights Subject to Attrition	6	5	10

Without *Net Inventory* Provision

	M	T	W
Hotel Sleeping Room Inventory	105	105	105
Less Occupancy	90	90	95
Equals Unsold Room Nights	15	15	10
Room Nights Subject to Attrition	6	5	10

With *Net Inventory* Provision

	M	T	W
Hotel Sleeping Room Inventory	105	105	105
Less Rooms Being Renovated	5	5	5
Equals Net Inventory	100	100	100
Less Occupancy	90	90	95
Less Unsold Rooms Other Group Paid Attrition On	10	5	0
Equals Unsold Room Nights	0	5	5
Room Nights Subject to Attrition	0	5	5

The *Net Inventory* provision removes: ❶ (a) sleeping rooms that cannot be sold by a hotel as a result of being out of order, under renovation, or due to repair, (b) sleeping rooms that a hotel chooses to not make available for sale because of preferred relationships (why should their preferred relationships impact a group representative negatively?), (c) sleeping rooms that the hotel decided to give away for free, and (d) unsold suites (because it's not uncommon for suites to go vacant). That's the inventory side of the equation. On the occupancy side, ❷ all sleeping rooms that a hotel was already compensated for (no matter the basis for compensation or the form of compensation) are counted as sold.

Hotels are generally accepting of this provision for purposes of the *Lowest Room Rate; Published or Confirmed* provision, but won't nearly be as accepting of it when they start thinking about its effect on attrition damages. That's one reason why the *Net Inventory* provision is located at this point in the MHSA and not in or around the *Attrition* provision—I don't want to attract attention to it. However, hotels do occasionally figure out the provision's effect on attrition damages and object. They do understand the reasonableness of the provision, so the group representative must push back hard on any objections and explain why not including the provision would allow the hotel to double-dip and, therefore, wouldn't be fair. A group representative can give on (d) since it's not that significant to affect the overall impact of the provision, but the group representative should fight for everything else. A group representative just needs to be able to explain the provision, which is why I've gone a little overboard in trying to explain it here.

> 5.2   <u>Net Inventory</u>. ❶Hotel shall not include in its guestroom inventory during the In-House Dates: (a) all guestrooms "out of order," being renovated, or repaired; (b) guestrooms held for last sale to Hotel's preferred customers; (c) "comped" guestrooms to third-parties; and, (d) any unsold suites. The resulting total of guestrooms shall be Hotel's Net Inventory. In addition, ❷all guestrooms billed to other groups or individuals for attrition, cancellation, or no-shows will be counted as sold guestrooms.

Dishonored Reservations

Imagine, after a long and arduous multi-leg flight, a group representative finally straggles into the lobby of the hotel where the group representative had made a reservation. The attractive, smiling clerk at the front desk welcomes the group representative, gathers the group representative's information, starts punching keys on the computer in front of her—and then frowns. What happens next is a part of the clerk's job that she hates the most. "Sir," she says, "We have you in the system but we don't have a room available for you. I'm sorry." It takes a second for the group representative's fatigued brain to register what the hotel employee just said, and another second for his blood pressure to start climbing...

A group representative doesn't want this to happen to him or her, but especially not to an attendee. But it can, it has, and it may happen again. For various reasons, such as over-booking, hotels must decline guests—even those who have confirmed reservations. When this happens, which is commonly referred to as "walking" an attendee or dishonoring a reservation, a group representative wants to make sure the hotel is on the hook to provide some sort of concession—which is the purpose of the *Dishonored Reservations* provision. The provision requires that, if a hotel dishonors a reservation, the walked attendee receives (a) through (e) and the group representative receives credit (f) toward the room block and toward comp rooms. Hotels rarely object to this provision, and, when they do, it's usually to eliminate or expand the one-mile limitation described in (a) and to somehow bound the hotel's exposure to (c) the cost of long-distance telephone calls (e.g.., by only agreeing to pay for one call).

6.   Dishonored Reservations. If Hotel is unable to provide a Guestroom to an Attendee holding a reservation, Hotel shall provide to each such Attendee, as the case may be, the following without charge: (a) comparable or superior guestroom (including room rate, tax, resort fee, and occupancy charge) at a comparable or superior Hotel no more than one (1) mile from the Meeting Location for the period of the applicable Guestroom Reservation; (b) transportation by the most convenient and efficient means possible for the Attendee or

Customer to and from the substitute Hotel; (c) long-distance telephone calls; (d) listing of Attendee's name with the Hotel switchboard or answering service, in order to facilitate the transfer of phone calls made to Attendee at Hotel to the alternate property; (e) its best efforts to bring the Attendee back after the first night and offer to relocate displaced Attendee back to Hotel; and, (f) credit Customer for any Attendees displaced toward the Room Pick-Up and toward the Comp Room credit.

Billing and Payment

The *Billing and Payment* section of the MHSA is limited to the mechanics of how and when payment is made, but, as one might expect, this section tends to get well-warranted scrutiny from hotels because it involves money. The provisions in this section of the MHSA are what hotels typically see from groups and the language is mostly innocuous. For that reason, the following MHSA provisions aren't discussed in this section because they're rarely, if ever, questioned or challenged: *Deposits, Additional Concessions, Exemption from Taxes.* However, there are some points of contention and other items worth worthy of discussion in this section.

Attendee Charges

The purpose of the *Attendee Charges* provision is to ensure that a group representative doesn't get hit with attendee charges that the group representative wasn't supposed to incur. The provision goes on to clarify that, ❶ if the hotel can't recover payment from an attendee, the hotel can't come after the group representative for that attendee's non-payment.

> 7.1 <u>Attendee Charges</u>. Except for individuals specifically designated by Customer in writing to Hotel, all Guestroom charges, taxes, incidentals, and all other charges and

expenses will be charged to Attendees. ❶Customer is not and shall not be liable for the non-payment by an Attendee for any such charges.

Master Account

The master account is established for a group representative to charge items that are intended to be paid for by the group representative and not by the attendees, such as food and beverage, audio-visual, and décor. The establishment of a master account frequently requires a credit application / authorization and security in the form of a credit card in lieu of a deposit (which is helpful for a group representative who may not have enough immediate funds for a deposit and who is relying on attendee registration fees to help defray expenses associated with a meeting). Hotels sometimes ignore the *Attendees Charges* provision or mistakenly charge the master account with attendee-originated charges and then—instead of reversing the charges and seeking payment from the appropriate attendee—demand that the group representative pay for the charges. To keep a group representative from being hit with such unanticipated charges, the provision states that the group representative and the hotel will review (preferably daily) charges posted to the master account and ❶ any category of charges (such as attendee room rates) not approved by the group representative will not be charged by the hotel to the master account. If such charges make their way to the master account, the group representative is entitled to "short-pay" the hotel invoice.

7.2   <u>Master Account</u>. For each <u>Exhibit A</u>, Hotel shall establish one or more accounts for charges to Customer (collectively and individually the "Master Account"). Customer will provide Hotel with appropriate credit information, in a form determined by Customer, to establish direct billing for the Master Account. Upon credit approval from Hotel, which approval shall not be unreasonably denied, withheld, or conditioned, a Master Account will be established for authorized charges. All charges to be posted to the Master Account will be reviewed by Hotel and the Customer Meeting Manager identified on an <u>Exhibit A</u>. ❶Only those categories of charges approved in writing by the Meeting Manager may be charged to the Master Account.

Payment

In my experience, I've been surprised to find that hotels aren't particularly timely about seeking payment. And, when a hotel finally does seek payment via an invoice, documentation to support the invoice is typically lacking. So, to help move hotels along in terms of invoicing, this provision ❶ requires that the hotel send its invoice and supporting documentation (such as a room pick-up report) within 30-days following the end of the associated meeting. The provision also implies ❷ that the hotel won't get paid until it provides a group representative with all of the supporting documentation the group representative needs, because payment is triggered upon "receipt" of such documentation. It doesn't mean a group representative doesn't have to pay if the hotel submits an invoice late, but the language at least gives the group representative the ability to complain to the hotel that it agreed to promptly invoice the group representative and failed to provide the group representative with the documentation that he or she needs to verify the charges. However, ❷ a group representative doesn't have to pay any charges on the invoice that the group representative disputes. Many hotels will want to tie "reasonableness" to the ability of a group representative to dispute charges, and that's perfectly alright. One part of the provision is a little unusual and that's the ❸ "convenience fee" part. I've actually had hotels try to charge me an extra percentage when I attempted to use a credit card to pay my master account. The hotels that have pulled this on me in the past argued that my use of the credit card was a "convenience" (it supposedly saves me the cost of having to cut and send the hotel a check) and that the hotel has to pay a credit card processing transaction fee for my convenience. Well, that's just tough, and hotels seem to be ready and willing to accept credit cards from attendees for their individual "master accounts." Hotels call it "convenience," I call it "baloney," and now the MHSA expressly prohibits convenience fees.

> 7.3   Payment. ❶Hotel agrees to submit charges associated with the applicable Meeting with all supporting or back-up documentation such as a post-meeting Room Pick-Up report within thirty (30) days of completion of a Meeting. Customer agrees to pay any ❷undisputed charges within sixty (60) days of receipt of invoice and post-Meeting Room Pick-Up and Meeting expenditure reports from Hotel. In the event there is any charge in dispute, only that charge in dispute shall be withheld from payment. ❸Customer shall not be required to pay a fee, such as a "convenience fee," should Customer choose to use a credit card to pay any charges. Invoices submitted by Hotel must specify an invoice number.

Service Charges / Gratuities

Definitions of gratuity almost universally include that a gratuity is something given *voluntarily*. Despite that, hotels frequently specify in their contracts that gratuities are mandatory. Certainly, where a hotel's wait staff or service employee performs at or above expectations, he or she is deserving of a gratuity. In that sense, gratuities should reward employees for performance and shouldn't be used by hotels as a salary substitute. This provision ❶ doesn't disallow mandatory gratuities (also called "service charges") on food and beverage or sleeping rooms, it just requires that the hotel be up front with them and that the mandatory gratuities be specified in an Exhibit A to the MHSA in order to be charged. In other words, unless otherwise specified in an Exhibit A to the MHSA, a hotel can't surprise a group representative with service charges or mandatory gratuities.

> 7.5 <u>Service Charges / Gratuities</u>. Gratuities, if any, shall be provided to deserving employees of Hotel in the sole discretion of Customer and Attendees. ❶Unless otherwise specified in an <u>Exhibit A</u>, under no circumstances will Hotel charge a mandatory gratuity or service charge on F&B or Guestrooms unless otherwise mandated by union agreement, provided such mandatory gratuity is disclosed in an <u>Exhibit A</u>.

No Other Fees

This provision is the catch-all for "no other fees"—just in case the MHSA misses some new fee that a hotel dreams up, this provision provides protection for a group representative and attendees. First, ❶ a hotel can't charge any fees that aren't specified in an Exhibit A to the MHSA unless a group representative agrees otherwise. Second, ❷ a hotel can't charge fees to one group that it's not charging to another group. An example of this I've seen in the past is where my attendees were being charged a resort fee that I discovered other guests weren't being charged with. Shame on me for not negotiating that resort fee out, but that was one of the reasons I drafted this provision.

Finally, and this part can become especially contentious, ❸ a hotel can't charge a fee (unless otherwise specified in an Exhibit A to the MHSA) for not utilizing those contractors recommended or required by the hotel. A common example of this is when a hotel charges a "patch fee" or "technical allocation" for a group's use of its own audio-visual contractor (instead of using the hotel's in-house or exclusive audio-visual contractor). The fee is also referred to by industry insiders in the slang as a "corkage fee." Patching means that a group's contractor connects (or patches in) external devices (such as microphones) into the internal system (e.g., the in-wall cabling) of a hotel. Sometimes the fee can be outrageous—in the thousands of dollars per day. Hotels have different excuses for charging the fee, usually centered around that a group's contractor is using the infrastructure of a hotel (usually mere cabling). One excuse is that a hotel needs to be compensated for the use of its infrastructure. Another excuse is that the fee is to help pay for any damage that a group's contractor may cause to a hotel's infrastructure. That's hogwash. The reason a hotel is charging a patch-in fee is to coerce the group representative into using the hotel's contractor—of which the hotel gets a big cut of the contractor's inflated rates. In my personal experience, using an in-house audio-visual contractor usually means paying anywhere from 25% to 50% more overall for the audio-visual service than I would have if I had used my own contractor. A hotel usually fails to mention that—as compared to external audio-visual contractors—the hotel's in-house contractor usually employs less experienced technicians, has less of a selection of equipment, and won't be dedicated to a group. If a hotel attempts to add such a fee, a group representative should refuse to allow it and the hotel will almost always cave. If a hotel doesn't cave, the group representative should get his or her audio-visual contractor to "make some calls" to the hotel about the hotel's fee and the demand for such a fee will usually evaporate.

7.8   No Other Fees. ❶ Hotel shall impose no fees for Services utilized by Customer, including, but not limited to, mandatory charges on Guestrooms, other than those specified in an

Exhibit A, without the prior written consent of Customer. ❷ If such fees are specified in an Exhibit A or subsequently agreed to by Customer, such fees shall not be imposed unless they are imposed on all guests using Hotel during the In-House Dates. Unless expressly stated to the contrary in an Exhibit A, ❸ Hotel shall impose no fees should Customer utilize contractors other than those recommended by Hotel to provide services such as audio-visual, decorating, security, and transportation.

Food and Beverage

From a contracting perspective, food and beverage is mostly straightforward. The ❶ details of any food and beverage to be provided by a hotel or a hotel contractor should be clearly specified in some sort of event schedule or description—commonly called a "program" or "program of events"—as a part of (or as an attachment to) an Exhibit A to the MHSA. The *Function Space Requirements* section contains an example program of events.[4]

Unlike room rates, which go up and down with the economy, or other factors which influence demand (such as pandemics), food and beverage prices seem to only go up. Considering that certain meetings are planned significantly in advance—in some cases, years—meeting planners have sought to minimize cost variability and improve budget predictability by asking hotels to lock-in food and beverage prices. Because there's enough margin in food and beverage prices (usually 20% or more of a profit margin) to mitigate any inflationary effects on a hotel's costs, most hotels have traditionally been willing to lock-in prices. To that end, the provision specifies that ❷ a hotel will guarantee the

---

[4] Note that "function" and "event" are frequently used to mean the same thing. An "event" is also a "function" for purposes of function space, food and beverage, and the like.

menu (meaning no bait-and-switch) and the menu prices at whatever was negotiated at the time the Exhibit A to the MHSA was executed. Occasionally, and particularly if the meeting will not be held within the next year or so, hotels want to redline this part of the provision to allow for some sort of escalation, such as "Hotel agrees to guarantee that the menu prices will not exceed five-percent (5%) per year." If a group representative can't get a hotel to back-down from this requested change and the hotel won't lock-in menu prices, refuse to redline the MHSA and instead include the menu price escalation limit in the Exhibit A to the MHSA.

While hotels will occasionally object to locking-in menu prices, hotels rarely object to guaranteeing the menu. If a hotel does object, it's unreasonable. If a hotel in Chattanooga, Tennessee has "The Pickle Barrel Club Sandwich" one year, there's no reason why the hotel's accomplished kitchen staff can't produce the same menu item two years later. If a hotel is obstinate about not guaranteeing its menu, the group representative should ask to speak with the hotel's executive chef who will likely tell the group representative that the chef can indeed produce the same menu regardless of the passage of time.

Similar to sleeping rooms, the concept of attrition is frequently applied by hotels to food and beverage. As a general concept in the hotel industry, attrition is merely a shortfall between something projected and that same something actualized. The concept can be as easily applied to food and beverage as it is to sleeping rooms. Not surprisingly, when food and beverage attrition occurs, hotels want to be made whole and, correspondingly, want liquidated damages for attrition to be specified in their contracts. However, if a group representative has sufficient negotiation leverage, attrition damages can be avoided. Considering that it's best to operate from a position of power, the version of the *Food and*

Beverage section that is contained in the MHSA specifies *no* attrition damages. The provision ❹ starts by indicating that it applies unless the corresponding Exhibit A to the MHSA specifies otherwise. It's very possible that a group representative has enough negotiation leverage for one meeting for which he or she can refuse food and beverage attrition damages and for another, subsequent meeting, the group representative may have to concede on attrition damages. The following provision provides that flexibility because the Exhibit A to the MHSA can include food and beverage attrition damages and not be in conflict with the overall *Food and Beverage* provision contained as-is in the MHSA. Another reason for the qualifier is to convince a hotel at the time the MHSA is being negotiated that the hotel isn't giving up on their right to food and beverage attrition damages in perpetuity—only for the meeting that is being negotiated at the same time the overall MHSA is being negotiated. Jumping ahead, the provision applies when a food and beverage function has ❺ less attendees than estimated or ❻ is cancelled. In either of those situations, ❼ the hotel isn't entitled to any remedy of any sort for attrition, ❽ including withdrawing previously granted concessions. Alternative language, which does specify attrition damages, can be found at the end of this section.

Some hotels charge for canned or bottled beverages that were ordered as a part of a food and beverage function but went unopened. The unopened beverages are then resold by the hotel to another group. The last part of the provision addresses this, and ❾ requires that bottled or canned beverages be provided on a "consumption basis" and that there is no charge for unopened beverages. Hotels that are honest and reasonable don't ask for this to be deleted—ones that aren't do ask.

8.　　**Food and Beverage.**　❶Where indicated in an <u>Exhibit A</u>, Hotel shall provide food and beverage ("F&B") to Customer as specified therein and in accordance with the following.

　　8.1　　<u>Fee for F&B</u>.　❷Hotel agrees to guarantee the menu and menu prices for the effective date indicated in an <u>Exhibit A</u>.

　　8.2　　<u>Attendee Minimum</u>. Unless otherwise specified in an <u>Exhibit A</u>, ❸for each F&B function, Customer shall provide Hotel with the estimated minimum number of Attendees no less than eight (8) hours in advance of the function and Hotel shall set for up to five percent (5%) over the estimated minimum number of Attendees, the specific percentage as directed by Customer.

　　8.3　　<u>F&B Attrition; Cancellation</u>.　❹Unless otherwise specified in an <u>Exhibit A</u>, Hotel acknowledges and agrees that it is ❼not entitled to any fees, charges, damages, or other forms of remedy, including the ❽withdrawal of any concessions by Hotel granted under this Agreement or an <u>Exhibit A</u> ❺where Customer holds a F&B function described in an <u>Exhibit A</u> but has less than the estimated number of Attendees or ❻where Customer cancels any F&B function described in an <u>Exhibit A</u>.

　　8.4　　<u>Beverage-Consumption Basis</u>.　❾All charges for beverages, including alcoholic beverages, provided by Hotel, if any, will be on a consumption basis with no charge for unopened bottles or cans. Hotel shall allow the Meeting Manager to be present when the consumption is being accounted for, or, at the request of Customer, provide a written accounting of the consumption.

A hotel may balk at not having any remedy if a group representative requests food and beverage as a part of a meeting and then cancels the food and beverage or the attendees don't materialize. It's debatable whether the hotel's position is legitimate or not. If a group representative notifies the hotel six-months in advance of the meeting that the food and beverage needs to be reduced or cancelled, the hotel hasn't purchased the food and beverage and hasn't suffered any damages (other than anticipated lost profits). On the other hand, if the hotel gets notice 24-hours before the food and beverage function is scheduled to be held, the hotel probably will suffer damages of some sort. The following, alternative language provides for food and beverage attrition damages. The provision is structured to consider food and beverage revenue over the entire meeting and not on a per-function basis. This gives a group representative the flexibility to modify (including reducing) food and beverage requirements on a per-function basis and not pay attrition damages provided that the group representative meets the minimum revenue amount for the total of the meeting.

If a group generates ❶ less than 80% of ❷ the minimum dollar amount of food and beverage that is specified in an Exhibit A to the MHSA, inclusive of service charges and other charges paid by the group that is associated with the food and beverage, the hotel is ❸ entitled to (but isn't compelled) to charge attrition damages. Note that the dollar amount of food and beverage doesn't include sponsor paid-for food and beverage when determining the minimum and that sponsor paid-for food and beverage *is* included for purposes of calculating the actualized food and beverage revenue. Thus, any sponsor paid-for food and beverage advantages a group representative in deflecting possible attrition damages. The attrition damages ❹ equal the difference between the food and beverage revenue that the group and its sponsors, if any, actually generated and 80% ❺ multiplied by 20%, which represents the lost profits. Hotels typically argue that they're out "100%" because they incurred costs associated with the food and beverage that they can't recoup (because they dispose of the un-used food and beverage) and they lost their expected profits. If a group representative negotiates anything less than 100%, he or she is doing well.

8.3   <u>F&B Attrition; Cancellation</u>. ❷Customer shall generate the minimum dollar amount of F&B revenue specified in an <u>Exhibit A</u>, if so specified, which shall include service charges and other charges associated with the F&B. Where the actual dollar amount of F&B revenue generated by Customer and its sponsors, if any, is ❶less than eighty percent (80%) of the minimum dollar amount of F&B revenue specified in an <u>Exhibit A</u>, Hotel is ❸entitled to request that Customer pay to Hotel attrition damages, as liquidated damages and not as a penalty. The attrition damages, if any, shall be ❹equal to the difference between the actual dollar amount of F&B revenue generated by Customer and its sponsors and eighty percent (80%) of the minimum dollar amount of F&B revenue specified in an <u>Exhibit A</u> ❺multiplied by twenty percent (20%). The attrition damages, if any, shall be non-taxable unless otherwise prohibited by law.

Function Space Requirements

Hotel function space such as ballrooms and breakout rooms is an integral part of most meetings held by groups. Clearly, if a hotel doesn't have function space which fits a wide variety of needs by a wide variety of groups, that hotel is going to have trouble filling its sleeping rooms with anything other than transient traffic. Second to destination, a hotel's function space is its most important asset for drawing business, filling its sleeping rooms, selling food and beverage, and driving ancillary revenue. Unless a group representative has the only group in a hotel over the meeting dates, the group representative is likely to be in competition for function space. In other words, function space is a hot commodity and it is as important to negotiate as room block and room rates.

To ensure that both a group representative and a hotel understand what function space is needed and when, and to avoid any unfortunate surprises, it's critical to communicate what events will be occurring, when they will be occurring, and in what function space. The typical method to ensure this common understanding is to ❶ include (or attach) a program of events (POE) as a part of an Exhibit A to the MHSA. A table is usually the best format for a POE. The following list is a simple example of the most basic of information needed for a POE:

- Event Name
- Date of Event
- Day of Event (helpful to have as a verification of the date)
- Start Time of Event
- End Time of Event
- Food and Beverage (if any)
- Audio-Visual (if any)
- Number of Attendees
- Room Set
- Room Name (include the name of the function space that has been assigned, if available at the time that the Exhibit A to the MHSA is being negotiated)

Once the MHSA and Exhibit A to the MHSA have been executed, a group representative should require that the hotel confirm the function space requirements (and all other associated requirements such as room sets) by providing the group representative with a banquet event order (BEO). A group representative should review each BEO carefully to ensure it matches the POE. BEOs also typically include anticipated charges, so a group representative should verify that the charges are appropriate before he or she acknowledges that a BEO is correct.

As a rule of thumb, a hotel will provide a group with roughly the same percentage of complimentary function space as the group occupies in sleeping rooms. For example, if a hotel has 1,000 sleeping rooms in its inventory and a group's room block is 500 sleeping rooms, the group representative will get *at least* 50% of the function space—on a *complimentary* basis. If a group's room block is 80% or more of a hotel's inventory, the group representative can expect up to 100% of the hotel's function space on a complimentary basis depending on whether there is another small group in the hotel or the remaining sleeping rooms in the hotel's inventory is allocated to transient traffic. The *Function Space Requirements* provision contemplates that ❷ all function space provided by a hotel for a group's meeting will be complimentary. It's unacceptable for a hotel to charge for function space unless there's a significant disparity in the room block-to-function space ratio.

Because function space is a hot commodity, hotels seek to maximize its use and its revenue-generation. It's not uncommon for a hotel to provide "rent-free" function space for a group during the day, then rent the same function space out in the evening for a banquet event unaffiliated with the group (such as a wedding party), and then have the same group from the day prior occupying the same function space the very next morning. Thus, there's a constant flow of groups in and out of function space and, inevitably, conflicts occur. Hotels can "accidentally" over-book function space, with two groups having overlapping times. A group can run late in vacating function space and cut into the next group's time. It's not uncommon for these conflicts to occur.

A "24-hour space hold" eliminates these conflicts, especially when a group representative needs the function space for multiple days. A group which has a 24-hour space hold on function space doesn't have to worry about another group or banquet event "stepping" on their time in the function space. A 24-hour space hold also eliminates the need for a group to set-up and break-down the function space each day (which takes time and money to do). Another benefit is that a group with a space hold has the flexibility to change the starting and ending times of events without having to worry about synching those times with function space availability. Hotels obviously don't like 24-hour space holds because, when a group isn't using the function space, the function space essentially becomes storage space and the hotel is precluded from obtaining additional revenue from the function space through rentals and food and beverage. A hotel will argue that its staff will tear-down the function space and set it back up exactly the way it was left. Clearly, that argument doesn't make sense when a group representative has the group's own contractors providing meeting support, such as setting up the audio/visual, because the group representative will end up paying for that additional labor. But let's say for the sake of argument that a group representative is using a hotel's staff exclusively and it won't cost him or her anything extra for daily set-up and tear-down. Should the group representative forget about the 24-hour space hold requirement and trust that the function space will be available when he or she needs it and that the function space will be set-up how it was when it was torn down? I did—a few times. Each time, I was sorry. One time I was hassled endlessly by a hotel to vacate the function space earlier than my event had been contracted to end because the hotel wanted extra time to set up for the next event in the function space. Another time the group that was in before my event didn't vacate when they were scheduled to vacate and caused my event to start late. Another time the hotel failed to re-set my function space correctly after the prior event which caused my event to start late. Never again for me. If a group representative buys into trusting a hotel and agrees to forego a 24-hour space hold, he or she should ask that the hotel include liquidated damages in the MHSA for each hour that the event starts late due to the function space not being available or not being set-up correctly. But, if a group representative is like me, he or she will want the ❸ 24-hour space hold that's specified in the *Function Space Requirements* provision. Lastly, with hotels trying to find revenue everywhere—including charging for room sets even if the group representative has no-charge function space—the provision stipulates ❹ that there is no charge for any function space set-up.

9. Function Space Requirements. If meeting or other function space requirements (collectively "Function Space") are specified in an Exhibit A or attached thereto and identified as the ❶Program of Events ("POE"), all such Function Space shall be ❷complimentary and ❸held on a twenty-four (24) hour space hold basis. In addition, there will be ❹no charge for Function Space setup if specified on an Exhibit A.

Function Space Changes; Hotel

As a part of maximizing its function space revenue, it's not uncommon for a hotel to shuffle function space assignments. I've been on the short end of such last-minute re-assignments in the past, and have been forced into function space that either didn't really work for my function or that was just down-right crummy compared to the function space that I had originally been assigned. I vowed I wouldn't let that happen again, and I added the *Function Space Changes; Hotel* provision to the MHSA. It specifies that a ❶ hotel cannot unilaterally change function space assignment. This implies that a group representative has been assigned function space—if that's not the case, the group representative shouldn't rely on the hotel to put the group into the hotel's best function space. If the group representative has been assigned function space, he or she should be sure to include the function space assignment in the POE. I've also been in situations where a hotel wanted to re-assign my previously-assigned function space and, instead of doing it unilaterally, the hotel requested the re-assignment. In some cases, because I was being disadvantaged, I had to say no. In other cases, I wasn't being disadvantaged but I had already printed signage and included the name of the function space in attendee literature. Surprisingly, in those situations, some (albeit very few) hotels have declined to pick-up the responsibility (and costs) associated with new signage and the like. To address this, I included language in the provision that requires the ❷ hotel to take on financial responsibility to notify attendees of the re-assignment if I do agree to a re-assignment.

> 9.1 <u>Function Space Changes; Hotel</u>. ❶Hotel shall not unilaterally change Function Space assignments. ❷Where Customer agrees to Hotel's request for a change in Function Space assignments, Hotel will assume the financial responsibility for such items as printing program agenda and signs, as may be needed to timely convey such change in assignment to Attendees.

Function Space for Storage

When requesting function space, a group representative is typically very diligent about ensuring that each function has assigned function space, a defined room set, food and beverage, audio-visual, and the like—all being typically described in a POE. What tends to get forgotten in terms of function space is the need for storage. Any reasonably sizeable group is going to need storage space for one thing or another, so it's important to identify those storage space needs. The *Function Space for Storage* provision is as much a reminder to a group representative to be sure to request function space for storage as it is anything else. The provision does, of course, serve as more than a reminder by specifying that ❶ any storage space provided by the hotel is without charge. The provision stipulates that the storage space will be provided over the in-house dates or for those dates specified in an Exhibit A to the MHSA. The reason for any dates other than in-house dates is to account for situations where a substantial amount of materials needs to be shipped to a hotel in advance of a meeting. In some situations I've experienced, the hotel wanted to be paid for labor associated with delivering my previously-shipped materials from their loading dock (or receiving area) to the function space—even when it was only a few boxes. Other times, when I've used outside contractors to assist in transporting materials (usually in exhibitor situations), the hotel wanted to charge a fee for allowing me to use their loading dock and freight elevator. If I have a ton of stuff that needs to be delivered, I can see a hotel wanting to be compensated for it—but I never have a ton of stuff without having my own staff (either my employees or contractors) available to transport it. That's the reason why the provision goes on to state ❷ a hotel has the obligation to assist in moving materials and won't charge fees for the group representative's use of his or her own staff. Some hotels disagree with having to provide no-charge moving services without knowing the scope, so I'll occasionally throw "Unless otherwise specified in an Exhibit A" in front of the language to appease the hotel.

9.2   Function Space for Storage. ❶There will be no charge for storing Customer's or Attendees' Meeting materials, publications, and equipment for the In-House Dates or as otherwise indicated in an Exhibit A. ❷Hotel staff shall assist in moving such materials, publications, and equipment at no charge to Customer or Attendees, and no fees will be imposed upon Customer for use of outside contractors for such purpose, if any.

Function Space Supplies

Function space is empty space. A group representative "fills" the function space with the needs specific to the function, such as chairs and tables. Other supplies are frequently needed to support the function in the function space, such as flip-charts and markers. Many hotels provide such supplies on a complimentary basis (and some do not). This provision requires that a ❶ hotel provide certain supplies (including chairs and tables) necessary to accommodate attendees in the function space and that the supplies be provided on a complimentary basis, ❷ including set-up, ❸ unless the supplies required are unusual. ❹ If the supplies or function space arrangement would cause unusual costs to a hotel such that it would be unreasonable for the supplies to be provided on a complimentary basis, the hotel is required to notify the group representative so that he or she can make a decision as to whether the group representative is willing to pay the costs or willing to change his or her requirements such that no unusual costs would be incurred. In addition to the foregoing, a ❺ hotel is obligated to provide a wired microphone and amplification equipment without charge, which is a common concession. Another common function space concession is for a ❻ hotel to provide complimentary telephones in the "meeting office" of a group representative as well as in the registration area for attendees. One catch in the past was that hotels would charge an "access" fee on top of any telephone calls—the provision prohibits this but does acknowledge that any long distance fees are to be charged to the master account.

> 9.3 <u>Function Space Supplies</u>. ❶Hotel shall provide, at no charge, Function Space supplies, including, but not limited to, chairs, tables, water, ice, blackboards, and easels with pads and markers, pads and pencils / pens, etc., in a

quantity sufficient to accommodate all anticipated Attendees related to the Function Space. ❷ Hotel shall impose no charge for Function Space set-up. ❸ This complimentary arrangement does not include unusual Function Space arrangements that would exhaust Hotel's normal in-house supplies to the point of requiring rental of additional supplies to accommodate Customer's or Attendees' needs. ❹ In the event of such an occurrence, Hotel shall notify Customer or Attendee and shall afford Customer or Attendee the opportunity to pay the rental cost for additional supplies or change the Function Space room arrangements to a more normal format, avoiding extra rental. ❺ In addition to the foregoing, Hotel shall provide one (1) microphone and amplification equipment in each Function Space at no cost to Customer or Attendee, and a ❻ complimentary telephone at Customer's Attendees' registration area and meeting office, if such Function Space is specified in an Exhibit A, with no access charges for local or long-distance telephone calls; long distance charges, if any, shall be billed to the Master Account.

Function Space Based on Room Block

Occasionally, hotels will want what is essentially the equivalent of a food and beverage or sleeping room attrition provision for function space. This is normally done through a complicated sliding-scale function space rental formula based on room pick-up. Based on the sliding-scale, if a group doesn't pick-up enough sleeping rooms, the group representative will have to pay the indicated rental fee for the function space. The less sleeping rooms that are picked up directly translate into a higher function space rental fee. Not only is this nit-picking by a hotel, it's double-dipping when the MHSA or Exhibit A to the MHSA includes a sleeping room attrition damages provision. In that case, where a hotel is being made whole through sleeping room attrition damages, the hotel is being unjustly enriched by also receiving a function space rental fee: the hotel had provided complimentary function space based on occupied sleeping rooms and attrition damages, when paid, equate to a head in a bed—so the hotel is in the same original position and is therefore whole. When attempting to account for this double-dipping within the sliding-scale formula so that the function space rental is only based on sleeping rooms not picked up within the permitted slippage, the sliding-scale formula becomes even more complicated. My solution is to absolutely refuse (via the following provision) any sort of sliding scale or any other form of remuneration for function space even if I'm not subject to a sleeping room attrition damages provision. If a hotel doesn't have enough flexibility to allow some sort of margin within the room block-to-function space ratio and instead demands a damages-based sliding-scale formula, that tells me the hotel is caught up in its own short-sighted yield management bureaucracy and that I should find an alternative hotel for my group. My tolerance for a sliding-scale formula is limited. If a hotel proposes it, I refuse it, and if the hotel insists, that's usually the end of the negotiations because there are many other hotels that are more flexible and don't require a mathematically-complex damages-based formula for function space.

> 9.4 <u>Function Space Based on Room Block</u>. Where "no-charge" Function Space is based on the Room Block and Customer has not achieved the Room Block, in no case shall Customer be liable to pay to Hotel a fee for such Function Space.

Internet Access

Internet access in a hotel's function space has been a very profitable source of revenue for hotels over the past few years. I've seen particularly greedy hotels charge hundreds of dollars per day to their captive groups for wired Internet "drops." That's outrageous, but, fortunately, wireless Internet is becoming more ubiquitous and even the greediest of hotels are too ashamed to charge extraordinary prices for wireless Internet in their function space (because a hotel can no longer justify the charges by claiming that it had to use labor to set up the access—which is a hotel's justification for wired drops). The following provision specifies that ❶ wireless Internet access in a hotel's function space be provided without charge. If a hotel doesn't yet have wireless Internet access in its function space, it's more likely that the hotel is afraid to lose its Internet revenue than for technical reasons. Regardless of the reason, the provision also specifies that ❷ the first five drops for Internet access are provided without charge and that subsequent drops are discounted. As "free" wireless Internet proliferates, this provision is becoming increasingly unnecessary. However, there are hotels still stuck in the last century that push back on having to provide wired Internet drops without charge or at a discounted rate.

> 9.5   <u>Internet Access</u>.   Where Hotel offers wireless Internet access in Hotel's Function Space, ❶Hotel agrees to provide such wireless Internet access to Customer over the In-House Dates without additional charge.   ❷For "wired" Internet access, Hotel agrees to provide "drops" for Internet access on a basis of the first five (5) drops at no charge and the remaining drops at fifty-percent (50%) of Hotel's lowest published rate, as specified in an <u>Exhibit A</u>.

Signage

Some hotels can be picky about signage; for example, certain hotels fret over placing sign stands on their beautiful, highly-polished natural stone floors. The following provision is to assuage the fears of such hotels and it merely points out that a group representative has the right to post signage for a meeting subject to a hotel's approval.

> 9.6 <u>Signage</u>. Unless otherwise specified in an <u>Exhibit A</u>, Hotel shall allow Customer or Attendee to post signs on the property concerning the Meeting. These signs shall be placed in locations and in a manner mutually agreeable to all parties.

Force Majeure; Excused Performance

The French-language term, "force majeure," literally means "greater force." More broadly, it refers to an event that is a result of the elements of nature or "acts of God," as opposed to an event caused by human behavior. A force majeure provision typically excuses a party from liability if some unforeseen event beyond the control of that party prevents it from performing its contractual obligations. Because contracting parties frequently desire to encompass excused performance for events that are caused by human behavior (such as wars), force majeure-type provisions are also referred to as "excused performance" or "excuse of performance" provisions. Whether or not a contract includes a force majeure and / or an excused performance provision, there are certain principles under contract law which may apply to a contract relating to excused performance: frustration of purpose, impossibility of performance, and impracticability of performance. Depending on the situation, one or more of these legal principles—again, even if not expressly included in a contract—may allow a party to terminate the contract or to discharge their obligated performance without liability. These legal principles are beyond the scope of this book, and may not be particularly relevant in that my general preference is to have certain legal principles express in my contract versus depending on contract law or legal doctrines which may or may not fill in contractual gaps. Consequently, and to the extent reasonable and fair, I expressly include elements of the legal principles of frustration, impossibility, and impracticability within the context of the *Force Majeure; Excuse of Performance* provision.

In the MHSA, excused performance *does* include certain human-caused events including events that are relevant to the hotel and travel industry. In the past couple of decades, there have been a variety of locally-based and global natural and human-caused events that have temporarily but adversely impacted the hotel and travel industries: Gulf War, 9/11, Iraq and Afghanistan wars, SARS, Katrina, H1N1, volcanic ash, Nashville floods, and the economy. While certain human-caused events, such as economic downturns, are arguably not appropriate to excuse the performance of either a hotel or a group, other events are entirely appropriate because the events materially frustrate the performance of a party.

Because a force majeure / excused performance provision provides an "out" for a group, it can be a hotly contested provision. However, the contention can be lessened by being more reasonable and more specific in including and describing the events that excuse non-performance. Another thing to keep in mind is that the provision is reciprocal and cuts both ways. A group representative doesn't want a hotel to use force majeure / excused performance as an out to dump the group if the hotel comes across better business.

A force majeure / excused performance provision is fact-specific and questions arise in terms of timing and the impact of a force majeure event. When can a party invoke the provision? What happens if the other party refutes that an event specified in the provision impacts performance? For example, after Hurricane Katrina, some hotels in New

Orleans were overly optimistic about the city's recovery and weren't accepting notices by groups to invoke force majeure. Groups were concerned whether New Orleans was really ready or not. Were there enough flights? Was there enough law enforcement? If groups invoked force majeure for their future meeting in New Orleans on the basis that they didn't think the city would be ready but hotels were arguing that the city would be ready, who's right? Unfortunately, even the most well-drafted force majeure / excused performance provision can't address every situation and a party must use its best business judgment in invoking the provision. In the case of New Orleans, if a group was scheduled to be there a few weeks after Hurricane Katrina, it likely would have been appropriate for a group to invoke force majeure regardless of what a hotel's position on "readiness" was. The hotel may have gone to court to enforce the contract, but it probably would have been an acceptable risk to the group because of the hotel's limited likelihood of prevailing on their claim. On the other hand, if the group was scheduled to be in New Orleans a year after Hurricane Katrina and the group attempts to invoke force majeure by notifying the hotel a week after the hurricane hit, that probably wouldn't be reasonable and would likely be legally risky. It comes down to what a group representative believes is in the best interests of the attendees and whether or not the position that the group representatives takes in invoking the force majeure event (and the timing of the force majeure event and the timing of the meeting) is legally defensible. "Legally defensible" would include the group representative having a reasonable and documented business continuity policy and plan relating to meetings, and the group representative having followed the policy and plan when electing to invoke force majeure or excused performance. Such a policy and plan would include factors that would play into a determination of force majeure or excused performance, such as attendee travel patterns, attendee demographics, meeting size, and proximity of the meeting to the force majeure event.

Excused Performance

While a force majeure / excused performance provision describes events that excuse a party's performance under a contract, it's unreasonable for the provision to be a catch-all of events, such as "any other cause beyond the control of a party," which allow a party to get out of a contract for nearly any reason. To reduce the potentially contentious nature of a force majeure / excused performance discussion in a negotiation, in my version of this provision, "less is more."

For the provision to be triggered, at least ❶ one of the described events[5] must occur or be imminent and written notice to the other party is required. Despite my "less is more" approach, hotels frequently attempt to restrict or further limit the events to some degree or another. The event most often changed by hotels is the event curtailing or interrupting travel, with the change almost always being limited to increasing the percentage of attendees impacted (usually to 50%) in order to trigger excused performance. Some of the objections from hotels are regionally-based. For example, hotels in Washington, D.C. often take issue with the "threatened" aspect of the terrorism force majeure event because the threat of terrorism is (according to the hotels) always imminent in the greater D.C. area. I would guess that hotels in New York City would have that same objection. Hotels in other areas generally don't take issue with the threat of terrorism force majeure event.

---

[5] The term "Force Majeure Event" is used in the MHSA even though it is technically incorrect in that it includes human-caused, and not just act of God, events.

Even though one of the described events does occur or is imminent, ❷ the event must make it inadvisable, impractical, or impossible for a party to perform in order for the performance to be excused. While "impossible" seems relatively clear, hotels occasionally take issue with "impractical" and more often take issue with "inadvisable." Their issue is that impractical and inadvisable are too subjective and that I could consider any force majeure event to have an impractical or inadvisable effect thereby excusing my performance. That's not a correct perspective, and with some education shared with a hotel, its concerns are typically allayed. That education involves an explanation of the reasonableness standard that must be applied. When determining where it is inadvisable, impractical, or impossible to perform, a commercially reasonable standard applies which requires objective consideration, made in good faith, from a commercial standpoint. In other words, when making my determination, I have to consider whether other reasonable business minds would come to the same conclusion and I have to make my determination in good faith. And a hotel is entitled to question how I came to my determination. In all likelihood, I would include the basis for my determination in the required written notice to the hotel. If it sounds like I didn't apply a reasonableness standard, the hotel can seek (through legal channels) to enforce my performance. It's common to include "illegal" along with inadvisable, impractical, and impossible but I exclude it on the basis that it's not likely to arise in reality (but it's an interesting academic legal discussion) and because, in my opinion, "impossible" includes "illegal" for purposes of hotel accommodations and purposes.

While a force majeure event may completely inhibit a party's ability to perform its contractual obligations, it also may only partially inhibit performance. The provision contemplates and ❸ permits partial performance or ❹ temporary suspension of performance. While it can be left up to the parties to agree upon what performance is still possible and when, there's an express provision, *Reduced-Sized Meetings*, that permits a meeting with reduced attendance or scope to be held without triggering any damages (e.g., attrition). Should a force majeure event be invoked, if there are any deposits or advance payments due back to a group representative from a hotel, the return of those monies is described in the *Deposits* provision.

10.1 <u>Excused Performance</u>. ❷Where any one or more of the following events (each, a "Force Majeure Event") make it inadvisable, impractical, or impossible for a party to perform, ❸in whole or in part, this Agreement or an <u>Exhibit A</u> as it relates to holding the Meeting, such party may ❹terminate, suspend, or partially perform its obligations under this Agreement or an <u>Exhibit A</u> without liability by written notice to the other party: ❶(a) acts of God (including fire, flood, earthquake, storm, hurricane or other natural disaster); (b) an advisory issued by any United States (federal or state) or international government entity (such as the United States Department of Homeland Security or the World Health Organization); (c) threatened or actual civil disorder, hostilities, war, or terrorism; or, (d) curtailment or interruption of transportation facilities unreasonably impeding at least twenty-five percent (25%) of Attendees from attending the Meeting.

Labor Disputes

A common characteristic of the hospitality industry is unionized staff. Because of the unpredictable and uncertain nature of the relationship between hotels and unionized staff, it's prudent for a group representative to include some sort of provision in his or her hotel contract to provide protection in the case of labor disputes. It's debatable as to whether the right of a group representative to terminate based on union staff issues should be in a termination for cause section or a force majeure / excused performance section. I chose the latter.

If there is any sort of ❶ threatened or actual work stoppage, boycott, or labor dispute that occurs within the 90-day period prior to a meeting, the hotel is required to notify the group representative. If the group representative ❷ determines that one of the described events will negatively impact the meeting, he or she can terminate the meeting ❸ completely or partially (partially meaning, perhaps, a reduced-sized meeting). If any ❹ one of the described events occurs while the meeting is being held and interferes with the meeting, the group representative is entitled to seek one of the remedies described in the *Remedy for Hotel Interference* provision.

Hotels rarely object to this provision, but when a hotel does it's usually because the hotel doesn't have union staff. The hotel's objection is that the provision doesn't apply and should be removed. I argue to keep the provision in the MHSA on the basis that the hotel's staff may be unionized in the future. Much more often than not, the provision remains.

> 10.2   Labor Disputes. Regardless of Hotel's union status, should there be ❶any threatened or actual strikes, lockouts, boycotts, labor disputes, or work stoppages within ninety (90) calendar days prior to the In-House Dates, Hotel shall immediately notify Customer in writing.   ❷If Customer reasonably determines that a strike, lockout, labor dispute, or work stoppage (each, also, a "Force Majeure Event") will adversely affect the success of the Meeting, Customer shall have the right to terminate an Exhibit A, ❸in whole or in part, without liability upon written notice to Hotel.   ❹If any strikes, lockouts, boycotts, labor disputes, or work stoppages occur over the In-House Dates that in any way interfere with Customer's or Attendees' use of Hotel, the same shall be deemed to be an interference for purposes of determining a

remedy associated with interference, as further described herein.

Reduced-Sized Meetings

Just in case the "in whole or in part" clauses in the *Excused Performance* and *Labor Disputes* provisions aren't clear, I've included the *Reduced-Sized Meetings* provision to be crystal clear. It's possible that a group representative will decide to still hold a meeting despite a force majeure event albeit a reduced-sized event because some number of expected attendees will not be attending (due to the force majeure event). ❶ If a group representative does decide to still hold a meeting despite a force majeure event, ❷ the group representative won't be liable to the hotel (e.g., for attrition damages) if the meeting is a reduced-sized meeting. It's also appropriate to include ❸ "lowest room rate guaranteed" language because the *Lowest Room Rate; Published or Confirmed* provision may not apply due to the reduced-sized group no longer meeting the required room block / hotel net inventory threshold. Hotels are generally encouraged by this provision because it shows intent by a group representative to still hold a meeting despite a force majeure event. I don't recall a hotel ever taking issue with the language.

> 10.3   <u>Reduced-Sized Meeting</u>. ❶Where Customer elects to hold the Meeting despite any Force Majeure Event, Hotel shall ❷waive any and all fees, liquidated damages, and other liabilities related to a reduced-sized Meeting and shall ❸offer Attendees any lower room rate offered to other guests during the In-House Dates.

Collective Bargaining Agreements

Should a hotel have union staff, there is a period of time corresponding with the expiration of a collective bargaining agreement during which there is an increased likelihood of some sort of labor dispute. Thus, should the expiration of a collective bargaining agreement be scheduled to occur near when a meeting will be held, there's a greater possibility that the meeting will be impacted by the negotiation (or stalemate) of the collective bargaining agreement. To ensure that a group representative is cognizant of the expiration of a collective bargaining agreement and the heightened risk to the success of a meeting, the following provision requires that a hotel notify a group representative of any such expiration that is scheduled to occur 90-days before or after the meeting. Since there's no obligation for a hotel to do anything other than notify a group representative under this provision, there are rarely any questions or objections from hotels regarding this provision.

> 10.4   <u>Collective Bargaining Agreements</u>.   Hotel shall promptly notify Customer in writing of any collective bargaining agreement expiring within ninety (90) calendar days prior to or after the In-House Dates.

Attrition

The *Attrition* provision is the most controversial provision in the MHSA—as it is in any hotel contract. In the context of sleeping rooms, attrition is the shortfall between the contracted room block and the room pick-up. When liquidated damages ("attrition damages") are involved, attrition can be a hotly contested point of negotiation between a hotel and a group representative. There is a nearly endless variety of methods to calculate attrition and attrition damages, but there are two primary types of provisions: ones that are favorable to hotels and ones that are favorable to groups.

Prior to the mid-1980s, the concept of sleeping room attrition and attrition damages didn't exist. The reason was based purely on supply and demand. In the early 1980s and prior, there were tax advantages and tax law loopholes that permitted hotel owners to use their properties as tax write-offs. Quite simply, hotel owners were rewarded for overbuilding hotels and they did just that. Consequently, it was a buyer's market for groups and group meetings. It wasn't uncommon back then for a group to enter into a contract with a hotel, shop its deal around to other hotels in a reverse auction manner, and then cancel the contract if the group came across a better deal. There was no economic disincentive for a group to stop it from cancelling and it's not as if the hotel that had gotten the short end of the stick had foregone any revenue. The hotel's holding of sleeping rooms for the group wasn't to the hotel's detriment—the hotel wouldn't have been able to sell the sleeping rooms to anyone else in the first place. Then came the Tax Recovery Act of 1986, which killed the tax advantages and closed the loopholes. Hotel construction halted practically overnight. It took a while—until the 1990s—for demand to catch-up with capacity and for hoteliers to be less forgiving when a group either cancelled or their attendance didn't actualize in a material way. Hotel investors and operators began demanding that groups meet their commitments under a hotel contract—and necessity, the mother of invention, gave birth to attrition. Since that time, the pendulum of attrition has swung widely both ways—from hotels to groups—depending on the economy and other factors that impact travel such as pandemics, terrorism, and war.

Most recently, in the economic heyday of 2004 – 2007, the pendulum swung too far in favor of hotels. When occupancy levels were going through the (hotel) roof, hoteliers were loathe to allow any flexibility in attrition and routinely didn't permit any slippage without attrition damages. This drove the behavior of meeting planners and group representatives to "under-block" their meetings. In other words, if a group representative thought his or her meeting would need 100 sleeping rooms for a particular night, the group representative would intentionally contract for 90 sleeping rooms instead to avoid attrition. If reservations picked-up more than what had been contracted for, the group representative would approach the hotel to ask for additional sleeping rooms at the negotiated room rate. When this practice started becoming widely used by group representatives to avoid the outrageous attrition damages provisions mandated by hotels and the practice subsequently became known to hotels, an industry relations executive for a prominent flag was unable to control his contempt for groups who were trying to protect themselves by under-blocking. He declared in the industry press that any groups asking for additional sleeping rooms over their contracted room block would not only not get their negotiated room rate, they wouldn't get anything less than the full rack rate (which no one pays) if they were lucky to be given additional sleeping rooms at all. It was a laughable, over-the-top threat because hotels had created the dilemma and it's absurd to think that the science of meeting attendance is so exact that meeting planners and group representatives can predict attendee room block needs and room pick-up with 100% accuracy. Fortunately or unfortunately, the hotel industry soon tanked along with the economy after that absurd threat and hoteliers realized the fallacy of 100% room block accuracy by again permitting reasonable slippage. That's not to say that the customer-gouging hotel heyday of the past and the power-hungry rants of hotel execs in the press won't come again—it may. For now, cooler heads have prevailed.

In this section, I present three *Attrition* provision alternatives. A group representative's ability to employ any one of the alternatives depends on many different factors, such as the timing of negotiations and the group representative's negotiation leverage. The provisions are presented in order of a group representative's negotiation leverage, from highest to lowest. The first alternative provision stipulates no attrition damages, implying that a group representative has a reasonable degree of negotiation leverage. The second alternative provision is a revenue-based model that—even if attrition is experienced—specifies attrition damages only in certain cases. The third alternative provision, the least favorable, is a more traditional attrition-damages-for-attrition model, but attempts to at least be reasonable. There are many variations in between that can be negotiated, and regarding the last and least favorable alternative provision, many worse. Again, whatever alternative or whatever variation a group representative is able to negotiate is directly linked to timing and leverage. If a group representative is subject under the MHSA (or a corresponding Exhibit A to the MHSA) to attrition damages, it's important that he or she understand the important impact and effect of the related *Obligation of Hotel to Mitigate Damages* provision, discussed later but which should be read in conjunction with the *Attrition* provision alternatives discussed in this section.

The negotiation position to start from, particularly when a group representative is competitively bidding out a meeting and has the greatest amount of leverage, is to exclude attrition damages. There's a legal debate as to whether being silent in a contract on attrition is sufficient to exclude a hotel from being entitled to attrition damages. One position is that if a hotel contract doesn't expressly describe attrition or attrition damages, and attrition occurs, the hotel *isn't* entitled to any damages. At least one court has supported this position, finding that a hotel will not be able to recover from a group for unused sleeping rooms in the absence of an attrition provision. The opposite position is that if a hotel contract doesn't expressly permit attrition, and attrition occurs, the hotel didn't realize the "benefit of the bargain" under the contract and may be entitled to damages. Regardless of which position one takes on the issue, I personally think it's helpful to have a provision that is express rather than being silent in the contract—that a hotel is not entitled to any damages or any other form of remedy in the case of attrition—merely because it helps to clarify the intent of the parties.

If a provision is included in a hotel contract that permits attrition but doesn't provide for a remedy to the hotel (such as liquidated damages), lawyers who represent hoteliers argue that such a provision voids the contract. Their argument centers on "consideration," which combined with offer and acceptance, is a mandatory element of basic contract formation. Under contract law, consideration is the value given in return for a promise, i.e., a benefit that the promisor received and a detriment that the promisee incurred. No contract is enforceable without consideration. What hoteliers' lawyers claim is that the consideration under a hotel contract is based on the hotel promising to hold sleeping rooms open for a group to the exclusion of all others (to the detriment of the hotel and to the benefit to the group) and the room rate paid by the group (to the detriment of the group and to the benefit of the hotel). These same lawyers then argue that if a hotel contract doesn't contain a provision specifying damages for attrition, there is no detriment to a group because the group could decide to not use any sleeping rooms and still not owe anything to the hotel. On that basis, the hoteliers' lawyers conclude there is a lack of consideration and the contract is therefore unenforceable. Therefore, the hoteliers' lawyers argue that groups should *want* a hotel contract that specifies damages for attrition because, if a contract doesn't contain such a provision, a hotel doesn't have to live up to their end of the agreement because the contract is unenforceable due to a lack of consideration. This means that a group could arrive on-site at a hotel, only to be told that the group doesn't have any sleeping rooms because the hotel decided not to perform the contract. The group wouldn't have any recourse because the hotel contract is unenforceable. Well, that legal theory might strike fear in the hearts of some groups and might hold water if all of the planets are aligned just right, but the reality is that there is likely enough "other" consideration under a hotel contract (such as food and beverage) that a court wouldn't hold a hotel contract to be unenforceable just because it didn't contain attrition damages. So, at the possibly slight risk of a lack of consideration, the following is an example of how a "no attrition damages" provision could be structured.

The provision ❶ starts by indicating that it applies unless the corresponding Exhibit A to the MHSA specifies otherwise. Similar to other provisions in the MHSA that have this qualifier, the purpose is to provide for flexibility from meeting to meeting since the MHSA is re-useable. It's very possible that a group representative has enough negotiation leverage for one meeting for which he or she can refuse sleeping room attrition damages and for another, subsequent meeting, the group representative may have to concede on sleeping room attrition damages. The following provision provides that flexibility because the Exhibit A to the MHSA can include attrition damages and not be in conflict with the following provision contained in the MHSA. Another reason for the qualifier is to convince a hotel at the time the MHSA is being negotiated that the hotel isn't giving up on their right to sleeping room attrition damages in perpetuity—only for the meeting that is being negotiated at the same time the overall MHSA is being negotiated—and that the hotel can request attrition damages be included in an Exhibit A to the MHSA for a future meeting. Jumping ahead, the provision caveats that ❷ it is the *adjusted* room block, which may not be the same as the contracted room block, that is the subject of the provision. That's really not necessary to caveat since there won't be any damages, but I like to include it anyway if a hotel later complains about the amount of attrition (which could be less significant if based on the final, adjusted room block). The provision stipulates that ❸ the hotel isn't entitled to any remedy of any sort for attrition, ❹ including withdrawing previously granted concessions.

11. Attrition. ❶Unless otherwise specified in an Exhibit A, Hotel acknowledges and agrees that it is ❸not entitled to any fees, charges, damages, or other forms of remedy, including the ❹withdrawal of any concessions by Hotel granted under this Agreement or an Exhibit A where Customer does not ❷fully utilize the total Room Nights represented by the Room Block, as the same may be adjusted as agreed upon by the parties or as otherwise permitted in this Agreement or an Exhibit A.

With attrition damages, a hotel is seeking to preserve its expected revenue—the hotel achieves its profit result through liquidated damages if a group fails to utilize the contracted room block. However, what happens if a hotel experiences occupancy higher than its normal, expected occupancy such that the adverse revenue impact caused by a group's attrition over the same room nights is negated? What happens if a group experiences sleeping room attrition but exceeds a hotel's revenue expectations in other areas (e.g., food and beverage or audio-visual) such that total overall revenue expectations are met or exceeded? Would it be fair in either of those cases for a group to be subject to sleeping room attrition damages? Some (hoteliers) would likely argue that it would be fair for a hotel to charge attrition damages and be enriched beyond its expectation in either or both of those cases.

In the first case, higher occupancy, it's very possible that the sleeping rooms sold by a hotel were in fact the very same that a group experienced attrition on. Simply, if the hotel didn't have the sleeping rooms available, the hotel wouldn't have been able to sell the sleeping rooms. In some ways, it's a fiction to say that the sleeping rooms that had been assigned to a group were actually the very same sleeping rooms resold by a hotel because it's difficult or impossible to make that determination—particularly when a hotel experiences normal occupancy. But what is a reality is that, when a hotel experiences higher occupancy than normal, at least some of the sleeping rooms left unoccupied by a group where certainly resold. A related scenario is where a hotel represented to others that it was "sold out" and / or refused to accept reservations. If a hotel was truly sold-out, then certainly the sleeping rooms assigned to a group were resold. If not, then the hotel failed to mitigate its damages by refusing to accept reservations for any unoccupied sleeping rooms. In any of these scenarios, it's clearly unfair for a hotel to charge a group for attrition damages.

In the second case, where a group exceeds expectations for other sources of revenue, a hotel has no damages. In fact, depending on how much the other sources of revenue have been exceeded, a hotel may have received even more revenue and profit than it had originally expected. For a hotel to then charge a group attrition damages and enrich itself beyond its expectations is not only unfair, it's unreasonable.

What *is* fair in either or both of those cases is for a hotel to be made whole. If a hotel hasn't suffered any real (or material) losses, then a group shouldn't have to pay any damages. The following *Attrition* provision alternative attempts to consider both of those cases in a fair and reasonable way.

I developed this provision after a particularly nasty attrition battle with a large hotel in New Orleans. Because of an ice storm in the middle of the country which affected the businesses of my attendees—arguably a force majeure event—attendance didn't materialize as expected. Unfortunately, the contract had been negotiated before my time and, in addition to a weak force majeure provision, had an attrition damages provision with a slippage percentage that was much lower than the industry norms of 20% – 30%. In short, even though I had an extremely large group, I had very little leeway in terms of slippage. To make matters worse, attrition damages were pegged at 100% of the room rate rather than the lower amount of room profit. Consequently, the hotel presented me with a bill for attrition damages in excess of $100,000. The first thing I did, which every group representative should do, is to ask the hotel for an audit (see the *Reporting by Hotel* section for more information) which ensures that all of my attendees were credited to my room pick-up. There were discrepancies, but not material enough to affect the attrition damages by more than a few thousand dollars. I tried to appeal to the hotel management's sense of fairness and argued that the attrition damages should be modified based on a slippage rate of 20% and a room rate profit margin of 80%. In other words, I was willing to be reasonable and pay some amount of attrition damages. No luck. I pointed out that we had a multi-year contract (my large group would be back at the hotel for three more meetings over the next ten years). No luck. I offered to hold other, future meetings at the hotel to compensate for the lost revenue. No luck. The negotiations dragged on for weeks and weeks with the hotel staunch in its position. As I tried to think of alternative after alternative in an effort to reduce the attrition damages (each met with resistance or a "no" from the hotel), I remembered a part of the audit which had information relating to my group's revenue performance in other categories. I hadn't paid much attention to the information at the time the audit was completed because I was focused on sleeping room revenue. In looking back at the information, it became immediately obvious that my group—despite the lower number of attendees—had dramatically exceeded the long-ago contracted minimums and hotel revenue expectations in non-sleeping room categories, particularly food and beverage and audio-visual. In significant excess of $100,000. In brief, armed with this new information and after significant (and tough) negotiations, the hotel acknowledged that I was due a credit of $7,000 (associated with double-dipping cancellation charges the hotel had hit my attendees with) from the hotel versus my owing the hotel $100,000 in attrition damages. That was fair—the hotel had gotten even more total revenue that it had expected despite the sleeping room attrition.

After reflecting on what had happened, I decided that it made sense to draft an attrition damages provision as an alternative when my negotiation leverage isn't sufficient to avoid attrition damages. In concept—similar to the outcome of the dilemma I just described as well as to cover the cases and scenarios I previously described—this alternative provision seeks to compare the expected revenue (actually profit) from sleeping rooms (considering a reasonable amount for slippage) against total revenue (for all categories of business) received by a hotel from a group to determine damages, if any. If the total revenue actually received exceeds the revenue amount that a hotel had expected to receive from sleeping rooms, the hotel has theoretically not been harmed and isn't owed any damages. The opposite result—if received revenue is less than expected revenue—means that a group is subject to paying damages to the hotel. There are nuances and arguably minor flaws in the provision. For example, the provision actually compares sleeping room profit (pegged at 80% of the room rate) to revenue of different categories of business which may or may not have profit margins that are less than 80%. However, the efficiency of the provision and its general effectiveness in making a hotel whole financially when the hotel has in reality been damaged over-shadows any nuances or minor flaws. However, be aware that hotels may attempt to use such nuances or minor flaws to chip away at the provision. The best reaction is to get the hotel to see the "big picture" and agree that, despite the mathematical machinations that could be introduced into the provision, it is, overall, easy to understand and reasonably fair for both parties. It's also better than the hotel not getting any attrition damages at all.

This provision begins by making it clear that ❶ the room block to serve as the measuring point for determining attrition is the total room nights (i.e., cumulative over the in-house dates for the meeting) based on the *adjusted* room block (if the contract permitted the contracted room block to be adjusted, for example, on a review date).

The provision then goes on to state that ❷ a hotel *may* ("entitled to request") charge attrition damages—but it isn't compelled to do so under the contract. I structured the provision in this way to allow me to appeal to a hotel as to why it shouldn't charge me attrition damages even though it is undisputed that the hotel was due attrition damages. Note that taxes are not payable on the attrition damages, if any, unless taxes are required by law.

The next step ❸ is to determine the minimum room block by applying the permitted slippage (which is 20%). This determination is made by multiplying the total room nights represented by the final adjusted room block by 80%.

Then ❹ the number of unsold sleeping rooms are determined by subtracting the sleeping rooms actually picked-up by the group and those sleeping rooms that are unoccupied but that the hotel has already been compensated for from the sleeping rooms that the hotel actually has available "for sale."

Next, ❺ the revenue that the hotel could have reasonably expected from sleeping rooms is calculated. This is done by using either the minimum room block calculated in ❸ or the unsold rooms calculated in ❹, whichever is lower. The argument for using unsold sleeping rooms (when lower) as opposed to the minimum room block is that the hotel hasn't been damaged to the extent that sleeping rooms have been occupied and paid for—regardless of who paid for the sleeping rooms. In essence, this is the case I previously described, where a hotel has achieved a level of occupancy that is higher than typical. The revenue is determined by using 80% of the room rate less any amount associated with commissions (which was payable to a third-party and not to the hotel). The reason for multiplying the room rate less commissions by 80% is to determine the hotel's lost *profit* for unoccupied sleeping rooms. It's reasonable to pay the profit, but not the revenue[6] (i.e., the room rate), since a hotel doesn't incur certain costs when a sleeping room is unoccupied (such as housekeeping)—a hotel shouldn't be compensated for those costs when the hotel hasn't incurred them. Further, liquidated damages under contract law are solely intended to make a party whole and anything greater becomes a "penalty"—which is generally not permitted under contract law. If 100% of the room rate were to be specified as damages in the *Attrition* provision, the hotel is receiving more than its lost profits (which looks like a penalty) and it's

---

[6] Even though the formula in the provision uses the technically incorrect term of "revenue" to refer to what is really sleeping room profit, the term "revenue" is used so as to be consistent and not confusing with other determinations of revenue such as food and beverage.

likely that the entire provision would be struck (voided) by a court in a lawsuit.

To determine the potential revenue loss, if any, to a hotel, the ❻ total actual revenue is first calculated by including all of the categories and sources of revenue realized by the hotel which are attributed to the group, including ❼ any cancellation or early departure fees.

Finally, ❽ the total actual revenue is compared to the potential expected sleeping room revenue calculated earlier in ❺. If ❾ the total actual revenue is less than the potential expected revenue, the hotel has experienced a revenue loss. Mirroring the language in ❷, the hotel ❾ has the right (but is not compelled) to seek attrition damages in the amount of the difference between the potential expected sleeping room revenue calculated earlier in ❺ and the revenue that was actually generated by the room pick-up. But this right to damages is ❿ subject to the hotel not having represented itself as being "sold out," having refused to accept reservations, having at least met its average occupancy level (as measured over the last three years) over the period that the meeting is being conducted, or the group electing to hold a future meeting (or meetings) at the hotel which has (have) a value equal to or greater than the liquidated damages (thereby making the hotel whole).

11.   Attrition. ❶Where Customer does not fully utilize the total Room Nights represented by the Room Block, as the same may be adjusted as agreed upon by the parties or as otherwise permitted in this Agreement, Hotel is ❷entitled to request that Customer pay to Hotel attrition damages, as liquidated damages and not as a penalty. The attrition damages, if any, shall be non-taxable unless otherwise prohibited by law and are calculated and subject to the following determinations.

11.1   ❸Determine the minimum Room Block commitment ("Minimum Room Block Commitment") by multiplying the total Room Nights represented by the final adjusted Room Block by eighty percent (80%).

11.2 ❹ Determine the number of unsold rooms ("Unsold Rooms") available for sale by Hotel by subtracting the Room Pick-Up and all guestrooms billed to other groups or individuals for attrition, cancellation, or no-shows from Net Inventory.

11.3 ❺ Determine the minimum commitment revenue ("Minimum Commitment Revenue") by multiplying eighty percent (80%) of the Room Rate less any commissionable amount by either the Minimum Room Block Commitment or Unsold Rooms, whichever is lower.

11.4 ❻ Determine the actual revenue ("Actual Revenue") by aggregating total revenue for all categories of business received by Hotel that is associated with the Meeting and Attendees, ❼ including any fees charged by Hotel for Attendee cancellations and early departures.

11.5 ❽ Determine the difference between the Actual Revenue and the Minimum Commitment Revenue. ❾ If the Actual Revenue does not meet or exceed the Minimum Commitment Revenue, Hotel is entitled to request that Customer pay to Hotel attrition damages, as liquidated damages and not as a penalty, in the amount of the difference between the Minimum Commitment Revenue less the revenue represented by the Room Pick-Up.

11.6 Notwithstanding the foregoing, ❿ Hotel acknowledges and agrees that it is not entitled to any fees, charges, damages, or other forms of remedy, including the withdrawal of any concessions by Hotel granted under this Agreement or an Exhibit A where Customer does not fully utilize the total Room Nights represented by the Room Block, as the same may be adjusted as agreed upon by the parties or as otherwise permitted in this Agreement or an Exhibit A where: (a) Hotel represented, in advance of the In-House Dates, to any other groups or to the general public that it was "sold out" or had no vacancies over the In-House Dates; (b) Hotel refused to accept guestroom reservations from other groups or from the general public over the In-House Dates; (c) Hotel met or exceeded its average occupancy level (as measured over the prior three years) for the period associated with the

In-House Dates; or, (d) Customer elects, within ninety (90) calendar days of being notified by Hotel of potential attrition damages, to contract with Hotel for a subsequent meeting or meetings of equal or greater value than the attrition damages.

If a group representative's negotiation leverage is such that he or she is forced to agree to a more traditional attrition damages provision, the group representative should at the very least be allowed some reasonable amount of slippage and should only be subject to damages based on sleeping room profit (not revenue). The following alternative provision provides for those allowances. The provision has been widely accepted in the hotel industry and is commonly known as an "80/80" attrition provision because it is based on something less than ❶ 80% room pick-up (meaning that a 20% slippage is permitted) and ❷ 80% of a non-commissionable room rate. However, the 80/80 ratio as a "standard" is likely to change over time based on a number of factors, with hotel supply and demand being the most impactful. If a group representative is able to negotiate anything less than the then-current standard[7], he or she has a favorable result. Anything more than the then-current standard is an unfavorable result and indicates that a hotel is being unreasonable. Keep in mind that if a group representative is able to negotiate review dates (as described in the *Adjustment of Room Block* provision), the following provision is even more favorable because it is based on the adjusted room block. Note that the provision also ❸ contains the same limitations as described in the prior alternative, subjecting the right to damages to the hotel not having represented itself as being "sold out," having refused to accept reservations, having at least met its average occupancy level (as measured over the last three years)

---

[7] For example, in the economic environment that this book was written, a "70/70" provision would be considered to be favorable for a group representative.

over the period that the meeting is being conducted, or the group electing to hold another meeting at the hotel which has a room block which at least meets the number of rooms represented by the attrition (thereby making the hotel whole).

11. <u>Attrition</u>. Where the Room Pick-Up is ❶less than eighty percent (80%) of the total Room Nights represented by the Room Block, as the same may be adjusted as agreed upon by the parties or as otherwise permitted in this Agreement, Hotel is entitled to request that Customer pay to Hotel attrition damages, as liquidated damages and not as a penalty. The attrition damages, if any, shall be non-taxable unless otherwise prohibited by law and are calculated and subject to the following determinations.

   11.1 The attrition damages shall be equal to the difference between the total Room Nights represented by the final adjusted Room Block and the Room Pick-Up multiplied by ❷eighty percent (80%) of the Room Rate less any commissionable amounts.

   11.2 Notwithstanding the foregoing, ❸Hotel acknowledges and agrees that it is not entitled to any fees, charges, damages, or other forms of remedy, including the withdrawal of any concessions by Hotel granted under this Agreement or an <u>Exhibit A</u> where Customer does not fully utilize the total Room Nights represented by the Room Block, as the same may be adjusted as agreed upon by the parties or as otherwise permitted in this Agreement or an <u>Exhibit A</u> where (a) Hotel represented, in advance of the In-House Dates, to any other groups or to the public that it was "sold out" or had no vacancies over the In-House Dates; (b) Hotel refused to accept guestroom reservations from other groups or from the public over the In-House Dates; (c) Hotel met or exceeded its average occupancy level (as measured over the prior three years) for the period associated with the In-House Dates; or, (d) Customer elects, within sixty (60) calendar days of being notified by Hotel of potential attrition damages, to contract with Hotel for a subsequent Meeting with a Room Block that equals or exceeds the attrition associated with the Meeting that is the subject of attrition hereunder, the In-

House Dates of such subsequent Meeting to be mutually agreed upon by the parties.

Termination; Cancellation

The *Termination; Cancellation* section serves as a "centralizing" area in the MHSA to describe a number of different termination rights for both a group representative and a hotel. However, where better described elsewhere, additional termination rights are contained within other MHSA provisions: *Force Majeure, Labor Disputes, No Interference; Incompatible Events, No Interference; Construction,* and *Deterioration in Quality.* While the name of this section includes "cancellation" in its title, cancellation is essentially termination for convenience and is therefore described in the MHSA in the context of termination: a meeting is "cancelled," but a contract is not—a contract is terminated for convenience when someone determines that a meeting needs to be cancelled. As with any other provision in the MHSA that allows a group representative to possibly terminate or decrease the scope of a meeting, this section of the MHSA receives a significant amount of scrutiny from hotels.

Termination for Cause; Customer

This provision describes events that allow a group representative to terminate the MHSA completely or to terminate a meeting (via an Exhibit A to the MHSA). This is the only provision within the *Termination; Cancellation* section that allows termination for cause, meaning that a hotel doesn't have a similar right. That raises the first contention that a hotel may bring up relating to this provision: the hotel will want a similar right. However, that doesn't make any sense. A group representative has very limited obligations under the MHSA or an

Exhibit A to the MHSA: namely, and most importantly, to pay. That limited obligation contrasts with the great number of obligations that a hotel has to a group representative and attendees. Thus, a hotel's termination for cause would be limited to where a group representative (and the group) doesn't fulfill its obligation of payment—which occurs roughly at the same time as a meeting (for payment of the sleeping rooms) and after (for payment of services other than sleeping rooms). Because payment is essentially made concurrently or in arrears, it doesn't make any sense for a hotel to terminate for cause for non-payment since the hotel has already materially performed. It's not as if a hotel can terminate for cause to stop any further performance or to limit any future losses—that time has already passed. Therefore, a hotel's right to terminate for cause would have a very limited scope, doesn't work from a time perspective, and doesn't provide any protections for the hotel.

The provision ❶ clarifies that it isn't the only provision that allows for termination and that it doesn't limit any other provisions that provide for termination rights. A group representative has the ❷ right to terminate the MHSA or a meeting (via an Exhibit A to the MHSA) without liability upon written notice to the hotel provided that one or more of the conditions described in the provision occur. Similar to other provisions in the MHSA where the parties have a "right," are "entitled," or "may" invoke some sort of remedy, a group representative isn't compelled to terminate for cause. An alternative would be to bargain for concessions instead.

The ❸ first condition is not unique to the MHSA and can be commonly found in any legal contract—the right to terminate for cause based on material breach. To ease a hotel's concern over this condition, I've doubled-up on materiality: there has to be a material breach of a material term. In other words, a group representative can't terminate for cause if a hotel insignificantly breaches a non-critical term. For example, if a hotel tells a group representative that the hotel can't live up to the *Guestroom Upgrades* provision because the hotel sold-out to another group on every suite, as much as that might make a group representative unhappy, that doesn't rise to the level of materiality. As a contrasting example, if a hotel approaches a group representative a year in advance of a meeting and says that the hotel can't live up to the contracted room rate, that's a material breach of a material term.

Later in the *Termination; Cancellation* section, the *Termination for Convenience; Hotel* provision requires that a hotel make a group representative whole where the hotel terminates for convenience. Knowing this, a sneaky hotel may refuse to perform (i.e., materially breach) a material term—hoping that the group representative will terminate for cause under the *Termination for Cause; Customer* provision—when in reality the hotel wants to avoid terminating for convenience and the associated liquidated damages. To address this possibility and to preserve the rights of a group representative to pursue damages for breach, the condition includes language that makes it clear, in addition to the right of termination for cause, all remedies at law and in equity are available to the group representative.

The ❹ next condition involves a change in a hotel's branding, affiliation, ownership, or management company. The condition itself doesn't require much explanation—a group representative entered into a contract with a hotel based on the attributes of that hotel at that specific point in time—not a different brand, owner, etc. If the hotel "changes," and isn't what the group representative "bought," it's only reasonable that a group representative have the option of terminating (or enforcing) the MHSA. This condition has been a point of negotiation contention in the past with hotels, since the changes described in the condition occur with some frequency. The contention associated with the condition may increase as consolidation in the hotel industry in tough economic times is likely. Hotels will likely argue that the change to a new management company or new owner will be seamless or transparent to a group representative. But that's not a legitimate basis for removing the condition. Instead, keep the condition, and if the hotel "changes," the hotel can then convince the group representative why he or she shouldn't terminate the MHSA.

While the *Assignment of Agreement* provision impliedly requires notice to a group representative in the case of any change in ownership, this condition expressly requires 30-days advance notice. The requirement of notice doesn't mean that a change in ownership isn't a condition of termination for cause (it is); actually, the requirement of notice is a notice of anticipatory breach. Again, a group representative isn't compelled to terminate for cause when this condition is met. If a hotel provides advanced notice of a change in ownership and assuming that no changes have been made to this provision or the *Assignment of Agreement* provision, the hotel has breached under this condition, breached under the ❸ first condition, and breached the *Assignment of Agreement* provision. A group representative can either terminate, or, if beneficial to the group representative or the group, bargain for concessions and enforce the MHSA. If a group representative does elect to enforce the MHSA, he or she should require assurances that the rights and obligations specified in the MHSA will be or have in fact been transferred to the new entity. Another point in considering this condition is to read it in conjunction with the *Assignment of Agreement* provision, which prohibits a hotel's assignment of an MHSA: if this condition is diluted during negotiations but the *Assignment of Agreement* provision is unchanged, where a hotel does "change" without the approval of a group representative, that would be a material breach of a material term (the *Assignment of Agreement* provision) and could be covered under the ❸ first condition.

The ❺ next condition is straightforward: if a hotel goes belly-up and goes into foreclosure or bankruptcy, a group representative can terminate. A hotel in this type of financial distress will likely suffer deficiencies in service, maintenance, and the like in such a way that attendees will be negatively impacted—which may not be acceptable at any room rate.

The ❻❼ next two conditions are related and are really only meant to address issues that result from a citywide, where a large venue such as convention center and overflow hotels are needed for a meeting. The ❻ first of the two related conditions addresses the inability to contract with the venue associated with the meeting. The "unable" part of this condition relates to venues which may not even be built yet (many cities are "sold" to groups on the basis of the city having some new, yet-to-be-constructed venue) and may not be completed on time or at all. The ❼ second of the two related conditions addresses the inability to obtain the necessary number of sleeping rooms for the entire meeting room block at other hotels (either the headquarters hotel or overflow hotels).

With a citywide, it's impossible for the venue, headquarters, and overflows to be contracted with at exactly the same time. The typical approach to a citywide is to book the venue first, the headquarters hotel (usually a big box connected to or located close to the venue) second, nearby overflow hotels (likely also big boxes) third, and the outlying overflow hotels last. Unfortunately, booking a citywide doesn't always follow that approach. Venues such as convention centers—especially in top tier cities—are notoriously difficult to negotiate with and the contracts tend to take a long time to get to the point to where they can be executed. Some hotels are pushy, wanting contracts and unwilling to provide a first option as a group representative works to piece together the needed room blocks. Sometimes a big box can only provide a second option and a group representative must wait to hear back as he or she works on other room blocks. My point is that a group representative can't operate sequentially, and might contract with overflows first, the venue second, and the headquarters last. Anywhere along the way, something can (and does) go wrong. Consequently, a group representative needs an out in order to unwind the citywide if the venue can't be contracted with or the group representative can't get enough hotels to build the necessary room block. More sophisticated hotels generally don't take issue with the language, but may ask that some time parameters be put around the ❻❼ two conditions, such as the conditions expiring as a basis for termination for cause six months prior to the meeting. A group representative still has a right to terminate via the *Termination for Convenience; Customer* provision, but there may be some liquidated damages associated with the termination. I believe that time-bounding the conditions could be reasonable (based on the timeframe) considering that a hotel is potentially foregoing business. Hotels in small towns or more rural areas, such as Columbus, Georgia, will likely object to these conditions and will want the conditions removed—which is reasonable. If a hotel objects to these conditions, is located where a citywide is possible, refused to give a solid first option and instead demanded a contract, and the group representative is in fact seeking to negotiate the MHSA as a part of a citywide, the hotel is being wholly unreasonable.

12.1   <u>Termination for Cause; Customer</u>. ❶Without limiting the rights of Customer to terminate for cause or convenience as otherwise provided for in this Agreement, ❷Customer shall have the right to terminate this Agreement or an <u>Exhibit A</u>

without liability upon the occurrence of any of the following conditions and upon written notice to Hotel.

12.1.1 ❸Hotel's material breach of any material term or condition of this Agreement or an <u>Exhibit A</u>. Customer's right of termination for cause shall be in addition to, and shall in no way limit, Customer's right to other remedies at law or in equity available to Customer for breaches of this Agreement; or,

12.1.2 ❹Any change at Hotel in branding, affiliation, ownership, or management company. In the case of any foregoing change, Hotel agrees to notify Customer in writing no later than thirty (30) calendar days prior to such change; or,

12.1.3 ❺Foreclosure by Hotel's creditors, or a petition in bankruptcy filed by or on behalf of Hotel or its creditors; or,

12.1.4 ❻The non-Hotel site, if applicable, for the Meeting is unwilling or unable to provide suitable facilities for the Meeting or such site shall not be available for whatever reason; or,

12.1.5 ❼An adequate number of sleeping rooms at other hotels within a reasonable distance of the Meeting Location to accommodate Customer and / or Customer attendees is not available or cannot be contracted for.

Termination for Convenience; Mutual

Should a group representative and a hotel mutually decide, for whatever reason, to terminate the MHSA or a meeting (via an Exhibit A to the MHSA), this provision permits such a termination without liability.

12.2 <u>Termination for Convenience; Mutual</u>. This Agreement or an <u>Exhibit A</u> may be terminated by mutual agreement between Customer and Hotel at any time without liability to the other party.

Termination for Convenience; Customer

The right of a group representative to terminate a meeting for convenience (commonly called cancellation) is a common provision in hotel contracts, so a hotel won't object to its presence within the MHSA. "Cancellation" provisions typically tie liquidated damages to the date of termination based on a sliding scale, and this provision is structured similarly. What a hotel may object to is how the liquidated damages are calculated and the time parameters.

The provision ❶ clarifies that the right of termination for convenience is in addition to the *Termination for Cause; Customer* provision and any other rights of termination specified in the MHSA. To exercise the right, ❷ a group representative must provide written notice to the hotel. The ❸ hotel is *entitled* (not compelled) to request the liquidated damages specified in the provision from the group representative, thereby giving a group representative an opportunity to try and bargain some or all of the liquidated damages away. Hotels sometimes redline this section of the provision, changing "Hotel shall be entitled to request from Customer" to "Customer shall pay to Hotel within thirty (30) calendar days of the date of termination notice" which has the effect of mandating payment and removes the negotiation leverage of the group representative that the original language provided. The amount of liquidated damages is based on the ❹ sliding scale described in the provision, with the liquidated damages increasing as the start of the meeting draws closer. The sliding scale part of the provision draws the most attention from hotels, with hotels frequently wanting to change the timeframes or the percentages of liquidated damages. The liquidated damages are set based on the calculation of "peak night room revenue," which is "peak night" multiplied by "room revenue." ❺ Peak night is based on the adjusted room block and ❼ excludes staff rooms and comp rooms (which are excluded because those sleeping rooms are provided by the hotel without charge). ❻ Room revenue is calculated as 60% of the room rate, with the 60% representing the lost profit. Hotels also frequently want to change the calculation (which has the effect of increasing the liquidated damages) by changing peak night to total room nights and room revenue to a higher percentage (usually 80%) of the room rate. A hotel may also object to the ❽ requirement in the provision that the liquidated damages be waived if the meeting that was canceled is replaced with one or more meetings that have total revenue equal to or greater than the amount of liquidated damages. Most hotels will agree to this requirement but typically redline it such that there is only partial credit of a future meeting against the liquidated damages and the future meeting (or meetings) must be scheduled and occur within a specified timeframe (usually a year).

12.3   Termination for Convenience; Customer. ❶Without limiting the rights of Customer to terminate for cause as otherwise provided for in this Agreement, ❷Customer shall have the right to terminate an Exhibit A for convenience upon written notice to Hotel and ❸Hotel shall be entitled to request from Customer, as liquidated damages and not as a penalty, an amount, if any, ❹based on the following sliding scale: (a) greater than one hundred and eighty (180) calendar days prior to the Official Dates: no liquidated damages or liability; (b) one hundred and seventy-nine (179) to ninety (90) calendar days prior to the Official Dates: fifty percent (50%) of peak night room revenue; (c) eighty-nine (89) to thirty (30) calendar days prior to the Official Dates: seventy-five percent (75%) of peak night room revenue; or, (d) less than thirty (30) calendar days prior to the Official Dates: one hundred (100%) of peak night room revenue. For purposes of this provision: (a) ❺"peak night" shall be determined based on the adjusted Room Block, if so adjusted; (b) ❻"room revenue" shall be calculated as sixty percent (60%) of the single standard Room Rate and shall exclude sales tax and other charges; and, (c) ❼Staff Rooms and Comp Rooms shall not be counted as part of the Room Block. ❽Hotel agrees that liquidated damages, if any, due from Customer hereunder shall be waived if Customer elects, within ninety (90) calendar days of the date of termination for convenience, to contract with Hotel for a subsequent meeting or meetings of equal or greater value than the liquidated damages.

An example of a redlined provision, which incorporates a hotel's "wish list" of changes, follows. This version doesn't include changes to the sliding scale, which could be changed in a variety of ways. Even without changing the sliding scale, this version of the provision is highly unfavorable and wholly unacceptable.

12.3　　Termination for Convenience; Customer. Without limiting the rights of Customer to terminate for cause as otherwise provided for in this Agreement, Customer shall have the right to terminate an Exhibit A for convenience upon written notice to Hotel and Hotel shall be entitled to request from Customer Customer shall pay to Hotel within thirty (30) calendar days of the date of termination notice, as liquidated damages and not as a penalty, an amount, if any, based on the following sliding scale: a) greater than one hundred and eighty (180) calendar days prior to the Official Dates: no liquidated damages or liability; (b) one hundred and seventy-nine (179) to ninety (90) calendar days prior to the Official Dates: fifty percent (50%) of peak night room revenuetotal room night revenue; (c) eighty-nine (89) to thirty (30) calendar days prior to the Official Dates: seventy-five percent (75%) of peak night room revenuetotal room night revenue; or (d) less than thirty (30) calendar days prior to the Official Dates: one hundred (100%) of peak night room revenuetotal room night revenue. For purposes of this provision: (a) "peaktotal room night" shall be determined based on the adjusted Room Block, if so adjusted; and (b) "room revenue" shall be calculated as sixtyeighty percent (6080%) of the single standard Room Rate and shall exclude sales tax and other charges; and, (c) Staff Rooms and Comp Rooms shall not

~~be counted as part of the Room Block~~. Hotel agrees that <u>twenty-five percent (25%) of the total</u> liquidated damages, if any, due from Customer hereunder shall be waived if Customer elects, within ~~ninety~~<u>thirty</u> (~~90~~<u>30</u>) calendar days of the date of termination for convenience, to contract with Hotel for a subsequent meeting ~~or meetings~~ of equal or greater value than the liquidated damages<u> provided that such meeting occurs within one (1) year following the date of notice of termination</u>.

Termination for Convenience; Hotel

While a hotel doesn't have the right to terminate for cause under the MHSA, the MHSA does provide a hotel with the unilateral ability to terminate for convenience. It might seem unusual to include this in the MHSA since a hotel's termination of a meeting would likely present serious consequences for a group representative. There are two origins as to why I've included this provision. The first origin is when I had a hotel in San Diego send me a letter saying that it was closing down for a major renovation and couldn't honor our contract as an overflow hotel. That put me in a huge bind because I had already booked every hotel within a reasonable distance of the convention center. Under the contract, the hotel didn't have a right to terminate for convenience. Thus, the hotel's refusal to perform was a material breach of the contract. That meant that I had legal remedies that I could pursue, such as the cost associated with finding another overflow hotel, additional transportation costs associated with a shuttle for attendees, and higher room rates. However, pursuing legal remedies would have taken time and focus I didn't have, so I ended up not doing anything other than expressing my outrage to the hotel. As a matter of practice, I try to include an easy-to-implement remedy for every major problem that might occur under a contract. That way, a remedy exists and is readily available—versus the lengthy and costly pursuit of my "rights and remedies at law or in equity" when I don't have an express remedy in my contract. After reflecting on the San Diego problem, I realized I could have avoided at least being left empty-ended by having a hotel-based termination for convenience with associated liquidated damages and other specified remedies. With that type of provision in my contract with the San Diego hotel, I would still have been tremendously inconvenienced and outraged, but I would've at least had a check to show for it.

The second origin is that I've had a number of hotels redline my MHSA in the past to include the ability for the hotel to terminate for convenience. When I did get those kinds of redlines, they were usually highly unfavorable, so I decided to include my own, more favorable language. It seems odd that a hotel would want to terminate a meeting for convenience (why would the hotel want to give up the business?), but they've asked enough for me to warrant including the provision in the MHSA. While a hotel can terminate for convenience, based on the timeframe in relation to the meeting, it could be a costly proposition for the hotel.

The provision is ❶ triggered when a hotel seeks to terminate for convenience, which is clarified to include termination without cause and cancellation, and ❷ includes an acknowledgement that termination for convenience will result in material harm to the group representative. If a hotel terminates ❸ prior to 180-calendar days (or whatever period is specified by the parties) before the start of the meeting, the hotel must ❹ return any monies pre-paid by a group representative with interest, ❺ reimburse the group representative for expenses incurred in anticipation of having a room block at the hotel (such as re-printing attendee materials), and ❻ pay for the relocation of the meeting to a similar or better property. If the hotel terminates for convenience ❼ after the specified period, the hotel has to do all of the foregoing and ❽ pay liquidated damages in the amount of 60% of the sleeping room revenue (based on multiplying the total room nights by the room rate). A ❾ list of example costs associated with relocating the meeting is given at the end of the provision.

Hotels are typically pleasantly surprised to see a provision that allows their termination for convenience, so objections are infrequent. When there are objections, the objections relate to not paying interest on deposits and somehow bounding the amount of out-of-pocket expenses or the costs of relocation. Additionally, hotels typically want to strike the allowance for ❽ liquidated damages or lower the stated percentage of 60% of the total sleeping room revenue. When I first included this provision in the MHSA, I set the percentage to 60% to be consistent with the *Termination for Convenience; Customer* provision, which pegs "room revenue" at the same percentage of the room rate. Interestingly, that has worked to my advantage when hotels argue that the percentage should be higher than 60% of room revenue when I seek to terminate for convenience. When I indicate to a hotel that we'll make the same adjustment for this provision, and the hotel balks, it makes for an interesting conversation as to why what's good for the goose isn't good for the gander. More often than not, after that conversation, the percentages in both provisions go unchanged. For that reason alone—to justify the 60% room revenue liquidated damages in the *Termination for Convenience; Customer* provision—the *Termination for Convenience; Hotel* provision is worth having in the MHSA. Also, it's a provision that a hotel won't likely invoke since there's no reason to (i.e., they have the business), so there's no compelling reason not to include it.

12.4   Termination for Convenience; Hotel. ❶In the event Hotel terminates for convenience (which shall include any termination without cause and cancellation), ❷ Hotel acknowledges that Customer would be materially harmed. Where Hotel terminates for convenience ❸ prior to the Hotel Termination Period specified in an <u>Exhibit A</u>, which, if not so specified, shall be one-hundred and eighty (180) calendar days prior to the Official Dates, within fourteen (14) calendar days of termination, Hotel agrees to: (a) ❹ pay Customer all deposits or monies forwarded to Hotel with interest calculated at a rate of one and one-half percent (1.5%) per month, but not to exceed eighteen percent (18%) per annum or the highest rate allowable by state law, whichever is less; (b) ❺ reimburse Customer for any documented out-of-pocket expenses incurred in reasonable expectation of conducting the Meeting; and, (c) ❻ pay for any costs associated with relocating the Meeting to a comparable or superior property, which has been approved by Customer. Where Hotel terminates for convenience ❼ following the Hotel Termination Period, within fourteen (14) calendar days of termination, Hotel agrees to: (a) pay Customer all deposits or monies forwarded to Hotel with interest calculated at a rate of one and one-half percent (1.5%) per month, but not to exceed eighteen percent (18%) per annum or the highest rate allowable by state law, whichever is less; (b) reimburse Customer for any documented out-of-pocket expenses incurred in reasonable expectation of conducting the Meeting; (c) pay for any costs associated with relocating the Meeting to a comparable or superior property, which has been approved by Customer; and, (d) ❽ pay to Customer, as liquidated damages and not as a penalty, sixty percent (60%) of the total Guestroom revenue, which shall be calculated by multiplying the total Room Nights resulting from the adjusted Room Block by the applicable Room Rates. ❾ Costs associated with relocating the Meeting include but are not limited to such items as differences in room rates, mailings, transportation, and other direct costs associated with changing the Meeting site.

Reporting By Hotel

There are two points in time that a group representative needs a hotel to report data relating to sleeping rooms: pre- and post-meeting. The purpose of the pre-meeting report is to assist the group representative in assessing room pick-up. If attendees are reserving sleeping rooms at a faster rate than anticipated, the group representative may need to negotiate with the hotel to increase the room block (at the group rate) or book an overflow hotel. If the opposite is true and sleeping rooms aren't being picked-up as quickly as expected by the group representative—which may imply potential attrition—actions can be taken to try and improve room pick-up (such as sending out additional marketing materials to prospective attendees). If the associated hotel contract contains an attrition damages provision, it may also be time for the group representative to reduce the room block (if permitted) or to begin "pre-negotiating" attrition damages with the hotel (even though actual room pick-up isn't truly known at this point, it still may be appropriate to start having discussions with the hotel). The purpose of the post-meeting report is to determine actual room pick-up. The report serves as history for the group and, if the associated hotel contract includes an attrition damages provision, determines whether attrition damages are triggered.

Pre-Meeting Room Pick-Up Reports

For pre-meeting room pick-up reports, the MHSA requires that ❶ a hotel provide a report to a group representative—in the form requested by the group representative, such as a spreadsheet—which shows ❷ the room block, sleeping rooms reserved by attendees to-date, the hotel's net inventory (essentially, in the pre-meeting context, the sleeping rooms in the hotel that are in-service), and the total sleeping rooms in the hotel that have been reserved by other groups or transient travelers. The data is to be provided by a hotel ❸ on a weekly basis six-months before the start of the meeting unless another timeframe is specified in the Exhibit A to the MHSA. Some hotels begin attrition damages discussions early (months or weeks before a meeting) and, likewise, the earlier that a group representative can get access to room pick-up performance, the better. In one case, with a San Diego hotel, the hotel sent me an invoice for attrition damages roughly 30-days before my meeting was scheduled to begin. The hotel didn't send any data to support its attrition claim; it just sent the invoice for the attrition damages. This occurred early in my negotiation experience with hotels and the event triggered me to include a number of provisions in the MHSA, including the pre-meeting reporting requirement, to avoid a future similar dilemma and to provide me with as much negotiation leverage as possible in a potentially adverse situation. I ended up not having to pay attrition damages to the San Diego hotel because my group did pick-up the room block; however, I wouldn't have been in such a panic if the hotel had provided me with some basic, pre-meeting reporting. With this reporting, a group representative can ascertain how the group is picking up the contracted room block as well as how the hotel is performing overall with its occupancy level. This comparison between group performance and hotel performance is helpful to facilitate discussions with a hotel if it appears attrition is looming. An example of pre-meeting negotiation leverage in a possible attrition situation is where a group is underperforming in its room pick-up but the hotel is experiencing higher-than-normal occupancy. In that situation, a group representative will have more bargaining power with the hotel (depending on the attrition damages provision) since the hotel may not be damaged by the group's potential attrition.

Hotels generally don't take issue with the language of the provision other than the timeframe, which can be adjusted via the Exhibit A to the MHSA, and the requirement that the report be in the form specified by the group representative. The form of the report can be a position of flexibility with a group representative—provided that the elements of data specified in the provision are included—since a hotel will likely provide the data in an electronic format that can be easily manipulated.

13.1   <u>Pre-Meeting Room Pick-Up Reports</u>.   ❶In the form requested by Customer, Hotel shall provide Customer with pre-Meeting Room Pick-Up reports on a ❸weekly basis starting six (6) months (or such other timeframe specified in an <u>Exhibit A</u>) prior to the Meeting, ❷which shall show Guestrooms blocked, Guestrooms reserved, Net Inventory, and total sleeping rooms left in Hotel that have not been reserved by other groups or transient guests.

Post-Meeting Reports

For post-meeting reports, the MHSA requires that ❶ a hotel provide a report to a group representative—again, in the form requested—which shows ❷ data elements on a daily basis not only related to room pick-up but also to revenue generated by a group. ❸ The report is to be provided by a hotel within 30-days following the meeting. In addition to the data elements listed in the provision (just in case anything was missed) ❹ a hotel is required to provide detailed data associated with attrition or cancellation (such as historical occupancy levels). Hotels rarely object to the language in this provision, and, when they do, it's typically directed to their reluctance to provide revenue data that is attendee-specific (e.g., room service) because of the additional effort required to supply the data. If this presents a major stumbling block in negotiations, the requirement for attendee revenue data can be limited to attrition or cancellation situations.

13.2 Post-Meeting Reports. ❸Within thirty (30) days following the Meeting, ❶in the form requested by Customer, Hotel shall provide Customer with a post-Meeting report, ❷which shall show, per-day over the In-House Dates, Guestrooms occupied per night, percentage of singles / doubles, Guestroom revenue, Comp Rooms to which Customer is entitled, Staff Rooms to which Customer is entitled, dishonored reservations, Attendee reservation cancellations, Attendee early departures, Hotel's Net Inventory, F&B activity (including room service and restaurant), audio-visual activity, and details relating to all other ancillary revenue. In addition to the foregoing, ❹Hotel shall provide detailed data to Customer to support any cancellation or attrition claims.

Customer Audit Rights

In a situation where attrition damages may be assessed, it's clearly important for a group representative to independently verify that the hotel's claims of attrition are accurate. For example, did the hotel really include all attendee reservations in the room pick-up, including those attendees that booked around the room block (such as through an alternative reservation method)? That type of verification, which includes auditing a hotel's records, is more invasive than the pre- and post-meeting reports previously described and can be a point of contention with hotels. Despite that contention, the *Customer Audit Rights* provision is important for a group representative to have in that the rights it confers can make the difference between attrition damages and no attrition damages. The ability to audit a hotel's records also helps in analyzing group behavior such as whether attendees routinely use room service, hotel restaurants, spa services, and the like. This data can help a group representative in planning a future meeting that is more tailored to the behaviors and needs of attendees.

As the world has become obsessed with privacy, some hoteliers have become sophisticated as it relates to the release of hotel records, establishing privacy policies at the flag level. These hoteliers typically want to replace the entire *Customer Audit Rights* provision with their policy. Provided that I have the same basic rights that my provision provides, I've been agreeable with replacing the language in my provision with a hotelier's policy. Be cautious, however, if the language that a hotel proposes contains an Internet link to its privacy policy. By referencing an Internet website in a hotel contract that is linked to a hotelier's privacy policy, the policy that a group representative first reviewed and found acceptable may not be the same privacy policy that applies when the group representative attempts to invoke his or her audit rights. Instead of a link, the privacy policy should be included within the body of the MHSA or as an attachment.

The provision starts off only slightly invasive, ❶ requiring that a hotel provide access to its records for purposes of determining room pick-up and charges to a group. If the records show that a sleeping room was occupied by an attendee but wasn't counted toward room pick-up (e.g., the attendee could have booked around the block), ❷ any missed occupied sleeping rooms will be included in the room pick-up and credited for a variety of purposes including determining comp rooms. Some hotels have proposed that they conduct the detailed audit. I've agreed to that provided the hotel allows me or my designee to be present when the hotel conducts the audit.

The provision then becomes more invasive. ❸ Where a group representative believes that a hotel has been keeping less-than-accurate records—as demonstrated by finding an unreasonable number of discrepancies—the hotel is required to provide guest-level data to the group representative (or a designee such as an accountant or a lawyer) for auditing purposes. Two points of contention with hotels regarding this provision in my past negotiations was that ❹ hotels almost universally required that the hotel's records be reviewed on-property and that some sort of confidentially agreement be signed in order for me to have access to the hotel's guest list. That wasn't an issue for me in the past, and for purposes of negotiation efficiency in the future, I included appropriate language in the provision. Some hotels will ask for an indemnification to be included to cover the hotel if I disclose or misuse hotel records or guest list information. That's also not an issue for me because I won't disclose or misuse the information, but hotels have to ask for the indemnification as a part of negotiating an MHSA. I haven't included the indemnification language for hotels in this provision as a part of the MHSA contract template—even though I'll agree to an indemnification if asked—because the indemnification does present legal risk to me.

❺ If a hotel has done a sloppy job of keeping records, its lack of attention to detail has likely resulted in unnecessary expense to a group representative who has performed an audit. For purposes of this provision, the MHSA defines "sloppiness" as a 2% margin of error. In that case, a hotel is on the hook to pay the costs of a group representative in conducting the audit. Not surprisingly, hotels occasionally object to the possibility of having to fund an audit. If I can't reason my way through the objections (e.g., but for the hotel's sloppiness, I wouldn't have conducted an audit), I'll trade it as a concession for another negotiation point that is more important for me.

13.3 <u>Customer Audit Rights</u>. ❶At Customer's request, Hotel shall provide Customer, or its designated representative, access to Hotel's books and records for the purposes of determining final Room Pick-Up and/or to audit any charges to Customer. ❷Any Guestroom occupied by an Attendee, but not credited to Customer by Hotel, will be credited to the Room Pick-Up and earned Comp Rooms, and such Guestrooms shall be commissionable to the Intermediary, if any.

13.3.1 <u>Discrepancy</u>. ❸If a discrepancy exists between Hotel's occupancy figures and the occupancy figures believed to be accurate by Customer, Hotel will furnish to Customer a record of individual names and companies occupying sleeping rooms in Hotel over the In-House Dates. ❹The record shall be viewed on Hotel's premises in the presence of Hotel and Customer, or its designated representative, who will sign a confidentiality agreement stating that the parties will not use private information gathered from Hotel's records for any other purpose than to independently ascertain Room Pick-Up and Hotel's occupancy. ❺If the numbers represented by Hotel before the audit are off by two percent (2%) or more, Hotel shall pay the reasonable expenses of Customer in conducting the audit, including the use of experts, if any.

No Interference

"Quiet enjoyment" is a concept in real estate and tenant law that, at its most basic, means an occupant has the right to be free from any interference in the use and enjoyment of the occupied real property. "Quiet" is not restricted to an absence of noise; it has been more broadly interpreted to mean freedom from interference. That same concept of "quiet enjoyment" (or "no interference") can be extended to the occupants of hotel sleeping rooms and function space, who have the right to expect that their meeting will be free from interference such as construction. This section of the MHSA includes not only a typical "quiet enjoyment" provision but provisions against interference caused by construction and incompatible groups (such as competitors).

No Interference; Quiet Enjoyment

The first provision in this section is a representation and warranty (essentially, a legal promise) of quiet enjoyment by a hotel. Specifically, a hotel agrees that there won't be any interferences under the hotel's control that will have a negative impact on a group's meeting. Hotels rarely take issue with this provision, and, when they do, it's normally to strike "represents and warrants" and replace it with "agrees" (because a hotel's lawyer told the hotel that "represents and warrants" is too high of a legal standard). These same hotels typically make similar changes throughout the MHSA as it relates to the words "represents," "representation," "warranty," and "warrants." In my opinion, their lawyers are dead wrong and the hotels are as much on the hook legally with the word "agrees" as they are with the words "represents and warrants." Granted, there are academic legal differences between the words, but since a hotel is still on the hook (in my opinion), I don't fall into the trap of an academic, time-wasting debate with a hotel's attorney and I agree to the change. With that said, I prefer "represents and warrants" because I prefer traditional legal terminology.

14.1 <u>No Interference; Quiet Enjoyment</u>. Hotel represents and warrants that there will be no distractions or disturbances within Hotel's control during the In-House Dates that could affect the ordinary use and quiet enjoyment of Hotel facilities by Customer or Attendees.

No Interference; Incompatible Events

In addition to a hotel's overall agreement of quiet enjoyment and no interference, it's common (subject to the size of a group) for hotel contracts to include a provision that specifically describes what are called "incompatible" events or groups. Unless a group is completely occupying a hotel, it's highly likely that one or more other groups will be in-house at the same time. There are a number of good reasons to include this type of provision. One example is where a group, such as a pharmaceutical company, doesn't want competitors in-house at the same time because of confidentiality concerns and potential corporate espionage. Another reason is where one group's values or ideals are incompatible with another group's. For example, if a group has a specific religious orientation, it's possible that the group won't want other groups in-house that have conflicting religious beliefs (or no religious beliefs at all). As a final example, a group may be having serious, keynote speakers and wouldn't want a loud and raucous corporate sales incentive meeting in the adjacent function space.

Under the provision, a ❶ hotel must immediately notify a group representative of *any* meetings or events (including, e.g., entertainment within the hotel's facilities) that are in-house at the same time as the meeting planned by the group representative. The ❷ group representative is obligated to then notify the hotel in writing if the other meeting or event is incompatible, and, ❸ if so, the group representative is entitled to terminate the meeting, either completely or partially, without liability.

Note that the provision states that a group representative is *entitled* to terminate. A group representative may elect to not terminate even if there is an incompatible event. I've only experienced one situation where a concurrent event was incompatible and I elected not to terminate. In that situation, a Las Vegas hotel followed their contractual obligations and notified me that it had booked some sort of "nude male revue" which the hotel felt might be incompatible with the conservative nature of my group. Unfortunately, the hotel booked the attraction without seeking my approval first in a "hoping for forgiveness instead of asking for permission" type of ploy. While I wasn't happy with that ploy, in discussions with the hotel regarding the location of the event and how the hotel was promoting the event within the hotel's facilities, I felt assured my attendees wouldn't be affected by the attraction. Rather than immediately seeking to terminate, I suggest that a group representative work with the hotel to determine if there are things that can be done (and additional concessions that can be made by the hotel) to negate any effects that may result from the incompatibility.

14.2 **No Interference; Incompatible Events**. ❶Hotel shall immediately notify Customer in writing of any concurrent or overlapping meetings, conventions, special events, or other attractions to be held in Hotel during the In-House Dates. Upon notification from Hotel, ❷Customer shall promptly notify Hotel if the concurrent or overlapping events will be incompatible to Customer or Attendees, at the sole determination of Customer, and ❸Customer shall be entitled to terminate the applicable Exhibit A, in whole or in part, without liability upon written notice to Hotel.

Keep in mind that this is a "size matters" type of provision. If there is a disparity between the size of a group and a hotel's inventory with the group size being small and the hotel's inventory being large, the hotel won't likely agree to this provision because the hotel doesn't want a small group dictating its flexibility in accepting a larger group. Rather than striking the provision completely, and as a compromise, I suggest redlining the provision as illustrated below by ❶ adding a group size threshold and leaving the remainder of the provision unchanged. If that still doesn't work, the provision can be ❷softened by specifying mutual agreement as to alternative arrangements and deleting the language that allows for unilateral termination.

> 14.2   No Interference; Incompatible Events. ❶Where Customer has booked more than fifty percent (50%) of Hotel's Net Inventory for a Meeting, Hotel shall immediately notify Customer in writing of any concurrent or overlapping meetings, conventions, special events, or other attractions to be held in Hotel during the In-House Dates. Upon ❷mutual determination of Customer and Hotel that alternate arrangements are necessary, such alternative arrangements shall be mutually agreed-upon between Customer and Hotelnotification from Hotel, Customer shall promptly notify Hotel if the concurrent or overlapping events will be incompatible to Customer or Attendees, at the sole determination of Customer, and Customer shall be entitled to terminate the applicable Exhibit A, in whole or in part, without liability upon written notice to Hotel.

No Interference; Construction

To maintain quality and condition, hotels undertake remodeling and renovation projects. Hotels also undertake various construction projects in an effort to expand their facilities and grow their business. While these various projects are admirable and good, no group wants to experience the construction activities and the accompanying noise, dust, smells, distractions, limited access, out-of-service amenities, and inconveniences.

I've invoked this type of provision in one form or another in the past. On almost every occasion I invoked it, it wasn't because the hotel advised me of the construction—I found out independently. I've also discovered, more than once, that a hotel was aware (at the time of contracting) of future constructions that would be concurrent with my meeting and the hotel neglected to disclose it. That's negotiating in bad faith and it makes me less "flexible" when I do invoke the provision. I would much rather that hotels be straightforward about their construction projects in order to find a mutually-agreeable solution well in advance of a meeting. A positive example I experienced was with a large hotel in Anaheim, California where I was booking practically the entire net inventory. After notification by the hotel and our working together on solutions, the hotel agreed to a number of concessions. These included reducing the working hours of construction and rearranging the construction project as much as practical to avoid noise-generating activities (such as jack-hammering). While there were some negligible signs of construction, my attendees were unaffected.

As a consequence of my experiences, this provision is particularly detailed. At the point a hotel and a group representative execute an Exhibit A to the MHSA for a meeting, the ❶ hotel is agreeing that there won't be any construction, which excludes normal maintenance, at the same time as the meeting. ❷ If there will be construction, the hotel must immediately notify the group representative and the notification must include information relating to what the construction is, why the construction must occur at the same time as the meeting, and whether the construction is thought to be material. ❸ The provision assists a hotel in determining materiality by providing an illustrative list: reduced service, conditions that interfere with or impede the meeting, or conditions that otherwise breach the right to quiet enjoyment granted by the *No Interference; Quiet Enjoyment* provision. The ❹ group representative is obligated to then notify the hotel in writing if the construction will interfere with the meeting, and, if so, ❺ the group representative is entitled to terminate the meeting, either completely or partially, without liability.

Similar to the *No Interference; Incompatible Events* provision, this provision states that a group representative is *entitled* to terminate. A group representative may elect to not terminate even if there is construction and can either accept the risk of disruptions or work with the hotel to minimize disruptions resulting from the construction. I suggest that, in addition to the hotel minimizing disruptions, a group representative seek other concessions such as reduced room rates and food and beverage prices.

Hotels frequently object to this provision on the basis that remodeling and renovations are often ongoing and are generally not disruptive. Their objections typically include redlines which define construction as being "substantial" and that disruptions be "material." I'm generally not agreeable to those types of redlines because I contracted with the hotel to be of a certain quality and in a certain condition—and that didn't include construction. The other reason is that the provision already covers "substantial" in that it excludes normal maintenance and it already covers "material" in that a hotel is given an opportunity to describe the materiality of the impact on me or my attendees. Another common redline is where a hotel excludes any construction which has a budget less than a certain dollar amount and that the hotel only has to notify me of construction above the dollar amount. That's a ruse since even low-dollar construction projects can generate tremendous amounts of noise, dust, smells, and inconvenience. My position in negotiating this provision is to not negotiate it at all. That may seem inflexible, but it's my meeting. I will, however, agree to non-substantive redlines.

14.3   No Interference; Construction. Upon ratification of an Exhibit A, such ❶ Exhibit A shall constitute Hotel's express warranty that no construction, remodeling or renovation, excluding normal maintenance, (collectively and individually "Construction") shall occur during the In-House Dates. ❷ In the event Construction is to occur during the In-House Dates, Hotel shall immediately notify Customer in writing: (a) the nature and scope of such Construction; (b) the reason or cause for such Construction during the In-House Dates; and, (c) whether such Construction may materially interfere with Attendees' or Customer's use of Hotel including, but not limited to: ❸ (i) reducing serviceability to areas reserved for Customer's or Attendees' use; (ii) noise, dust, smells, or temperature conditions that would interrupt or disrupt Customer's or Attendees' operations or otherwise impede the operations of the Meeting; or, (iii) breach Customer's or Attendees' right of quiet enjoyment. Upon notification from Hotel, ❹ Customer shall promptly notify Hotel if the Construction will interfere with the Meeting, at the sole determination of Customer, and ❺ Customer shall be entitled to terminate the applicable Exhibit A, in whole or in part, without liability upon written notice to Hotel.

An example of a less-detailed and less group-favorable (therefore less contentious) "no construction" provision follows. While I don't suggest the use of this provision, it's better than not having a "no construction" provision at all.

14.3   No Interference; Construction. Hotel shall immediately notify Customer of any significant construction, remodeling, or renovation, excluding normal maintenance, that materially impacts the Meeting (collectively and individually "Construction"). Should Hotel prepare for or undertake any Construction during the In-House Dates, Hotel agrees that such Construction will not interfere with the Meeting. Customer shall be entitled to terminate the applicable Exhibit A, in whole or in part, without liability upon written notice to Hotel where Hotel and Customer mutually agree that

Construction is substantial and would materially interfere with the Meeting.

Remedy for Interference

Should a group representative desire an alternative to terminating a meeting (as permitted by the *No Interference; Incompatible Events* and *No Interference; Construction* provisions), the *Remedy for Interference* provision provides those alternative remedies. In the case of ❶ any interference, disturbances, or distractions which inhibit the use of a hotel, ❷ a group representative can ❸ select from one of three remedies. The first remedy requires the hotel to relocate the meeting to another comparable hotel at the same or lower cost. The second remedy is similar to the first except that the relocation occurs in the same hotel versus a different hotel (this would obviously only be applicable to a large hotel, compound-type of hotel, or a resort). The last remedy is that the group stays in the hotel, endures the inconveniencies, but gets the benefit of lower room rates and costs. ❹ Any credits or reduced charges due to a group representative are jointly negotiated between the hotel and the group representative.

> 14.4 <u>Remedy for Interference</u>. In the event of ❶interference, unreasonable disturbance, or any other distractions not caused by Customer or Attendees which inhibit Customer's or Attendees' peaceful use and enjoyment of Hotel, Hotel shall, ❷at the sole election of Customer: ❸(a) arrange for comparable or superior guestrooms (at the same Room Rates or lower) and any required function space at no charge to Customer at a nearby, comparable hotel acceptable to Customer with Hotel being responsible for any reasonable and necessary costs associated with relocating the Meeting to the alternate hotel; (b) arrange for comparable or superior guestrooms (at the same Room Rates or lower) and any required function space within Hotel

at no charge to Customer with Hotel being responsible for any reasonable and necessary costs associated with relocating the Meeting within Hotel; or, (c) reduce the Room Rates and charges owed or previously paid to Hotel by an amount proportionate to the inconvenience suffered by Customer or Attendees. Hotel and Customer shall ❹jointly decide the appropriate amount of a credit or reduced charges Customer is entitled to under such circumstances, after consultation in good faith.

Hotels frequently redline this provision, most commonly as follows. The ❶ limitation to events of interference isn't problematic in that, by including disturbances and distractions, I was perhaps over-reaching by expanding the scope of the provision to cover situations that may not be covered by the *No Interference; Incompatible Events* and *No Interference; Construction* provisions. The ❷ mutuality of determining the remedy is obviously not favorable, particularly considering that ❸ remedies other than reduced room rates and charges have been eliminated—but considering that a group representative still has the option to terminate the meeting, a hotel has a greater incentive to be "mutually" agreeable. Again, because of my prior experiences, I don't generally agree to changes to this provision unless they're minor, but, if I don't have the negotiation leverage to keep the provision in the MHSA as-is, I would consider something similar to the following as being acceptable.

14.4 Remedy for Interference. In the event of interference ❶, unreasonable disturbance, or any other distractions not caused by Customer or Attendees which inhibit Customer's or Attendees' peaceful use and enjoyment of Hotel, Hotel shall, ❷upon the mutual determination of Hotel and Customer, ❸at the sole election of Customer: (a) arrange for comparable or superior guestrooms (at the same Room Rates or lower) and any required function space at no

~~charge to Customer at a nearby, comparable hotel acceptable to Customer with Hotel being responsible for any reasonable and necessary costs associated with relocating the Meeting to the alternate hotel; (b) arrange for comparable or superior guestrooms (at the same Room Rates or lower) and any required function space within the Hotel at no charge to Customer with Hotel being responsible for any reasonable and necessary costs associated with relocating the Meeting within Hotel; or, (c)~~ reduce the Room Rates and charges owed or previously paid to Hotel by an amount proportionate to the inconvenience suffered by Customer or Attendees. Hotel and Customer shall jointly decide the appropriate amount, if any, of a credit or reduced charges Customer is entitled to under such circumstances, after consultation in good faith.

Deterioration in Quality

Without proper maintenance and necessary renovations, the quality and condition of a hotel will deteriorate over time. If a group representative elects to contract with a hotel based on its quality and condition—and at a corresponding price point—it would be unreasonable for the group representative to be held to the contract or the price point if the hotel fails to keep up its end of the bargain by not maintaining the same level of quality or condition.

The purpose of the *Deterioration in Quality* provision, sometimes referred to as a "condition of premises" provision, is to ensure that a group representative has a remedy if a hotel fails to maintain the same level of quality and physical condition at the time of a meeting as when the hotel contract was first entered into. This type of provision is oriented to a meeting that is scheduled to occur in the long-term versus the short-term where material deterioration is unlikely. With a large or important meeting scheduled significantly in advance, it's common for a group representative to conduct a site inspection which, among other things, re-examines hotel quality and condition.

Under the provision, ❶ a hotel warrants that the quality of the services that it is contracted to provide and the physical condition of its facilities will be the same at the time of a meeting as when the meeting was originally contracted. The group representative must ❷ notify the hotel if he or she determines, from a site inspection as an example, of any deficiencies in quality or condition which are material. If the hotel ❸ doesn't or won't timely correct the deficiencies to the satisfaction of the group representative, the group representative may seek either or both of the stated remedies. The remedies are the ❹ right to terminate the meeting, in whole or in part, and a ❺ reduced room rate and reduced costs for other contracted services (both as measured against other, comparable hotels). Unfortunately, I've had to rely on the remedies in this provision more than once, but, fortunately, I had the provision in the MHSA which enabled my ability to obtain a remedy.

Some hotels request that normal aging and normal wear and tear be excepted as deficiencies that rise to the level of materiality. That request may sound like a reasonable one, but it's not. The quality and condition of a hotel *is* its business. A hotel has an obligation to groups it contracts with to maintain itself, normal aging and normal wear and tear *not* excepted. I've been in hotels built hundreds of years ago that are in a condition as good (or maybe even better) as when the hotels were first built. There's no reason why other hotels can't do the same and there's no reason why any quality or condition exception should be granted to a hotel. In a way, an exception is already built into most deterioration in quality provisions—as is this one—which requires that the change in quality or condition be material. For all of the foregoing reasons, exceptions for normal aging and normal wear and tear are unreasonable.

Hotels occasionally object to this provision on the basis that it's too subjective and hotels will seek to introduce what they think creates objectivity, such as a reduction in "stars" (e.g., Forbes Travel Guide) as a basis for materiality. Hotel rating schemas might be a bit more objective, but there must be a significant drop in quality or condition to warrant degrading a hotel's rating—which is too forgiving in terms of defining materiality and, therefore, unacceptable. Hotels also occasionally object to the remedy of termination, preferring to offer a lower room rate and lower charges as the sole remedy.

15. <u>Deterioration in Quality</u>. Upon ratification of an <u>Exhibit A</u>, such <u>Exhibit A</u> shall constitute ❶ Hotel's express warranty that the quality of the Services and the physical condition of Hotel, Guestrooms, and any Function Space over the In-House Dates shall be the same or better than on the date of ratification of the <u>Exhibit A</u>. ❷ Customer shall promptly notify Hotel if Customer determines, at the sole determination of Customer, that there are material deficiencies in quality or condition. Should ❸ Hotel be unable or unwilling to correct the identified deficiencies to the satisfaction of Customer within a commercially reasonable time, Customer may elect to: (a) ❹ terminate the <u>Exhibit A</u>, in whole or in part, without liability; and / or, (b) ❺ reduce the Room Rate and the cost of any other Services by an amount equivalent to the decline in quality or condition as evidenced by the cost of similar rooms or services at other hotels comparable to Hotel.

Americans with Disabilities Act Compliance

While the MHSA does contain the *Compliance with Laws* provision that requires a hotel to comply with various laws and regulations, the Americans with Disabilities Act of 1990 (ADA) has unique characteristics and obligations that warrant a compliance provision specific to the ADA. The ADA, as amended, is a wide-ranging civil rights law that prohibits, under certain circumstances, discrimination based on disability. Disability is defined by the ADA as "a physical or mental impairment that substantially limits a major life activity." Title III of the ADA, which the U.S. Department of Justice has implemented regulations for and which can be found in the Code of Federal Regulations (C.F.R.) at 28 C.F.R. Part 36, applies to public accommodations. Under Title III, no individual may be discriminated against on the basis of disability with regards to the full and equal enjoyment of the goods, services, facilities, or accommodations of any place of public accommodation. As defined by the regulations, "public accommodations" includes "[a]n inn, hotel, motel, or other place of lodging…." There are exceptions, such as historic properties which must comply with the provisions of Title III to the "maximum extent feasible" unless following the usual standards would "threaten to destroy the historic significance of a feature of the building." In such a case, alternative standards may be used.

Under Title III, all "new construction" (construction, modification, or alterations) after the 1992 effective date of the ADA must be fully compliant with the Americans with Disabilities Act Accessibility Guidelines found at 28 C.F.R. Part 36, Appendix A. Title III also applies to existing facilities. One of the definitions of "discrimination" under Title III is a "failure to remove" architectural barriers in existing facilities. This means that even facilities that have not been modified or altered in any way after the effective date of the ADA was passed still have obligations. The standard is whether "removing barriers" (typically defined as bringing a condition into compliance with the Americans with Disabilities Act Accessibility Guidelines) is "readily achievable," defined as "easily accomplished without much difficulty or expense." Additionally, under Title III, hotels have a duty to provide "auxiliary aids and services"[8] to individuals where necessary to ensure effective communication with individuals with disabilities. Hotels must

---

[8] 28 C.F.R. Part 36.303(c) lists examples of aids and services.

also make reasonable modifications to policies, practices, or procedures, when the modifications are necessary to afford goods, services, facilities, privileges, advantages, or accommodations to individuals with disabilities. An example would be that a hotel's "no pets" policy be modified to allow for service animals used by disabled individuals.

The provision begins by specifying that ❶ both a hotel and a group representative will comply with the ADA, the implementing regulations, and any guidelines (such as the Americans with Disabilities Act Accessibility Guidelines). The provision ❷ collectively identifies all of the foregoing as the "ADA" for purposes of the provision, and adds the qualifier, "as amended." That qualifier is important in that the ADA must be complied with in its then-current form. For example, there were significant changes to Title III in 2010 that will eventually (after a grace period) impact hotels and require, among other things, that hotels ensure "accessible" rooms and other guest amenities (such as fitness areas and pools) meet new construction guidelines. The ❸ ADA is a U.S. law and doesn't apply to hotels located outside of the U.S. Therefore, the provision makes it clear that only U.S.-based meetings are covered. Among other requirements that a hotel must comply with under the ADA, the provision ❹ enumerates three major requirements of the ADA in (a) through (c). These three requirements have been lifted practically word-for-word from the ADA regulations. If a hotel attempts to redline (a) through (c) by changing the language, that's completely unacceptable and the hotel's redlines should be summarily refused along with the advice that the hotel "read the regs." To facilitate ensuring that the needs of disabled individuals are accommodated, the provision ❺ requires cooperation between a hotel and a group representative. Should a group representative know or become aware of the special needs of a disabled individual, he or she is required to notify the hotel. Similarly, if the hotel becomes aware of the special needs of a disabled individual from a source other than the group representative, the hotel is required to notify the group representative.

It's not uncommon for an ADA compliance provision to contain an indemnification. Instead of including it here, I elected to include a broader indemnification in the *Compliance with Laws* provision which addresses the hotel's failure to comply with any laws or regulations, including the ADA.

16. Americans with Disabilities Act Compliance. ❶Each of Customer and Hotel warrants that it shall comply with the Americans with Disabilities Act of 1990, all relevant regulations, and all relevant guidelines (collectively, the "ADA," ❷as amended) applicable to the Meeting provided that the Meeting is ❸located in the United States, its territories, or its possessions. Hotel acknowledges and agrees that ❹it is responsible for: (a) the "readily achievable" removal of physical barriers to access to Hotel's premises; (b) the provision of auxiliary aids and services where necessary to ensure that no disabled individual is treated differently by Hotel than other individuals; and, (c) the modification of Hotel's policies, practices, and procedures as necessary to provide goods, services, facilities, privileges, advantages, or accommodations to disabled individuals. ❺Customer shall attempt to identify in advance any special needs of disabled Attendees and will notify Hotel of such needs for accommodation as soon as they are identified by Customer. ❻Hotel shall notify Customer of requests for accommodation made by Attendees which it may receive otherwise than through Customer to facilitate identification by Customer of its own accommodation obligations.

My preference is to use the short, reciprocal version of the provision above, but hotels occasionally want my obligations relating to accommodations (such as ensuring that my exhibits, room sets, stages, and so on are ADA-compliant) to be expressly included in the MHSA. A longer version of the provision follows, which clearly identifies obligations by party.

16. <u>Americans with Disabilities Act Compliance</u>. Each of Customer and Hotel warrants that it shall comply with the <u>Americans with Disabilities Act</u>, all relevant regulations, and all relevant guidelines (collectively, the "ADA," as amended) applicable to the Meeting provided that the Meeting is located in the United States, its territories, or its possessions.

16.1 <u>Compliance by Hotel</u>. Hotel acknowledges and agrees that it shall be responsible for complying with the public accommodations requirements of the ADA not otherwise allocated to Customer herein, including: (a) the "readily achievable" removal of physical barriers to access to Hotel's premises; (b) the provision of auxiliary aids and services where necessary to ensure that no disabled individual is treated differently by Hotel than other individuals; and, (c) the modification of Hotel's policies, practices, and procedures as necessary to provide goods, services, facilities, privileges, advantages, or accommodations to disabled individuals.

16.2 <u>Compliance by Customer</u>. Customer acknowledges and agrees that it shall be responsible for complying with the following public accommodations requirements of ADA: (a) the "readily achievable" removal of physical barriers within the meeting rooms utilized by Customer which Customer would otherwise create (e.g., set-up of exhibits in an accessible manner) and not controlled or mandated by Hotel; (b) the provision of auxiliary aids and services where necessary to ensure effective communication of the content of the Meeting to disabled Attendees; and, (c) the modification of Customer's policies, practices and procedures applicable to the Meeting as necessary to enable disabled Attendees to participate equally in the Meeting.

16.3 <u>Mutual Cooperation in Identifying Special Needs</u>. Customer shall attempt to identify in advance any special needs of disabled Attendees requiring accommodation by Hotel, and will notify Hotel of such needs for accommodation as soon as they are identified to Customer. Whenever possible, Customer shall provide to Hotel any correspondence between Customer and Attendees who indicate special needs requiring accommodation. Hotel shall notify Customer of requests for accommodation made by Attendees which it may receive otherwise than through Customer to facilitate identification by Customer of its own accommodation obligations.

For meetings that are held outside of the U.S., the following non-law-specific provision addresses the accommodation of disabled attendees in an international context and can be included as a part of the MHSA or included in an Exhibit A to the MHSA for the specific meeting.

XX.   Accommodation of Disabled Attendees. Where the Meeting is located outside of the United States, its territories, or its possessions, with respect to disabled Attendees, Hotel agrees to: (a) the removal of physical barriers which inhibit access by disabled Attendees to Hotel's premises; (b) the provision of auxiliary aids and services where necessary to ensure that disabled Attendees have the best possible guest experience; and, (c) provide its staff with training and guidance in order to enhance its staff's understanding of the services necessary to accommodate disabled Attendees.

Indemnification; Liability; Insurance

While words like "indemnification," "liability," and "insurance" may just sound like a lot of legalese, they're worth paying attention to since they'll help to keep a group representative out of legal and financial hot water. Without these important provisions, a group representative might be on the hook to pay a hotel for damages caused by an attendee or to pay an attendee for damages caused by the hotel. Pay close attention to any changes requested by a hotel to any of the provisions contained in this section.

Also, be cognizant that there is a relationship between the *General Indemnification, Limitation of Liability,* and *Insurance* provisions contained in the MHSA. If a group representative is unfamiliar with these types of provisions, it may make sense to read the explanations below and then re-read this paragraph to better understand the interplay between the provisions. While an indemnity serves as a substantial risk mitigation tool for buyers, its usefulness can be eroded by the limitation of liability and (lack of) insurance. For example, if a limitation of liability provision is structured such that the obligation of indemnification is substantially limited, a buyer has no real safety because the seller has a limited dollar amount that it is responsible for. Further, even if an indemnification provision is not substantially limited by the limitation of liability provision, a seller may be "judgment-proof" if it has limited insurance or no insurance. In other words, if a seller has no insurance or has no substantial assets by which to draw from to pay for any claims resulting from the seller's obligation of indemnification, the obligation is meaningless. Therefore, limitation of liability and insurance provisions are critical to consider in conjunction with the indemnification provision.

If a group representative is unsure of the impact of any changes made by a hotel to the provisions contained in this section or doesn't feel comfortable negotiating the legalese, it would be prudent to seek qualified legal counsel.

General Indemnification

Indemnification might at first glance appear to be intimidating and hard to understand, but it's really a simple concept. When one party agrees to indemnify another party, the indemnifying party is agreeing to provide compensation, either directly or by reimbursement, for any loss or damage sustained by the indemnified party as a result of a stated set of circumstances. Broad indemnification provisions can also include an agreement by the indemnifying party to legally defend the indemnified party against any claim asserted by a third party. An indemnification provision usually stipulates that the indemnity does not apply to the extent that the claim resulted from the acts or omissions caused by the party seeking indemnification. I think about the concept of indemnification even more simply—when something goes wrong under a contract, and it wasn't my fault, the other party is going to defend me and make me whole.

Under a buyer-seller contract, the buyer typically seeks a unilateral general indemnification provision (where only the seller is the indemnifying party) on the basis that the buyer is the only party likely to have a significant claim asserted against it as a result of the contract and as a result of the seller's performance. On the other hand, the seller is not likely to have a claim asserted against it as a result of the buyer's performance because, arguably, a buyer's only substantial obligation to the seller under a buyer-seller contract is payment. Under an MHSA, the relationship between the buyer (the group representative) and the seller (the hotel) is a bit more intertwined than the typical buyer-seller relationship. For example, it's common for a group representative to have contractors, guest speakers, and others onsite at a hotel and working within the hotel's facilities. That means that a hotel is exposed to substantially more risk than the risk of non-payment. Consequently, instead of using a unilateral indemnification provision, the MHSA acknowledges the more intertwined relationship and contains mutual indemnification. A group representative could always start negotiations with a unilateral indemnification provision but it's highly likely that almost every hotel would ask for mutuality—which is entirely reasonable—and it's therefore more efficient to start with a mutual provision.

While this provision provides for mutuality, it does so by including two separate unilateral provisions. One reason for this is because the indemnifications aren't entirely balanced—meaning that the hotel's obligation of indemnification is more beneficial than the indemnification that it gets from the group representative. Another reason for this is because the parties being indemnified are different based on whether it's the hotel or the group representative. It's typical to indemnify a party and that party's officers, directors, employees, representatives, and agents. Under an MHSA, however, there are additional parties involved because of the innkeeper-guest relationship. In the case of a hotel's indemnification of the "Customer," ❶ the Customer parties include contractors, vendors, guests (e.g., speakers), and attendees where there is some sort of liability created by the "Hotel," and the Hotel parties ❷ include other guests of the hotel. In other words, if something happens to the attendees as a result of another hotel guest, the hotel is responsible for indemnifying the group representative. Just to be clear—and this doesn't limit the hotel's obligation of indemnification— the hotel is on the hook if ❸ there's any damage, injury, or death resulting from the hotel's equipment, premises or fixtures, or its sale of alcohol. In the case of a group representative's (the "Customer") indemnification of the "Hotel," ❹ the Hotel parties *don't* include other guests of the Hotel where there is some sort of liability created by the "Customer," and the Customer parties ❺ *don't* include the attendees. In other words, if something happens to the Hotel parties (including other guests) as a result of one of the attendees, the group representative is *not* responsible for indemnifying the hotel. A hotel might object to this, but it's reasonable that a group representative not be responsible for the individual actions of the attendees—that's between the hotel and whoever else may be damaged by an attendee and that damaged party can seek their own legal recourse.

17.1 General Indemnification.

17.1.1 By Hotel. Hotel shall indemnify, defend, and hold harmless ❶Customer, its officers, directors, partners, employees, contractors, vendors, guests, volunteers, representatives, agents, and Attendees (each, a "Customer Indemnitee") from any and all demands, charges, claims, damages, losses, and liabilities, including reasonable attorneys' fees and expenses (collectively "Claims") that any Customer Indemnitee may or does incur arising out of or caused by the act, error, omission, negligence, misconduct, or wrongdoing of ❷Hotel, its officers, directors, partners, employees, contractors, vendors, representatives, agents, or guests in connection with this Agreement or an Exhibit A. ❸Hotel's indemnification of a Customer Indemnitee shall include, but not be limited to, any damage or injury (including death) arising out of the failure of Hotel equipment, defects in Hotel's premises or fixtures, and the sale or service of alcohol by Hotel. The foregoing indemnity shall not apply to the extent that the applicable Claim resulted from the act, error, omission, negligence, misconduct, or wrongdoing of a Customer Indemnitee. Customer is not deemed to have waived, by reason of this provision, any defense that it may have with respect to any Claim.

17.1.2 By Customer. Customer shall indemnify, defend, and hold harmless ❹Hotel, its officers, directors, partners, employees, contractors, vendors, and agents (each, a "Hotel Indemnitee") from any and all Claims that any Hotel Indemnitee may or does incur arising out of or caused by the act, error, omission, negligence, misconduct, or wrongdoing of ❺Customer, its officers, directors, partners, employees, contractors, vendors, guests, volunteers, representatives, or agents in connection with this Agreement or an Exhibit A. The foregoing indemnity shall not apply to the extent that the applicable Claim resulted from the act, error, omission, negligence, misconduct, or wrongdoing of a Hotel Indemnitee. Hotel is not deemed to have waived, by reason of this provision, any defense that it may have with respect to any Claim.

Liquor Liability

A group representative should take appropriate and responsible measures to ensure that attendees don't become intoxicated and aren't put into situations where they can cause damage to themselves or others. Examples of such measures include providing no- or low-alcohol beverage options, providing food items in addition to alcohol, and closing alcohol service well before the scheduled end of the event. However, it's impossible for a group representative to monitor and ensure that a hotel is being responsible in its serving of alcohol to attendees. Consequently, it's appropriate that a hotel take on liability for its failure to be responsible. Many states have what are called "dram shop" laws which hold commercial servers of alcohol (including hotels) liable for damages caused by an intoxicated patron. The term "dram shop" comes courtesy of 18th century England when establishments sold gin by the spoonful, called a dram. In states that have enacted dram shop laws there is significant variation. Some states have very limited dram shop laws and only find liability where an illegal sale of alcohol was involved (such as to a minor). Other states take a stricter position, extending liability to non-commercial social hosts. Since some states haven't enacted dram shop laws and since there is significant variation from state-to-state where such laws have been enacted, it makes sense to include the *Liquor Liability* provision in the MHSA in order to ensure appropriate and consistent allocation of liability.

Hotels infrequently take issue with the following provision, and, when they do, it's usually to point out that the ❶ indemnification section of the provision is redundant with the *General Indemnification* provision. I like to call it "clarification" instead of "redundant," but that section of the provision really is redundant since the *General Indemnification* provision would capture the hotel's breach of the *Liquor Liability* provision. Therefore, if a group representative has to concede on the deletion of the indemnification section in this provision, there's no real harm in doing so.

17.2   Liquor Liability. At all functions that are catered by Hotel where alcohol is served, Hotel shall be responsible for exercising reasonable care in its service of alcohol to Attendees. Hotel shall be responsible for adhering to state and local laws regulating the sale and service of alcoholic beverages and shall not serve alcohol to Attendees that are either noticeably intoxicated or underage. Hotel represents and warrants to Customer that it has adopted a written policy requiring bartenders, staff serving tables, and other Hotel personnel regarding the service of alcoholic beverages to guests, including, but not limited to, discontinuance of service of alcoholic beverages to any person who appears to be intoxicated. Hotel represents and warrants that all Hotel personnel have undergone adequate training to prevent any incidents that could result in claims of liquor liability.

17.2.1   Liquor Liability Indemnification. Notwithstanding any other provisions in this Agreement, ❶Hotel shall indemnify, defend, and hold harmless any Customer Indemnitee from any and all Claims that any Customer Indemnitee may or does incur arising out of or caused by Hotel's sale or service of alcoholic beverages.

Limitation of Liability

Limitation of liability is perhaps the single most important provision in any contract from the perspective of risk mitigation. Quite simply, the limit which is described in a limitation of liability provision constitutes the maximum financial damages recoverable by one party against the other party. Properly drafted, the provision can provide protection against significant liability (for the party that has to pay up) and too little liability (for the party that has been damaged). Limitation of liability provisions are easy to spot in most contracts because of the capitalized text used to ensure that the provision is conspicuous and to avoid any argument that the limitation was "hidden" by embodying it among less critical provisions.

Limitation of liability provisions are usually comprised of four sections that can be found in different order from contract to contract. ❶ The first section is referred to as the "exculpation" from the limitation of liability. When a contract is breached, the recognized remedy for the non-breaching party is the recovery of damages that result *directly* from the breach. Consequential damages (also sometimes referred to as special or indirect damages) are those damages that do not directly result from a breach but are a consequence of the breach (such as lost profits). Because consequential damages in many cases are not "reasonably foreseeable," parties typically agree that no party will be liable for these types of damages. ❷ The second section of a typical limitation of liability provision contains an "exclusion" to the exculpation. Under the exclusion, a party *will* be liable for consequential damages where the party caused the damage through their negligence and misconduct. ❸ The third section is the actual limitation of liability, which is the core of the provision. This section of the provision states that a party is liable for direct damages up to the stated limitation. The limitation can be specified quantitatively by stating an exact dollar amount (such as one million dollars) or be described qualitatively such as "fees paid or payable under the Agreement." ❹ The fourth section is called an "exception" to the limitation of liability. An exception means that, for the stated exception, there is no limitation of liability and a party's liability relating to the exception will be unlimited. Commonly, a party's obligation of indemnification, damages caused by a party's negligence or misconduct, or a breach of a party's obligation of confidentiality are exceptions to the limit and, therefore, there is no limitation with respect to the exceptions. Since the MHSA doesn't contain a confidentiality provision, the obligation of confidentiality only arises by virtue of a separate agreement (such as under the *Customer Audit Rights* provision).

In some cases, where the parties have unequal negotiation leverage or one party is more sophisticated than the other, the limitation of liability may be unilateral—meaning that one party has limited liability and the other party has unlimited liability. With hotels, the negotiation leverage is clearly unequal (a group representative or a hotel may have the negotiating advantage based on the situation) but it's more efficient to start with a mutual limitation of liability since both parties are generally sophisticated (especially after reading this book). If a hotel's legal representative gets involved in the negotiation of the MHSA, that individual will likely have some sort of "input" relating to the *Limitation of Liability* provision. That input will inevitably entail a lower limit for the hotel and / or a higher limit for the group representative (as the payor). Read and consider all requested changes carefully.

17.3   Limitation of Liability. NOTWITHSTANDING ANY OTHER PROVISION SET FORTH HEREIN, ❶NEITHER PARTY SHALL BE LIABLE FOR ANY INDIRECT, SPECIAL, AND/OR CONSEQUENTIAL DAMAGES, ARISING OUT OF OR IN CONNECTION WITH THIS AGREEMENT; PROVIDED, HOWEVER, THAT ❷THE FOREGOING EXCULPATION OF LIABILITY SHALL NOT APPLY WITH RESPECT TO DAMAGES INCURRED AS A RESULT OF THE GROSS NEGLIGENCE OR WILLFUL MISCONDUCT OF A PARTY. ❸A PARTY SHALL BE LIABLE TO THE

OTHER FOR ANY DIRECT DAMAGES ARISING OUT OF OR RELATING TO ITS PERFORMANCE OR FAILURE TO PERFORM UNDER THIS AGREEMENT; PROVIDED, HOWEVER, THAT THE LIABILITY OF A PARTY, WHETHER BASED ON AN ACTION OR CLAIM IN CONTRACT, EQUITY, NEGLIGENCE, TORT, OR OTHERWISE FOR ALL EVENTS, ACTS, OR OMISSIONS UNDER THIS AGREEMENT SHALL NOT EXCEED ONE MILLION UNITED STATES DOLLARS ($1,000,000), AND PROVIDED, FURTHER, THAT ❹THE FOREGOING LIMITATION SHALL NOT APPLY TO: (A) A PARTY'S OBLIGATIONS OF INDEMNIFICATION, AS FURTHER DESCRIBED IN THIS AGREEMENT; (B) DAMAGES CAUSED BY A PARTY'S GROSS NEGLIGENCE OR WILLFUL MISCONDUCT; OR, (C) A PARTY'S BREACH OF ITS OBLIGATIONS, IF ANY, OF CONFIDENTIALITY.

Insurance

Where a party to a contract causes some sort of damage or injury to the other party or to a beneficiary to the contract (in the case of an MHSA, a beneficiary would be an attendee), the party at fault will generally be responsible for such damage or injury subject to the terms and conditions of the contract (such as the *General Indemnification* and *Limitation of Liability* provisions). While hotels are usually well-capitalized and typically have tangible assets, it's always helpful to have the peace of mind that, should anything go awry, a hotel has the funds in the form of insurance to cover any liabilities that might arise. There's always the possibility that a hotel doesn't have any liquid assets or, for that matter, any assets at all, to cover any liabilities. In that case, if a hotel doesn't have insurance, good luck collecting on any claim or judgment a group representative or one of the attendees may have against the hotel. Thus, requiring insurance of both parties to the MHSA is just a prudent measure to take.

Hotels rarely take issue with the following insurance language, which also requires that a hotel provide ❶ "special" coverage due to the nature of the hotel's business (such as liquor liability insurance). If a hotel wants to tweak the language a bit, that's probably fine, but be sure to examine any changes—such as coverage limitations—carefully. If a hotel makes any substantive changes, doing so should raise a big, red flag and the group representative needs to question why the hotel isn't willing to provide the required insurance coverage.

> 17.4   <u>Insurance</u>. Each party shall obtain, maintain, and provide evidence of insurance in amounts sufficient, unless such amounts are otherwise specified herein or in an <u>Exhibit A</u>, to provide coverage for any liabilities arising out of or resulting from the respective obligations pursuant to this Agreement and an <u>Exhibit A</u>, as the case may be.
>
> > 17.4.1   <u>Additional Insurance; Hotel</u>.   In addition to comprehensive general liability insurance, Hotel shall carry ❶crime, liquor liability, property or hazard, and other insurance in such dollar amount as is necessary to protect itself against any claims arising from the performance of this Agreement or an <u>Exhibit A</u>, including Hotel's indemnification obligations herein.

General

Like many other contracts, the MHSA contains a section of "boilerplate" contract provisions. While I won't explain each of the boilerplate provisions in the MHSA because some are relatively straightforward, there are certain provisions that are unique to the MHSA and some other boilerplate provisions that have nuances worth highlighting.

Claims; Disputes; Informal Resolution

When there's a dispute or breach under a contract, the contracting parties can informally negotiate the resolution before having to resort to other forms of dispute resolution such as arbitration or litigation. Informal dispute resolution is usually more effective, almost always more cost-efficient, and clearly less disruptive to a business relationship than formal dispute resolution. In certain contracts, such as an MHSA, where there are a lot of little things that can go wrong, I like to specify the requirement and procedure for the parties to at least try to informally resolve most issues. Even if the contract specifies some sort of remedy for a particular breach, the non-breaching party is "stayed" from implementing the specified remedy until the informal dispute resolution procedure is followed. An example is where an MHSA specifies liquidated damages for attrition and there is a subsequent meeting where the room pick-up is less than the permitted slippage, thus triggering attrition damages. In that example, it's clear that the liquidated damages are payable by the group representative to the hotel. Without the *Claims; Disputes; Informal Resolution* provision, a group representative has to pay up if the hotel demands it. With the provision, the hotel can't immediately demand the liquidated damages, which gives the group representative some time to try and bargain the liquidated damages away. But the provision works both ways—if a hotel breaches, the group representative is also required to work through the informal dispute resolution procedure. So, if a group representative prefers having the leverage of being able to threaten litigation when something goes wrong (there's nothing wrong with that, and I prefer that sort of leverage in other types of contracts), then just remove this provision from the MHSA. In fact, some hotels feel the same way and want the provision deleted.

The provision requires that ❶ the parties appoint a representative at the director-level (with the implication that the representative can make decisions for his or her employer) for the purpose of resolving the dispute. ❷ The representatives then meet as needed to resolve the dispute and share, as necessary, information that's not confidential or privileged. ❸ If the representatives can't come to a resolution within a 30-day period, then the remedy specified in the MHSA can be invoked or, if there isn't any specified remedy, the complaining party can proceed to another form of dispute resolution. There are certain situations ❹ where the requirement to follow the informal dispute resolution procedure shouldn't apply and where immediate relief is permitted: indemnification and an obligation of confidentiality (if any). For example, if a hotel negligently (allegedly) served alcohol to a minor attendee, it doesn't make any sense for director-level staff of the hotel and group representative to get together for up to 30-days to talk about a resolution—the hotel is required to indemnify the group representative immediately. Finally, ❺ during the period that the parties are working through the informal dispute resolution, the hotel must fulfill its obligations under the MHSA and any Exhibit A to the MHSA. That removes any leverage that a hotel could gain over a group representative by refusing to perform.

18.1   Claims; Disputes; Informal Resolution. In the event of any material dispute or disagreement between the parties with respect to the interpretation of any provision of this Agreement or an Exhibit A, or with respect to the performance of either party hereunder, ❶each party shall appoint director-level staff (each, a "Representative") who shall meet in good faith for the purpose of resolving the dispute or disagreement. ❷The Representatives shall meet as often as the parties reasonably deem necessary in order to gather and furnish to each other all essential, non-privileged information that the parties believe germane to resolution of the matter at issue. During the course of these non-judicial dispute resolution procedures, documents used to resolve the dispute or disagreement shall be limited to essential, non-privileged information. All requests shall be made in good faith and be reasonable in light of the economics and time efficiencies intended by the dispute resolution procedures. ❸Where the Representatives cannot come to resolution of the matter at issue within thirty (30) calendar days following the event resulting in the dispute or disagreement, the remedy provided for herein, if any, associated with such dispute, shall be enforced. ❹A dispute pertaining to a party's obligations of indemnification and confidentiality, if any, shall not be subject to this Section nor shall the provisions of this Section preclude either party from obtaining temporary injunctive relief in order to preserve its rights hereunder. Hotel acknowledges that the timely and complete performance of its obligations pursuant to this Agreement is critical to the business and operations of Customer. Accordingly, in the event of a dispute or disagreement between Hotel and Customer, ❺Hotel shall continue to perform its obligations hereunder in good faith during the resolution of such dispute or disagreement unless and until this Agreement or an <u>Exhibit A</u> is terminated in accordance with the provisions hereof. This provision shall survive the termination of this Agreement and an <u>Exhibit A</u>.

Obligation of Hotel to Mitigate Damages

Under the mitigation of damages doctrine, a contracting party who has the potential to suffer damages or has suffered damages caused by the other party's breach of contract must take reasonable steps to avoid or reduce the damages. The failure to take such reasonable steps will reduce any amount of recovery. The obligation to mitigate damages is implied under contract law and doesn't need to be expressly stated in a contract. However, in the MHSA, the mitigation of damages doctrine is expressly stated as the *Obligation of Hotel to Mitigate Damages* provision.

I had a large event scheduled in Las Vegas in the mid-2000s while the hotel business was still booming and before the economy went bust. At the time, Las Vegas was one of the hottest destinations for groups and the hotels were gouging everyone with outrageous room rates, inflated food and beverage minimums, and 100% attrition damages. I had "inherited" the contracts for the Las Vegas meeting, which had been negotiated years earlier. Unfortunately, the contracted room blocks were way more than what I needed. Because I knew this significantly in advance, I mailed letters to the appropriate hotels roughly six months in advance and advised the hotels of the exact reductions in room blocks I needed to make. With this significant advance notice and because Las Vegas was so hot, the hotels would have had little trouble reselling the sleeping rooms I didn't need. This reselling of sleeping rooms was clearly a means by which the hotels could mitigate their damages. So, what did these hotels do? The hotels either ignored me or sent back some sort of communication (either a letter or an e-mail) advising me that I wasn't contractually permitted to reduce the room block (which was true). Instead of attempting to resell the sleeping rooms, the hotels did nothing. Consequently, after the meeting, the hotels promptly sent me notices indicating the amounts of attrition damages. I was faced with hundreds of thousands of dollars in attrition damages. Unfortunately, for the hotels, they were on shaky legal footing because they had been given significant advance notice and they failed to reasonably mitigate their damages. Sparing all of the ensuing details, months later I ended up paying only a small fraction of the attrition damages. After Las Vegas, even though the obligation is implied in a contract, I decided to include an express provision in the MHSA requiring a hotel to mitigate damages. Even if an MHSA doesn't specify attrition damages, this provision can remain since the provision is only trigged "if any" damages are incurred.

Not surprisingly, hotels don't like this provision but they can't complain too much because it merely mirrors well-established contract law that the hotels are ultimately subject to.

> 18.2 <u>Obligation of Hotel to Mitigate Damages</u>. For the purposes of unused Guestrooms, Hotel shall undertake all reasonable efforts to resell unused Guestrooms and will credit the revenues against the liquidated damages, if any, in an amount not to exceed the full amount of such damages.

Relationship between Customer and Hotel

It's typical in buyer-seller contracts to include a provision that describes the relationship between the parties. One significant reason is to avoid "co-employment" issues. Co-employment is a legal doctrine which applies when two legally distinct employers have an employer-employee relationship with the same person. If that occurs, a seller's employee may be deemed to be an employee of the buyer for legal purposes such as employee benefits. The *Relationship between Customer and Hotel* provision in the context of co-employment is over-kill because of the short duration of an Exhibit A to the MHSA (i.e., the duration of the meeting). However, the provision is helpful in that ❶ it specifies that the parties are completely independent and that a hotel doesn't have the authority to bind a group representative. Also, the provision makes clear that ❷ a hotel doesn't hold any special relationship to a group representative. If a hotel does attempt to bind a group representative or does act, for example, as an unauthorized agent, the hotel—and not the group representative—will be liable for any damages.

> 18.3 <u>Relationship between Customer and Hotel</u>. Hotel represents and warrants that ❶it is an independent contractor with no

authority to contract for Customer or in any way to bind or to commit Customer to any agreement of any kind or to assume any liabilities of any nature in the name of or on behalf of Customer. ❷Under no circumstances shall Hotel, or any of its staff, hold itself out as or be considered an agent, employee, joint venture, or partner of Customer. In recognition of Hotel's status as independent contractor, Customer shall carry no Workers' Compensation insurance or any health or accident insurance to cover Hotel or Hotel's agents or staff. Customer shall not pay any contributions to Social Security, unemployment insurance, United States Federal or state withholding taxes, any other applicable taxes whether United States Federal, state, or local, nor provide any other contributions or benefits which might be expected in an employer-employee relationship. Neither Hotel nor its staff, shall be eligible for, participate in, or accrue any direct or indirect benefit under any other compensation, benefit, or pension plan of Customer.

Governing Law

This provision—also called a "choice of law" provision—specifies the body of law of a particular state or jurisdiction which governs the rights and responsibilities of parties under an MHSA. Strategically, a group representative would prefer that the governing law of an MHSA be the law of the jurisdiction in which the group representative is located because the cost to litigate a contract dispute in a hotel's (distant) jurisdiction is inherently higher and because the other jurisdiction may be potentially hostile to a group representative's claim or defense. Within limits, parties may choose which jurisdiction's law will govern matters related to contract formation, interpretation, and enforceability. A governing law provision includes both the substantive law to apply to a contract as well as the procedural law. For example, one jurisdiction's law could govern a contract and another jurisdiction could serve as the place (forum / venue) where the substantive law is applied. For example, contracting parties could agree that Maryland law applies but that Florida will be the forum state. In this example, the Florida courts would apply Maryland law. Mostly, a court will apply whatever governing law was selected provided that the governing law does not conflict with the public policy of the forum state. However, if the selected governing law is different than the state of domicile for the parties, a court in the forum state generally requires some sort of nexus between the selected governing law, the forum, and the parties.

For the same reason that a group representative wants his or her state's law to govern an MHSA, a hotel will want its state law to apply particularly considering that it's more likely for a hotel to be sued under an MHSA than a group representative (because a hotel is doing more "performing" under an MHSA and has more exposure to something going wrong). In cases where neither party will budge on the governing law, as a compromise, it's common for the parties to agree to either New York or Illinois law to govern the contract. New York is a common compromise because of its position as one of the world's major financial and commercial centers—meaning that New York has well-established and balanced case law. The same goes for Illinois, and Chicago also makes sense as a geographic compromise.

18.4   Governing Law. This Agreement shall be governed by and construed in accordance with the laws of the State of Maryland and the Federal laws of the United States of America. The parties hereby consent and submit to the jurisdiction and forum of the state and United States Federal courts in the State of Maryland in all questions and controversies arising out of this Agreement.

Compliance with Laws

A provision that requires the parties to a contract to comply with all laws and regulations is fairly common. Because of the nature of their business, hotels are subject to many different laws and regulations. Therefore, it makes sense to have an affirmation in the MHSA that a hotel will comply accordingly. This provision also includes ❶ an indemnification by a hotel where it fails to comply. The indemnification is arguably overkill considering the *General Indemnification* provision covers the same subject matter (i.e., failure to comply under this provision would certainly constitute "wrongdoing" as described in the *General Indemnification* provision). The reason I include an indemnification here as well is to serve as a "backup" in case the *General Indemnification* provision gets watered down during contract negotiations. Assuming that the *General Indemnification* provision doesn't get watered down and a hotel objects to the indemnification section in this provision as being redundant or duplicative, removing the indemnification section wouldn't have any detrimental impact on a group representative's protections under the MHSA.

18.5 <u>Compliance with Laws</u>. Both parties agree to comply with all applicable United States Federal, state, and local laws, executive orders and regulations issued, where applicable. ❶Without limiting Hotel's other obligations of indemnification herein, Hotel shall defend, indemnify, and hold Customer Indemnitees harmless from and against any and all Claims, including reasonable expenses suffered by, accrued against, or charged to or recoverable from Customer, on account of the failure of Hotel to perform its obligations imposed herein.

Advertising and Logos

Under a buyer-seller contract, sellers frequently seek to market their business relationships with high-profile buyers as means to gain more business. Mostly, buyers are reluctant to allow sellers to do so because the buyer doesn't want to appear to be endorsing the products or services of the seller. Consequently, it's fairly typical to restrict a party's use of the other party's trademarks, service marks, logos, and other intellectual property in advertising and marketing. The MHSA contains such a provision, but the provision recognizes that ❶ a group representative must be able to advertise and communicate where a meeting is to be held. Hotels will rarely make changes to this provision, and, when they do, the changes typically involve the requirement that a hotel pre-approves any materials or medium using their intellectual property—which is reasonable.

> 18.6   Advertising and Logos. Hotel recognizes that Customer's and Attendees' names, trademarks, service marks, and logos represent valuable intellectual property of Customer or Attendee. Unless otherwise specified in an Exhibit A, Hotel agrees not to use such names, trademarks, service marks, or logos in any advertising or promotional materials without the prior written consent of Customer or Attendee, as the case may be. Customer agrees to accept the same restrictions with respect to the use of Hotel's name, trademarks, service marks and logos; ❶provided, however, that Customer shall have the right to use Hotel's name, trademarks, service marks and logos for the sole purpose of promoting and communicating a Meeting to prospective Attendees. This provision shall survive the termination of this Agreement and an Exhibit A.

Assignment of Agreement

Another common provision in buyer-seller contracts, and one that is particularly important for the MHSA, is the *Assignment of Agreement* provision. The concept is that a buyer selected the seller, and not someone else, to do business with and the buyer wants to have a say if the seller wishes to assign the contract to another party. When a group representative selects a hotel for a meeting, the hotel has likely been selected for many different reasons such as customer service, amenities, and facility conditions. If a hotel is sold to another owner, one or more of those many different reasons might be in jeopardy under the new ownership. Consequently, it makes sense that a group representative provides consent to any assignment of the MHSA and has the ability to void the MHSA if the group representative believes that the assignment isn't in the best interest of the meeting's attendees. On the other hand, a hotel shouldn't really care if the group representative assigns the MHSA to a different party—the hotel cares about "heads in a bed"—so the provision ❶ permits the "Customer" to assign the agreement to a succeeding company.

> 18.9 <u>Assignment of Agreement</u>. This Agreement and the obligations of Hotel hereunder are personal to Hotel and its staff. Neither Hotel nor any successor, receiver, or assignee of Hotel shall directly or indirectly assign this Agreement or the rights or duties created by this Agreement, whether such assignment is effected in connection with a sale of Hotel's assets or stock or through merger, an insolvency proceeding or otherwise, without the prior written consent of Customer. ❶ Customer, at Customer's sole election, may assign any and all of its rights and obligations under this Agreement to any company that succeeds to substantially all of Customer's business.

Hotels are bought and sold fairly frequently, and these types of provisions can be burdensome for hotels. Consequently, hotels will often take issue with this provision and want it removed. A common compromise is to limit the requirement of consent to assignments when the hotel changes "flags" (meaning hotel management company or brand), i.e., changing from a Marriott to a Starwood hotel, and not have any requirement of consent to changes in *ownership* under a flag. Changes of ownership under the same flag should be less of a concern to a group representative because the new owner must comply with the requirements of the hotel management company or be at risk of being de-flagged. If the new owner doesn't keep up the hotel, the group representative still has an out via the *Deterioration in Quality* provision. The following revision is an acceptable example.

> 18.9 <u>Assignment of Agreement</u>. This Agreement and the obligations of Hotel hereunder are personal to Hotel and its staff. <u>In the event of a change in Hotel's management company, n</u>Neither Hotel nor any successor, receiver, or assignee of Hotel shall directly or indirectly assign this Agreement or the rights or duties created by this Agreement <u>to the successor management company</u>, whether such assignment is effected in connection with a sale of Hotel's assets or stock or through merger, an insolvency proceeding or otherwise, without the prior written consent of Customer. Customer, at Customer's sole election, may assign any and all of its rights and obligations under this Agreement to any company that succeeds to substantially all of Customer's business.

Appendix I ~ Master Hotel Services Agreement

The Master Hotel Services Agreement (MHSA) contract template that is included in this appendix can be downloaded in an electronic, editable form without charge at www.stephenguth.com.

The MHSA does not constitute, or substitute for, legal advice. The MHSA is provided "AS IS" without warranty of any kind. ALL EXPRESS OR IMPLIED REPRESENTATIONS AND WARRANTIES, INCLUDING ANY IMPLIED WARRANTY OF MERCHANTABILITY, FITNESS FOR A PARTICULAR PURPOSE, OR NON-INFRINGEMENT, ARE HEREBY EXCLUDED. AUTHOR SHALL NOT BE LIABLE FOR ANY DAMAGES ARISING OUT OF OR SUFFERED AS A RESULT OF THE USE OF THE MHSA.

MASTER HOTEL SERVICES AGREEMENT

This agreement ("Agreement") is entered into, to be effective as of August 16, 2010 ("Effective Date"), by and between **GUTH VENTURES LLC** ("Customer"), with its principal place of business located at 16141 Cobb Island Road, Newburg, MD 20664, and **OLD NORTHEAST HOTEL AND SPA** ("Hotel"), with its principal place of business located at 625 17th Avenue N.E., St. Petersburg, FL 33704.

RECITALS

WHEREAS, Hotel has experience and expertise in the business of providing certain hospitality-related services that may include accommodations, housing, function space, and food and beverage (such services and similar services shall be individually and collectively referenced herein as the "Services");

WHEREAS, Customer conducts various events, conventions, and meetings (each, a "Meeting," as further described in an Exhibit A attached or to be attached hereto) that are critical to the business operations of Customer and its members;

WHEREAS, Hotel acknowledges the importance to Customer of Hotel's Services in support of a Meeting;

WHEREAS, Hotel acknowledges that non-performance of the Services may result in loss of revenue to Customer, negative impact upon the credibility and good will of Customer, and other financial and non-financial harm to Customer;

WHEREAS, Customer desires to have Hotel provide Services to Customer; and,

WHEREAS, Hotel desires to supply Services to Customer on the terms and conditions contained herein.

NOW THEREFORE, in consideration of the mutual promises and covenants contained herein, and for other good and valuable consideration, Hotel and Customer hereby agree as follows:

1. Hotel Services. Hotel agrees to provide, in accordance with the terms of this Agreement, the Services for the Meeting on the Official and In-House Dates and at the room rate(s) ("Room Rate" or "Room Rates") and other fees, if any, as set forth in an Exhibit A (sequentially numbered) in the form of the Exhibit A attached hereto or in other scope of services exhibits or attachments containing substantially similar information and identified as an Exhibit A. The dates that the actual Meeting will be held shall be known as the "Official Dates," as further described in an Exhibit A.

    1.1 Service and Staffing Requirements. Hotel represents and warrants that it shall assign an adequate number of trained staff to perform its obligations under this Agreement and an Exhibit A in accordance with industry standards and Hotel facilities of similar size and quality as Hotel.

    1.2 Health and Safety. Hotel represents and warrants that, at all times during the In-House Dates, Hotel shall comply with all local, state, and United States Federal fire and life safety laws, regulations, codes, and ordinances including but not limited to the requirements of the Hotel and Motel Fire Safety

Act of 1990, requiring, among other things, hard-wired smoke detectors in each guestroom and an automatic sprinkler system. Hotel further represents and warrants that it maintains procedures and policies concerning fire safety and other life safety issues and Hotel shall make all such procedures and policies available to Customer upon request. Failure of Customer to request a copy of such policies and procedures shall not relieve or alleviate Hotel's responsibility to comply with the terms of this provision. Hotel further represents that Hotel shall have: (a) at least one (1) person trained in cardio pulmonary resuscitation on premises at all times; and, (b) an automated external defibrillator on premises.

1.3 Security. Hotel represents and warrants that it provides adequate security (the same or better than hotel properties of similar size and quality) for Attendees by ensuring that, among other things, corridors, parking lots, recreational and public areas are adequately monitored. Hotel also agrees to provide adequate security and secured areas for setups in Function Spaces, such as locked-facilities or security guards. Hotel agrees to promptly notify Customer of any criminal incident of personal injury (including death) or theft of personal property valued at over Five Hundred Dollars ($500.00) involving a Hotel guest or employee that occurs within six (6) months of the start of the In-House Dates.

1.4 Attendees. For the purpose of this Agreement, the term "Attendee" means any individual, group or entity associated with a Meeting, including Customer and its directors, employees, members, representatives, agents, speakers, exhibitors, members, delegates, guests, invitees, contractors, and subcontractors with reservations at Hotel, regardless of how the guestroom reservations ("Guestroom Reservations") were made or accepted by Hotel, including, without limitation, Guestroom Reservations accepted through Customer's designated Housing Coordinator, if described in an Exhibit A, Hotel's reservation system, any Web sites and e-commerce sites on the Internet / World Wide Web, travel agents and corporate travel departments, or any other reservation portals.

2. Room Block. In consideration of Customer selecting Hotel to provide the Services and host the Meeting, Hotel agrees to hold the room

block ("Room Block") for the type of accommodations (each a "Guestroom") as specified in an Exhibit A.

2.1 Adjustment of Room Block. Hotel and Customer shall review the Room Block periodically, if so specified in an Exhibit A, on the review dates ("Review Dates") indicated therein. Unless otherwise provided in an Exhibit A, Customer shall have the right to adjust the Room Block, if necessary, without liability on the Review Dates or at anytime where Review Dates are not so indicated. Such adjustments, if any, shall be provided by Customer to allow Hotel to receive Room Block estimations with reasonable advance notice, when possible, in order for Hotel to resell rooms unused by Customer. Based upon availability and subject to Hotel's approval, Customer may increase the Room Block at the Room Rate specified in the applicable Exhibit A. In no case shall Hotel unilaterally reduce the Room Block prior to the reservation cut-off date ("Reservation Cut-Off Date") set forth in an Exhibit A, if any, without the prior written consent of Customer.

2.2 Check-In Time / Check-Out Time. Hotel guarantees that Attendees' Check-In Time shall be 3:00 P.M. Hotel local time and Check-Out Time shall be Noon Hotel local time, unless such times are otherwise specified in an Exhibit A. For Attendees who arrive prior to Check-In Time, Hotel will assign rooms, as they become available. Hotel will use its best efforts to provide early check-in for Attendees. Hotel will accommodate late check-out on a complimentary basis, up to four (4) hours for Attendees, subject to space availability.

2.2.1 Early Check-Out. Where an Attendee elects to depart Hotel earlier than the Attendee's original check-out date, Hotel agrees that Attendee shall not be required to pay any additional fee for such early check-out.

2.2.2 Cancellation fees shall be waived and all deposits will be refunded immediately to no-show Attendees who cancel because of an emergency. Such emergency cancellation requests will be reviewed by Hotel and a determination will be made by Hotel on a case by case basis.

3.   Room Rates.

    3.1   Room Rates. Room Rates shall be described in an Exhibit A for the Room Block. The Room Rate shall be offered and available to all Attendees for the three (3) days prior to and three (3) days after the In-House Dates. There will be no additional charge for persons under the age of twenty-one (21) staying in the same room with a parent, relative, or guardian Attendee.

        3.1.1   Commissionable Room Rates. If so specified by Customer, where third-party intermediary ("Intermediary") is designated to act on behalf of Customer in booking a Meeting with Hotel, and unless an Exhibit A expressly states to the contrary, Hotel agrees that: (a) Hotel shall pay a ten percent (10%) commission to such Intermediary on the actualized room revenue; (b) such Intermediary shall be paid such commission within thirty (30) days following the In-House Dates; and, (c) the commission due to such Intermediary is not transferable to another party or agency.

        3.1.2   Rebated Room Rates. If so specified by Customer, and unless an Exhibit A expressly states to the contrary, Hotel agrees that where no Intermediary is designated to act on behalf of Customer, Hotel shall provide a ten-percent (10%) rebate to Customer based on the actualized room revenue. Such rebate shall be: (a) applied against any amounts due to Hotel from Customer; or, (b) where such rebate cannot be consumed in the context of the applicable Meeting, Hotel shall remit a rebate to Customer for such corresponding value. Such rebate shall be due to Customer no more than thirty (30) days following the In-House Dates.

    3.2   Taxes. If Room Rates are subject to state and local sales tax or an occupancy fee, all such taxes and/or fees shall be stated in an Exhibit A. Customer shall not pay any taxes on gratuities unless such tax on gratuity is set forth in an Exhibit A and in all cases only to the extent required by law.

    3.3   Lowest Room Rate; Published or Confirmed. Where Customer has booked more than twenty-five percent (25%) of Hotel's net inventory ("Net Inventory," as further defined herein) on the peak night described in an Exhibit A, Hotel agrees not to advertise or offer any lower group, leisure, or promotional room rate lower than the Room Rate via any booking media, including but not limited to the Internet / World Wide Web, toll-free numbers, consolidators, or otherwise during the In-House dates and the thirty (30) calendar day periods before and after such In-House Dates. In the event that Hotel offers lower room rates to any party during the In-House Dates or the thirty (30) calendar day period preceding a Meeting the Room Rate shall automatically adjust to such lower room rate; in such event, an Exhibit A is deemed to have been revised and amended to reflect such lower room rate. In the event that Attendees have not received the lowest published or confirmed room rates, Hotel agrees that Customer shall be due the total of the difference between such lower room rates and the Room Rates for all room nights ("Room Nights") during the In-House Dates, and Hotel shall, at the sole election of Customer remit payment of such amount due to the Attendees or Customer, as the case may be, within fourteen (14) calendar days following the Meeting. The foregoing provision does not apply to qualified discounts such as government, corporate, or crew rates previously negotiated with Hotel.

3.4   Staff Rooms. Hotel will provide the number of staff (inclusive of contracted staff of Customer such as speakers) rooms (each a "Staff Room") indicated in an Exhibit A on a complimentary, no-charge basis (unless otherwise specified to the contrary in such Exhibit A). Customer shall provide Hotel with a list of staff members staying at Hotel on or before the Reservation Cut-Off Date. Staff Rooms shall be included as part of the Room Pick-Up.

3.5   Complimentary Rooms. Unless otherwise specified in an Exhibit A, Hotel shall provide one (1) complimentary Guestroom (each a "Comp Room") per night for every thirty-five (35) Room Nights associated with the Meeting on a cumulative, and not daily, basis. For purposes of determining the number of Comp Rooms, each room in a suite will count as a separate Room Night. In the event Comp Rooms earned are not used, Hotel agrees to: (a) apply the corresponding value of the applicable single standard Room Rate against any amounts due to Hotel; or, (b) where such corresponding value cannot be consumed in the context of the applicable Meeting, Hotel shall remit to Customer such corresponding value.

3.6 Guestroom Upgrades. At the request of Customer, Hotel shall upgrade no less than two (2) Comp Rooms to suite (parlor and sleeping room) Guestrooms.

3.7 VIP Suites. In addition to any complimentary Suite upgrades, unless otherwise specified in an Exhibit A, Hotel agrees to provide to Customer a minimum of four (4) suites (parlor and sleeping room) at the single Room Rate for a standard Guestroom.

3.8 Complimentary Planning Rooms. In addition to Comp Rooms, Staff Rooms, and complimentary upgrades, unless otherwise specified in an Exhibit A, Hotel agrees to furnish, on a space available basis, a minimum of two (2) complimentary guestrooms for a period of two (2) Room Nights for Meeting planning visits to Hotel. Additional Guestrooms beyond the two (2) complimentary planning Guestrooms Customer may require for meeting planning attendees will be charged at the applicable Room Rate and any required Function Space will be complimentary.

4. Reservation Procedures. Unless otherwise specified in an Exhibit A, the following reservation procedures shall apply.

4.1 Acceptance of Reservations after Reservation Cut-Off Date. Hotel shall hold the Room Block until 11:59 P.M. Hotel local time on the Reservation Cut-Off Date, such date being twenty-one (21) calendar days prior to the In-House Dates, or as otherwise specified in an Exhibit A if longer or shorter than twenty-one (21) calendar days. After the Reservation Cut-Off Date, Hotel agrees to accept Guestroom Reservations on a space available basis at the Room Rate.

4.2 Substitution of Attendees. Hotel agrees to allow Customer, at the sole discretion of Customer, Attendee, or the Housing Coordinator to simultaneously substitute Attendees at the Room Rate for Guestrooms canceled by Attendees with confirmed reservations both before and after the Reservation Cut-Off Date through to the first day of the Meeting.

4.3 Housing Coordinator. Where designated in an Exhibit A, Customer's housing coordinator ("Housing Coordinator") will manage Guestroom Reservations and Hotel shall pay the Housing Coordinator the fee designated in the relevant

Exhibit A.   Hotel will work directly with the Housing Coordinator, Meeting Manager and staff on all matters relating to Hotel's provision of Guestrooms for the Meeting. Except as specifically expressed in an Exhibit A, the Housing Coordinator shall have no authority to bind Customer. In the event that Customer initially designates a Housing Coordinator in an Exhibit A and subsequently elects not to use such Housing Coordinator, then the Room Rate shall adjust down to the extent of Housing Coordinator fees not payable by Hotel.

4.4   Over-booking by Hotel. In the event Hotel over-books prior to the Reservation Cut-Off Date and where Hotel has provided at least ninety percent (90%) of the Room Block: (a) within fourteen (14) calendar days of the occurrence of the over-booking, Hotel shall pay to Customer as liquidated damages, and not as a penalty, an amount equal to thirty percent (30%) of the average Room Rate for each Guestroom Reservation that Hotel is unable to accept prior to the Reservation Cut-off Date; and, (b) Hotel will include the displaced Room Nights caused by over-booking in the Room Pick-Up report; and, (c) Customer will not be liable for damages, if any, for any resulting reduction or shortfall in the Room Pick-Up. In the event that Hotel over-books prior to the Reservation Cut-off Date and where Hotel is unable to provide at least ninety percent (90%) of the Room Block, for the purposes of this Agreement, such over-booking shall be deemed to be a termination for convenience by Hotel of an Exhibit A.

5.   Room Pick-Up.

5.1   Room Pick-Up Calculation. All of the following shall be counted, calculated in terms of Room Nights over the In-House Dates, in the Room Block pick-up (the "Room Pick-Up"), whether such Guestrooms were reserved before or after the Reservation Cut-Off Date: (a) Guestrooms used by Attendees; (b) Guestrooms canceled by Attendees, where the Attendee has paid an "early departure" or other such fee for the cancellation; (c) displaced Guestrooms resulting from Hotel's over-booking; (d) Comp Rooms; (e) Staff Rooms; and, (f) Dishonored Reservations. Where a Guestroom consists of more than one room, each room shall be counted as a separate Guestroom for the purposes of the Room Pick-Up calculation (for example, a Guestroom consisting of a sleeping room and a parlor shall be counted as two (2) Guestrooms).

5.2 <u>Net Inventory</u>.   Hotel shall not include in its guestroom inventory during the In-House Dates: (a) all guestrooms "out of order," being renovated, or repaired; (b) guestrooms held for last sale to Hotel's preferred customers; (c) "comped" guestrooms to third-parties; and, (d) any unsold suites. The resulting total of guestrooms shall be Hotel's Net Inventory. In addition, all guestrooms billed to other groups or individuals for attrition, cancellation, or no-shows will be counted as sold guestrooms.

6.   <u>Dishonored Reservations</u>. If Hotel is unable to provide a Guestroom to an Attendee holding a reservation, Hotel shall provide to each such Attendee, as the case may be, the following without charge: (a) comparable or superior guestroom (including room rate, tax, resort fee, and occupancy charge) at a comparable or superior Hotel no more than one (1) mile from the Meeting Location for the period of the applicable Guestroom Reservation; (b) transportation by the most convenient and efficient means possible for the Attendee or Customer to and from the substitute Hotel; (c) long-distance telephone calls; (d) listing of Attendee's name with the Hotel switchboard or answering service, in order to facilitate the transfer of phone calls made to Attendee at Hotel to the alternate property; (e) its best efforts to bring the Attendee back after the first night and offer to relocate displaced Attendee back to Hotel; and, (f) credit Customer for any Attendees displaced toward the Room Pick-Up and toward the Comp Room credit.

7.   <u>Billing and Payment</u>.

7.1 <u>Attendee Charges</u>.   Except for individuals specifically designated by Customer in writing to Hotel, all Guestroom charges, taxes, incidentals, and all other charges and expenses will be charged to Attendees. Customer is not and shall not be liable for the non-payment by an Attendee for any such charges.

7.2 <u>Master Account</u>. For each <u>Exhibit A</u>, Hotel shall establish one or more accounts for charges to Customer (collectively and individually the "Master Account").   Customer will provide Hotel with appropriate credit information, in a form determined by Customer, to establish direct billing for the Master Account. Upon credit approval from Hotel, which approval shall not be unreasonably denied, withheld, or conditioned, a Master Account will be established for authorized charges. All charges to be posted to the Master Account will be reviewed by Hotel and the Customer Meeting Manager identified on an Exhibit A. Only those categories of charges approved in writing by the Meeting Manager may be charged to the Master Account.

7.3   Payment. Hotel agrees to submit charges associated with the applicable Meeting with all supporting or back-up documentation such as a post-meeting Room Pick-Up report within thirty (30) days of completion of a Meeting. Customer agrees to pay any undisputed charges within sixty (60) days of receipt of invoice and post-Meeting Room Pick-Up and Meeting expenditure reports from Hotel. In the event there is any charge in dispute, only that charge in dispute shall be withheld from payment. Customer shall not be required to pay a fee, such as a "convenience fee," should Customer choose to use a credit card to pay any charges. Invoices submitted by Hotel must specify an invoice number.

7.4   Deposits. Unless expressly stated to the contrary in an Exhibit A, all deposits or advance payments held by Hotel on behalf of Customer or an Attendee shall be refunded to Customer or the Attendee (in the same manner of payment by Attendee or Customer, if possible) within: (a) 48 (forty-eight) hours of Guestroom Reservation cancellation, if such cancellations are received by Hotel prior to the Reservation Cut-Off Date; (b) within fifteen (15) calendar days from receipt of notification of termination under the termination provisions of this Agreement; or, (c) within fifteen (15) calendar days from receipt of notification of a Force Majeure Event (as further described herein). If unpaid deposit or advance payment balances remain due to Customer or an Attendee fifteen (15) calendar days after cancellations are received by Hotel, or receipt of notification of termination, interest will accrue to the benefit of those owed refunds at the rate of one and one-half percent (1.5%) per month, but not to exceed eighteen percent (18%) per annum or the highest rate allowable by state law, whichever is less. Customer shall have the right to re-instate "no-show" Attendees and will guarantee such rooms to the Master Account, if so re-instated. This provision shall survive the termination of this Agreement and an Exhibit A.

7.5 Service Charges / Gratuities. Gratuities, if any, shall be provided to deserving employees of Hotel in the sole discretion of Customer and Attendees. Unless otherwise specified in an Exhibit A, under no circumstances will Hotel charge a mandatory gratuity or service charge on F&B or Guestrooms unless otherwise mandated by union agreement, provided such mandatory gratuity is disclosed in an Exhibit A.

7.6 Additional Concessions. Hotel will provide the additional concessions specified in an Exhibit A, if any, without charge to Customer.

7.7 Exemption from Taxes. Hotel agrees that should Customer meet the requirements for an exemption from sales tax in the jurisdiction in which the Meeting shall be held, no sales tax shall be charged to Customer, provided that Customer provides Hotel with appropriate proof of exemption.

7.8 No Other Fees. Hotel shall impose no fees for Services utilized by Customer, including, but not limited to, mandatory charges on Guestrooms, other than those specified in an Exhibit A, without the prior written consent of Customer. If such fees are specified in an Exhibit A or subsequently agreed to by Customer, such fees shall not be imposed unless they are imposed on all guests using Hotel during the In-House Dates. Unless expressly stated to the contrary in an Exhibit A, Hotel shall impose no fees should Customer utilize contractors other than those recommended by Hotel to provide services such as audio-visual, decorating, security, and transportation.

8. Food and Beverage. Where indicated in an Exhibit A, Hotel shall provide food and beverage ("F&B") to Customer as specified therein and in accordance with the following.

8.1 Fee for F&B. Hotel agrees to guarantee the menu and menu prices for the effective date indicated in an Exhibit A.

8.2 Attendee Minimum. Unless otherwise specified in an Exhibit A, for each F&B function, Customer shall provide Hotel with the estimated minimum number of Attendees no less than eight (8) hours in advance of the function and Hotel shall set for up to five percent (5%) over the estimated minimum number of Attendees, the specific percentage as directed by Customer.

8.3   F&B Attrition; Cancellation. Unless otherwise specified in an Exhibit A, Hotel acknowledges and agrees that it is not entitled to any fees, charges, damages, or other forms of remedy, including the withdrawal of any concessions by Hotel granted under this Agreement or an Exhibit A where Customer holds a F&B function described in an Exhibit A but has less than the estimated number of Attendees or where Customer cancels any F&B function described in an Exhibit A.

8.4   Beverage-Consumption Basis. All charges for beverages, including alcoholic beverages, provided by Hotel, if any, will be on a consumption basis with no charge for unopened bottles or cans. Hotel shall allow the Meeting Manager to be present when the consumption is being accounted for, or, at the request of Customer, provide a written accounting of the consumption.

9.   Function Space Requirements. If meeting or other function space requirements (collectively "Function Space") are specified in an Exhibit A or attached thereto and identified as the Program of Events ("POE"), all such Function Space shall be complimentary and held on a twenty-four (24) hour space hold basis. In addition, there will be no charge for Function Space setup if specified on an Exhibit A.

9.1   Function Space Changes; Hotel. Hotel shall not unilaterally change Function Space assignments. Where Customer agrees to Hotel's request for a change in Function Space assignments, Hotel will assume the financial responsibility for such items as printing program agenda and signs, as may be needed to timely convey such change in assignment to Attendees.

9.2   Function Space for Storage. There will be no charge for storing Customer's or Attendees' Meeting materials, publications, and equipment for the In-House Dates or as otherwise indicated in an Exhibit A. Hotel staff shall assist in moving such materials, publications, and equipment at no charge to Customer or Attendees, and no fees will be imposed upon Customer for use of outside contractors for such purpose, if any.

9.3   Function Space Supplies. Hotel shall provide, at no charge, Function Space supplies, including, but not limited to, chairs, tables, water, ice, blackboards, and easels with pads and markers, pads and pencils / pens, etc., in a quantity sufficient to accommodate all anticipated Attendees related to the Function Space. Hotel shall impose no charge for Function Space set-up. This complimentary arrangement does not include unusual Function Space arrangements that would exhaust Hotel's normal in-house supplies to the point of requiring rental of additional supplies to accommodate Customer's or Attendees' needs. In the event of such an occurrence, Hotel shall notify Customer or Attendee and shall afford Customer or Attendee the opportunity to pay the rental cost for additional supplies or change the Function Space room arrangements to a more normal format, avoiding extra rental. In addition to the foregoing, Hotel shall provide one (1) microphone and amplification equipment in each Function Space at no cost to Customer or Attendee, and a complimentary telephone at Customer's Attendees' registration area and meeting office, if such Function Space is specified in an Exhibit A, with no access charges for local or long-distance telephone calls; long distance charges, if any, shall be billed to the Master Account.

9.4   Function Space Based on Room Block. Where "no-charge" Function Space is based on the Room Block and Customer has not achieved the Room Block, in no case shall Customer be liable to pay to Hotel a fee for such Function Space.

9.5   Internet Access. Where Hotel offers wireless Internet access in Hotel's Function Space, Hotel agrees to provide such wireless Internet access to Customer over the In-House Dates without additional charge. For "wired" Internet access, Hotel agrees to provide "drops" for Internet access on a basis of the first five (5) drops at no charge and the remaining drops at fifty-percent (50%) of Hotel's lowest published rate, as specified in an Exhibit A.

9.6   Signage. Unless otherwise specified in an Exhibit A, Hotel shall allow Customer or Attendee to post signs on the property concerning the Meeting. These signs shall be placed in locations and in a manner mutually agreeable to all parties.

10.   Force Majeure; Excused Performance.

10.1   Excused Performance. Where any one or more of the following events (each, a "Force Majeure Event") make it inadvisable, impractical, or impossible for a party to perform, in whole or in part, this Agreement or an Exhibit A as it relates to holding the Meeting, such party may terminate, suspend, or partially perform its obligations under this Agreement or an <u>Exhibit A</u> without liability by written notice to the other party: (a) acts of God (including fire, flood, earthquake, storm, hurricane or other natural disaster); (b) an advisory issued by any United States (Federal or state) or international government entity (such as the United States Department of Homeland Security or the World Health Organization); (c) threatened or actual civil disorder, hostilities, war, or terrorism; or, (d) curtailment or interruption of transportation facilities unreasonably impeding at least twenty-five percent (25%) of Attendees from attending the Meeting.

10.2   <u>Labor Disputes</u>. Regardless of Hotel's union status, should there be any threatened or actual strikes, lockouts, boycotts, labor disputes, or work stoppages within ninety (90) calendar days prior to the In-House Dates, Hotel shall immediately notify Customer in writing. If Customer reasonably determines that a strike, lockout, labor dispute, or work stoppage (each, also, a "Force Majeure Event") will adversely affect the success of the Meeting, Customer shall have the right to terminate an <u>Exhibit A</u>, in whole or in part, without liability upon written notice to Hotel. If any strikes, lockouts, boycotts, labor disputes, or work stoppages occur over the In-House Dates that in any way interfere with Customer's or Attendees' use of Hotel, the same shall be deemed to be an interference for purposes of determining a remedy associated with interference, as further described herein.

10.3   <u>Reduced-Sized Meeting</u>. Where Customer elects to hold the Meeting despite any Force Majeure Event, Hotel shall waive any and all fees, liquidated damages, and other liabilities related to a reduced-sized Meeting and shall offer Attendees any lower room rate offered to other guests during the In-House Dates.

10.4   <u>Collective Bargaining Agreements</u>. Hotel shall promptly notify Customer in writing of any collective bargaining agreement expiring within ninety (90) calendar days prior to or after the In-House Dates.

11.   <u>Attrition</u>. Unless otherwise specified in an <u>Exhibit A</u>, Hotel acknowledges and agrees that it is not entitled to any fees, charges, damages, or other forms of remedy, including the withdrawal of any

concessions by Hotel granted under this Agreement or an <u>Exhibit A</u> where Customer does not fully utilize the total Room Nights represented by the Room Block, as the same may be adjusted as agreed upon by the parties or as otherwise permitted in this Agreement or an <u>Exhibit A</u>.

12. <u>Termination; Cancellation</u>.

    12.1   <u>Termination for Cause; Customer</u>. Without limiting the rights of Customer to terminate for cause or convenience as otherwise provided for in this Agreement, Customer shall have the right to terminate this Agreement or an <u>Exhibit A</u> without liability upon the occurrence of any of the following conditions and upon written notice to Hotel.

        12.1.1   Hotel's material breach of any material term or condition of this Agreement or an <u>Exhibit A</u>. Customer's right of termination for cause shall be in addition to, and shall in no way limit, Customer's right to other remedies at law or in equity available to Customer for breaches of this Agreement; or,

        12.1.2   Any change at Hotel in branding, affiliation, ownership, or management company. In the case of any foregoing change, Hotel agrees to notify Customer in writing no later than thirty (30) calendar days prior to such change; or,

        12.1.3   Foreclosure by Hotel's creditors, or a petition in bankruptcy filed by or on behalf of Hotel or its creditors; or,

        12.1.4   The non-Hotel site, if applicable, for the Meeting is unwilling or unable to provide suitable facilities for the Meeting or such site shall not be available for whatever reason; or,

        12.1.5   An adequate number of sleeping rooms at other hotels within a reasonable distance of the Meeting Location to accommodate Customer and / or Customer attendees is not available or cannot be contracted for.

    12.2   <u>Termination for Convenience; Mutual</u>. This Agreement or an <u>Exhibit A</u> may be terminated by mutual agreement between Customer and Hotel at any time without liability to the other party.

12.3   Termination for Convenience; Customer. Without limiting the rights of Customer to terminate for cause as otherwise provided for in this Agreement, Customer shall have the right to terminate an Exhibit A for convenience upon written notice to Hotel and Hotel shall be entitled to request from Customer, as liquidated damages and not as a penalty, an amount, if any, based on the following sliding scale: (a) greater than one hundred and eighty (180) calendar days prior to the Official Dates: no liquidated damages or liability; (b) one hundred and seventy-nine (179) to ninety (90) calendar days prior to the Official Dates: fifty percent (50%) of peak night room revenue; (c) eighty-nine (89) to thirty (30) calendar days prior to the Official Dates: seventy-five percent (75%) of peak night room revenue; or, (d) less than thirty (30) calendar days prior to the Official Dates: one hundred (100%) of peak night room revenue. For purposes of this provision: (a) "peak night" shall be determined based on the adjusted Room Block, if so adjusted; (b) "room revenue" shall be calculated as sixty percent (60%) of the single standard Room Rate and shall exclude sales tax and other charges; and, (c) Staff Rooms and Comp Rooms shall not be counted as part of the Room Block. Hotel agrees that liquidated damages, if any, due from Customer hereunder shall be waived if Customer elects, within ninety (90) calendar days of the date of termination for convenience, to contract with Hotel for a subsequent meeting or meetings of equal or greater value than the liquidated damages.

12.4   Termination for Convenience; Hotel. In the event Hotel terminates for convenience (which shall include any termination without cause and cancellation), Hotel acknowledges that Customer would be materially harmed. Where Hotel terminates for convenience prior to the Hotel Termination Period specified in an Exhibit A, which, if not so specified, shall be one-hundred and eighty (180) calendar days prior to the Official Dates, within fourteen (14) calendar days of termination, Hotel agrees to: (a) pay Customer all deposits or monies forwarded to Hotel with interest calculated at a rate of one and one-half percent (1.5%) per month, but not to exceed eighteen percent (18%) per annum or the highest rate allowable by state law, whichever is less; (b) reimburse Customer for any documented out-of-pocket expenses incurred in reasonable expectation of conducting the Meeting; and, (c) pay for any costs associated with relocating the Meeting to a comparable or superior property, which has been approved by Customer. Where Hotel terminates for convenience following the Hotel Termination Period, within fourteen (14) calendar days of termination, Hotel agrees to: (a) pay Customer all deposits or monies forwarded to Hotel with interest calculated at a rate of one and one-half percent (1.5%) per month, but not to exceed eighteen percent (18%) per annum or the highest rate allowable by state law, whichever is less; (b) reimburse Customer for any documented out-of-pocket expenses incurred in reasonable expectation of conducting the Meeting; (c) pay for any costs associated with relocating the Meeting to a comparable or superior property, which has been approved by Customer; and, (d) pay to Customer, as liquidated damages and not as a penalty, sixty percent (60%) of the total Guestroom revenue, which shall be calculated by multiplying the total Room Nights resulting from the adjusted Room Block by the applicable Room Rates. Costs associated with relocating the Meeting include but are not limited to such items as differences in room rates, mailings, transportation, and other direct costs associated with changing the Meeting site.

13. Reporting by Hotel.

13.1 Pre-Meeting Room Pick-Up Reports. In the form requested by Customer, Hotel shall provide Customer with pre-Meeting Room Pick-Up reports on a weekly basis starting six (6) months (or such other timeframe specified in an Exhibit A) prior to the Meeting, which shall show Guestrooms blocked, Guestrooms reserved, Net Inventory, and total sleeping rooms left in Hotel that have not been reserved by other groups or transient guests.

13.2 Post-Meeting Reports. Within thirty (30) days following the Meeting, in the form requested by Customer, Hotel shall provide Customer with a post-Meeting report, which shall show, per-day over the In-House Dates, Guestrooms occupied per night, percentage of singles / doubles, Guestroom revenue, Comp Rooms to which Customer is entitled, Staff Rooms to which Customer is entitled, dishonored reservations, Attendee reservation cancellations, Attendee early departures, Hotel's Net Inventory, F&B activity (including room service and restaurant), audio-visual activity, and details relating to all other ancillary revenue. In addition to the foregoing, Hotel shall provide detailed data to Customer to support any cancellation or attrition claims.

13.3 <u>Customer Audit Rights</u>. At Customer's request, Hotel shall provide Customer, or its designated representative, access to Hotel's books and records for the purposes of determining final Room Pick-Up and/or to audit any charges to Customer. Any Guestroom occupied by an Attendee, but not credited to Customer by Hotel, will be credited to the Room Pick-Up and earned Comp Rooms, and such Guestrooms shall be commissionable to the Intermediary, if any.

13.3.1 <u>Discrepancy</u>. If a discrepancy exists between Hotel's occupancy figures and the occupancy figures believed to be accurate by Customer, Hotel will furnish to Customer a record of individual names and companies occupying sleeping rooms in Hotel over the In-House Dates. The record shall be viewed on Hotel's premises in the presence of Hotel and Customer, or its designated representative, who will sign a confidentiality agreement stating that the parties will not use private information gathered from Hotel's records for any other purpose than to independently ascertain Room Pick-Up and Hotel's occupancy. If the numbers represented by Hotel before the audit are off by two percent (2%) or more, Hotel shall pay the reasonable expenses of Customer in conducting the audit, including the use of experts, if any.

14. <u>No Interference.</u>

14.1 <u>No Interference; Quiet Enjoyment</u>. Hotel represents and warrants that there will be no distractions or disturbances within Hotel's control during the In-House Dates that could affect the ordinary use and quiet enjoyment of Hotel facilities by Customer or Attendees.

14.2 <u>No Interference; Incompatible Events</u>. Hotel shall immediately notify Customer in writing of any concurrent or overlapping meetings, conventions, special events, or other attractions to be held in Hotel during the In-House Dates. Upon notification from Hotel, Customer shall promptly notify Hotel if the concurrent or overlapping events will be incompatible to Customer or Attendees, at the sole determination of Customer, and Customer shall be entitled to terminate the applicable Exhibit A, in whole or in part, without liability upon written notice to Hotel.

14.3   No Interference; Construction. Upon ratification of an Exhibit A, such Exhibit A shall constitute Hotel's express warranty that no construction, remodeling or renovation, excluding normal maintenance, (collectively and individually "Construction") shall occur during the In-House Dates. In the event Construction is to occur during the In-House Dates, Hotel shall immediately notify Customer in writing: (a) the nature and scope of such Construction; (b) the reason or cause for such Construction during the In-House Dates; and, (c) whether such Construction may materially interfere with Attendees' or Customer's use of Hotel including, but not limited to: (i) reducing serviceability to areas reserved for Customer's or Attendees' use; (ii) noise, dust, smells, or temperature conditions that would interrupt or disrupt Customer's or Attendees' operations or otherwise impede the operations of the Meeting; or, (iii) breach Customer's or Attendees' right of quiet enjoyment. Upon notification from Hotel, Customer shall promptly notify Hotel if the Construction will interfere with the Meeting, at the sole determination of Customer, and Customer shall be entitled to terminate the applicable Exhibit A, in whole or in part, without liability upon written notice to Hotel.

14.4   Remedy for Interference. In the event of interference, unreasonable disturbance, or any other distractions not caused by Customer or Attendees which inhibit Customer's or Attendees' peaceful use and enjoyment of Hotel, Hotel shall, at the sole election of Customer: (a) arrange for comparable or superior guestrooms (at the same Room Rates or lower) and any required function space at no charge to Customer at a nearby, comparable hotel acceptable to Customer with Hotel being responsible for any reasonable and necessary costs associated with relocating the Meeting to the alternate hotel; (b) arrange for comparable or superior guestrooms (at the same Room Rates or lower) and any required function space within Hotel at no charge to Customer with Hotel being responsible for any reasonable and necessary costs associated with relocating the Meeting within Hotel; or, (c) reduce the Room Rates and charges owed or previously paid to Hotel by an amount proportionate to the inconvenience suffered by Customer or Attendees. Hotel and Customer shall jointly decide the appropriate amount of a credit or reduced charges Customer is entitled to under such circumstances, after consultation in good faith.

15. Deterioration in Quality. Upon ratification of an Exhibit A, such Exhibit A shall constitute Hotel's express warranty that the quality of the Services and the physical condition of Hotel, Guestrooms, and any Function Space over the In-House Dates shall be the same or better than on the date of ratification of the Exhibit A. Customer shall promptly notify Hotel if Customer determines, at the sole determination of Customer, that there are material deficiencies in quality or condition. Should Hotel be unable or unwilling to correct the identified deficiencies to the satisfaction of Customer within a commercially reasonable time, Customer may elect to: (a) terminate the Exhibit A, in whole or in part, without liability; and / or, (b) reduce the Room Rate and the cost of any other Services by an amount equivalent to the decline in quality or condition as evidenced by the cost of similar rooms or services at other hotels comparable to Hotel.

16. Americans with Disabilities Act Compliance. Each of Customer and Hotel warrants that it shall comply with the Americans with Disabilities Act of 1990, all relevant regulations, and all relevant guidelines (collectively, the "ADA," as amended) applicable to the Meeting provided that the Meeting is located in the United States, its territories, or its possessions. Hotel acknowledges and agrees that it is responsible for: (a) the "readily achievable" removal of physical barriers to access to Hotel's premises; (b) the provision of auxiliary aids and services where necessary to ensure that no disabled individual is treated differently by Hotel than other individuals; and, (c) the modification of Hotel's policies, practices, and procedures as necessary to provide goods, services, facilities, privileges, advantages, or accommodations to disabled individuals. Customer shall attempt to identify in advance any special needs of disabled Attendees and will notify Hotel of such needs for accommodation as soon as they are identified by Customer. Hotel shall notify Customer of requests for accommodation made by Attendees which it may receive otherwise than through Customer to facilitate identification by Customer of its own accommodation obligations.

17.   Indemnification; Liability; Insurance.

    17.1   General Indemnification.

        17.1.1 By Hotel. Hotel shall indemnify, defend, and hold harmless Customer, its officers, directors, partners, employees, contractors, vendors, guests, volunteers, representatives, agents, and Attendees (each, a "Customer Indemnitee") from any and all demands, charges, claims, damages, losses, and liabilities, including reasonable attorneys' fees and expenses (collectively "Claims") that any Customer Indemnitee may or does incur arising out of or caused by the act, error, omission, negligence, misconduct, or wrongdoing of Hotel, its officers, directors, partners, employees, contractors, vendors, representatives, agents, or guests in connection with this Agreement or an Exhibit A. Hotel's indemnification of a Customer Indemnitee shall include, but not be limited to, any damage or injury (including death) arising out of the failure of Hotel equipment, defects in Hotel's premises or fixtures, and the sale or service of alcohol by Hotel. The foregoing indemnity shall not apply to the extent that the applicable Claim resulted from the act, error, omission, negligence, misconduct, or wrongdoing of a Customer Indemnitee. Customer is not deemed to have waived, by reason of this provision, any defense that it may have with respect to any Claim.

        17.1.2 By Customer. Customer shall indemnify, defend, and hold harmless Hotel, its officers, directors, partners, employees, contractors, vendors, and agents (each, a "Hotel Indemnitee") from any and all Claims that any Hotel Indemnitee may or does incur arising out of or caused by the act, error, omission, negligence, misconduct, or wrongdoing of Customer, its officers, directors, partners, employees, contractors, vendors, guests, volunteers, representatives, or agents in connection with this Agreement or an Exhibit A. The foregoing indemnity shall not apply to the extent that the applicable Claim resulted from the act, error, omission, negligence, misconduct, or wrongdoing of a Hotel Indemnitee. Hotel is not deemed to have waived, by reason of this provision, any defense that it may have with respect to any Claim.

17.2   Liquor Liability. At all functions that are catered by Hotel where alcohol is served, Hotel shall be responsible for exercising reasonable care in its service of alcohol to Attendees. Hotel shall be responsible for adhering to state and local laws regulating the sale and service of alcoholic beverages and shall not serve alcohol to Attendees that are either noticeably intoxicated or underage. Hotel represents and warrants to Customer that it has adopted a written policy requiring bartenders, staff serving tables, and other Hotel personnel regarding the service of alcoholic beverages to guests, including, but not limited to, discontinuance of service of alcoholic beverages to any person who appears to be intoxicated. Hotel represents and warrants that all Hotel personnel have undergone adequate training to prevent any incidents that could result in claims of liquor liability.

17.2.1   Liquor Liability Indemnification. Notwithstanding any other provisions in this Agreement, Hotel shall indemnify, defend, and hold harmless any Customer Indemnitee from any and all Claims that any Customer Indemnitee may or does incur arising out of or caused by Hotel's sale or service of alcoholic beverages.

17.3   Limitation of Liability. NOTWITHSTANDING ANY OTHER PROVISION SET FORTH HEREIN, NEITHER PARTY SHALL BE LIABLE FOR ANY INDIRECT, SPECIAL, AND/OR CONSEQUENTIAL DAMAGES, ARISING OUT OF OR IN CONNECTION WITH THIS AGREEMENT; PROVIDED, HOWEVER, THAT THE FOREGOING EXCULPATION OF LIABILITY SHALL NOT APPLY WITH RESPECT TO DAMAGES INCURRED AS A RESULT OF THE GROSS NEGLIGENCE OR WILLFUL MISCONDUCT OF A PARTY. A PARTY SHALL BE LIABLE TO THE OTHER FOR ANY DIRECT DAMAGES ARISING OUT OF OR RELATING TO ITS PERFORMANCE OR FAILURE TO PERFORM UNDER THIS AGREEMENT; PROVIDED, HOWEVER, THAT THE LIABILITY OF A PARTY, WHETHER BASED ON AN ACTION OR CLAIM IN CONTRACT, EQUITY, NEGLIGENCE, TORT, OR OTHERWISE FOR ALL EVENTS, ACTS, OR OMISSIONS UNDER THIS AGREEMENT SHALL NOT EXCEED ONE

MILLION UNITED STATES DOLLARS ($1,000,000), AND PROVIDED, FURTHER, THAT THE FOREGOING LIMITATION SHALL NOT APPLY TO: (A) A PARTY'S OBLIGATIONS OF INDEMNIFICATION, AS FURTHER DESCRIBED IN THIS AGREEMENT; (B) DAMAGES CAUSED BY A PARTY'S GROSS NEGLIGENCE OR WILLFUL MISCONDUCT; OR, (C) A PARTY'S BREACH OF ITS OBLIGATIONS, IF ANY, OF CONFIDENTIALITY.

17.4   Insurance. Each party shall obtain, maintain, and provide evidence of insurance in amounts sufficient, unless such amounts are otherwise specified herein or in an Exhibit A, to provide coverage for any liabilities arising out of or resulting from the respective obligations pursuant to this Agreement and an Exhibit A, as the case may be.

      17.4.1   Additional Insurance; Hotel. In addition to comprehensive general liability insurance, Hotel shall carry crime, liquor liability, property or hazard, and other insurance in such dollar amount as is necessary to protect itself against any claims arising from the performance of this Agreement or an Exhibit A, including Hotel's indemnification obligations herein.

17.5   Each of the foregoing provisions shall survive the termination of an Exhibit A and this Agreement.

18.   General.

18.1   Claims; Disputes; Informal Resolution. In the event of any material dispute or disagreement between the parties with respect to the interpretation of any provision of this Agreement or an Exhibit A, or with respect to the performance of either party hereunder, each party shall appoint director-level staff (each, a "Representative") who shall meet in good faith for the purpose of resolving the dispute or disagreement. The Representatives shall meet as often as the parties reasonably deem necessary in order to gather and furnish to each other all essential, non-privileged information that the parties believe germane to resolution of the matter at issue. During the course of these non-judicial dispute resolution procedures, documents used to resolve the dispute or disagreement shall be limited to essential, non-privileged information. All requests shall be made in good faith and be reasonable in light of the economics and time efficiencies intended by the dispute resolution procedures. Where the Representatives cannot come to resolution of the matter at issue within thirty (30) calendar days following the event resulting in the dispute or disagreement, the remedy provided for herein, if any, associated with such dispute, shall be enforced. A dispute pertaining to a party's obligations of indemnification and confidentiality, if any, shall not be subject to this Section nor shall the provisions of this Section preclude either party from obtaining temporary injunctive relief in order to preserve its rights hereunder. Hotel acknowledges that the timely and complete performance of its obligations pursuant to this Agreement is critical to the business and operations of Customer. Accordingly, in the event of a dispute or disagreement between Hotel and Customer, Hotel shall continue to perform its obligations hereunder in good faith during the resolution of such dispute or disagreement unless and until this Agreement or an Exhibit A is terminated in accordance with the provisions hereof. This provision shall survive the termination of this Agreement and an Exhibit A.

18.2   Obligation of Hotel to Mitigate Damages. For the purposes of unused Guestrooms, Hotel shall undertake all reasonable efforts to resell unused Guestrooms and will credit the revenues against the liquidated damages, if any, in an amount not to exceed the full amount of such damages.

18.3   Relationship between Customer and Hotel. Hotel represents and warrants that it is an independent contractor with no authority to contract for Customer or in any way to bind or to commit Customer to any agreement of any kind or to assume any liabilities of any nature in the name of or on behalf of Customer. Under no circumstances shall Hotel, or any of its staff, hold itself out as or be considered an agent, employee, joint venture, or partner of Customer. In recognition of Hotel's status as independent contractor, Customer shall carry no Workers' Compensation insurance or any health or accident insurance to cover Hotel or Hotel's agents or staff. Customer shall not pay any contributions to Social Security, unemployment insurance, United States Federal or state withholding taxes, any other applicable taxes whether United States Federal, state, or local, nor provide any other contributions or benefits which might be expected in an employer-employee relationship. Neither Hotel nor its staff, shall be eligible for, participate in, or accrue any direct or indirect benefit under any other compensation, benefit, or pension plan of Customer.

18.4 **Governing Law.** This Agreement shall be governed by and construed in accordance with the laws of the State of Maryland and the Federal laws of the United States of America. The parties hereby consent and submit to the jurisdiction and forum of the state and United States Federal courts in the State of Maryland in all questions and controversies arising out of this Agreement.

18.5 **Compliance with Laws.** Both parties agree to comply with all applicable United States Federal, state, and local laws, executive orders and regulations issued, where applicable. Without limiting Hotel's other obligations of indemnification herein, Hotel shall defend, indemnify, and hold Customer Indemnitees harmless from and against any and all Claims, including reasonable expenses suffered by, accrued against, or charged to or recoverable from Customer, on account of the failure of Hotel to perform its obligations imposed herein.

18.6 **Advertising and Logos.** Hotel recognizes that Customer's and Attendees' names, trademarks, service marks, and logos represent valuable intellectual property of Customer or Attendee. Unless otherwise specified in an Exhibit A, Hotel agrees not to use such names, trademarks, service marks, or logos in any advertising or promotional materials without the prior written consent of Customer or Attendee, as the case may be. Customer agrees to accept the same restrictions with respect to the use of Hotel's name, trademarks, service marks and logos; provided, however, that Customer shall have the right to use Hotel's name, trademarks, service marks and logos for the sole purpose of promoting and communicating a Meeting to prospective Attendees. This provision shall survive the termination of this Agreement and an Exhibit A.

18.7 **No Waiver.** The failure of either party at any time to require performance by the other party of any provision of this Agreement shall in no way affect that party's right to enforce such provisions, nor shall the waiver by either party of any breach of any provision of this Agreement be taken or held to be a waiver of any further breach of the same provision. An effective waiver under this Agreement must be in writing signed by the party waiving its right.

18.8   Notices. Any notice given pursuant to this Agreement shall be in writing and shall be given by personal service or by United States certified mail, return receipt requested, postage prepaid to the addresses appearing at the end of this Agreement, or as changed through written notice to the other party. Notice given by personal service shall be deemed effective on the date it is delivered to the addressee, and notice mailed shall be deemed effective on the third day following its placement in the mail.

18.9   Assignment of Agreement. This Agreement and the obligations of Hotel hereunder are personal to Hotel and its staff. Neither Hotel nor any successor, receiver, or assignee of Hotel shall directly or indirectly assign this Agreement or the rights or duties created by this Agreement, whether such assignment is effected in connection with a sale of Hotel's assets or stock or through merger, an insolvency proceeding or otherwise, without the prior written consent of Customer. Customer, at Customer's sole election, may assign any and all of its rights and obligations under this Agreement to any company that succeeds to substantially all of Customer's business.

18.10   Entire Agreement. This Agreement and its attached exhibits, if any, constitute the entire agreement between the parties and supersede any and all previous representations, understandings, discussions, or agreements between Customer and Hotel as to the subject matter hereof. This Agreement may only be amended by an instrument in writing signed by Customer and Hotel. Customer and Hotel each acknowledge that it has had the opportunity to review this Agreement with its legal counsel. From time to time, the parties hereto may execute one or more supplements as exhibits to this Agreement. Such exhibits, when signed by a representative of each of the parties, shall be incorporated herein and references to particular exhibits herein shall apply to such supplemental exhibits. Unless expressly provided for in the applicable exhibit, in the event of a conflict between the provisions contained in this Agreement and those contained in any exhibit to this Agreement, the provisions contained in the Agreement, as the case may be, shall prevail.

18.11   Cumulative Remedies. All rights and remedies of Customer herein shall be in addition to all other rights and remedies available at law or in equity, including, without limitation, specific performance for the enforcement of this Agreement, and temporary and permanent injunctive relief.

18.12 <u>Counterparts; Facsimile</u>. This Agreement may be executed in one or more counterparts, each of which shall be deemed an original, but all of which together shall constitute one and the same Agreement. The parties agree that an electronic signature shall have the same force and effect as an original signature.

Executed on the dates set forth below by the undersigned authorized representatives of the parties to be effective as of the Effective Date.

GUTH VENTURES LLC (**"Customer"**)	**OLD NORTHEAST HOTEL AND SPA** (**"Hotel"**)
By: _____	By: _____
Name: Stephen R. Guth	Name: Ronald J. Guth
Title: Chief Corporate Counsel	Title: General Manager
Date:	Date:

Address for Notice:
Guth Ventures LLC
Attn: Stephen R. Guth
16141 Cobb Island Road
Newburg, MD 20664

Address for Notice:
Old Northeast Hotel and Spa
Attn: Mr. Mineaux
625 17th Avenue N.E.
St. Petersburg, FL 33704

EXHIBIT A-___

Scope of Hotel Services

This Exhibit A - Scope of Hotel Services shall be incorporated in and governed by the terms of that certain Master Hotel Services Agreement by and between **CUSTOMER** ("Customer") and **OLD NORTHEAST HOTEL AND SPA** ("Hotel") dated August 16, 2010, as amended (the "Agreement"). Unless expressly provided for in this Exhibit A, in the event of a conflict between the provisions contained in the Agreement and those contained in this Exhibit A, the provisions contained in the Agreement shall prevail.

1.   **Meeting Name:**

2.   **Hotel Name:**

3.   **Meeting Location.**

4.   **In-House Dates:**

5.   **Official Dates:**

6.   **Sales Tax:**

7.   **Occupancy Fee:**

8.   **Other Fees:**

9.   **Room Block.**

Room Block:							
Day:							
Date:							
Run of House:							
1 Bedroom Suites:							
Club / Other Upgrades:							
Total Room Nights:							

10.   **Review Dates.**

11.   **Room Rates.**

12.   **Check-In / Check-Out Times.**

13. **Customer Meeting Manager:**

14. **Housing Coordinator.**

15. **Reservation Procedures.**

16. **Reservation Cut-off Date:**

17. **Function Space.**

18. **Food and Beverage.**

19. **Comp Room Ratio:**

20. **Staff and Speaker Rooms.**

21. **Rewards Program.**

22. **Hotel Termination Period.**

23. **Additional Concessions.**

24. **Prepared By.**

Executed on the dates set forth below by the undersigned authorized representatives of the parties to be effective as of the later of the dates below.

<table>
<tr><td align="center">GUTH VENTURES LLC
("Customer")</td><td align="center">OLD NORTHEAST HOTEL AND SPA
("Hotel")</td></tr>
</table>

By: _____   By: _____

Name: FOR REFERENCE ONLY   Name: FOR REFERENCE ONLY

Title: FOR REFERENCE ONLY   Title: FOR REFERENCE ONLY

Date: Date:

EXHIBIT A-1

Scope of Hotel Services

This Exhibit A - Scope of Hotel Services shall be incorporated in and governed by the terms of that certain Master Hotel Services Agreement by and between **GUTH VENTURES LLC** ("Customer") and **OLD NORTHEAST HOTEL AND SPA** ("Hotel") dated August 16, 2010, as amended (the "Agreement"). Unless expressly provided for in this Exhibit A, in the event of a conflict between the provisions contained in the Agreement and those contained in this Exhibit A, the provisions contained in the Agreement shall prevail.

1. **Meeting Name:** Guth Ventures Annual Meeting

2. **Hotel Name:** Old Northeast Hotel and Spa

3. **Meeting Location.** 625 17th Avenue N.E., St. Petersburg, FL

4. **In-House Dates:** *Thursday, February 20, 2020* through and including *Monday, February 24, 2020*

5. **Official Dates:** *Friday, February 21, 2020* through and including *Sunday, February 23, 2020*

6. **Sales Tax:** 10% State and City Taxes

7. **Occupancy Fee:** Not Applicable

8. **Other Fees.**

   None.

   Hotel will provide complimentary Internet access for all Guestrooms, and, if applicable, Function Space.

9. **Room Block.**

Room Block:							
Day:							
Date:							

Run of House:							
1 Bedroom Suites:							
Club / Other Upgrades:							
Total Room Nights:							

10. **Review Dates.** *Friday, October 25, 2019. Friday, December 13, 2019.*

On the date(s) specified above Customer will evaluate the Guestroom, Function Space, and F&B commitments. Based on such evaluation, Customer may adjust any one or all of the same without penalty on the date(s) listed above. Based on availability, Customer may increase the Room Block on the date(s) specified above at the Room Rate, such increase being confirmed in a writing and signed by the parties.

11. **Room Rates.**

$1,500, "The Pier" Suite
$99, Run of House

12. **Check-In / Check-Out Times.** Check-in: 4:00 pm local Hotel local time. Check-out: 11:00 am local Hotel local time.

13. **Customer Meeting Manager:**

14. **Housing Coordinator.**

Customer has designated [To Be Determined] as its Housing Coordinator for the Meeting and requires that all Guestroom Reservations made by the Attendees through such Housing Coordinator.

Customer will provide Hotel with the name of its Housing Coordinator and contact information no later than sixty (60 days) prior to the Reservation Cut-Off Date. Hotel will work directly with the Housing Coordinator, Meeting Manager specified herein, and Customer staff designated by the Meeting Manager on all matters relating to Hotel's provision of Guestrooms. The Housing Coordinator will manage Guestroom Reservations and Hotel will pay to Housing Coordinator a fee of twenty-four dollars ($24.00) per actualized reservation on all paid and occupied Guestrooms, once the Customer Master Account and all other undisputed amounts due from Customer have been paid. No such fees are payable on discounted Staff Rooms. The Housing Coordinator will send the rooming list directly to Hotel via electronic transmission or specified courier. Reservations shall be entered by Hotel into the Hotel reservation system electronically within two (2) business days following receipt of the rooming list.

15.   Reservation Procedures.

Each Guestroom Reservation will be accompanied by an Attendee credit card. Hotel will charge a one night room deposit equal to the applicable Room Rate for each Guestroom Reservation (the "Deposit"). Where an Attendee cancels a reservation after the Reservation Cut-Off Date specified in this Exhibit A and prior to Hotel's forty-eight (48) hour Guestroom Reservation cancellation policy, Hotel will credit such Deposits to Customer immediately following the completion of the Meeting in the form of a credit to the Customer Master Account or of a payment to Customer. If Attendee cancellations are made after Hotel's individual reservation cancellation policy (as stated above), the Deposit will not be payable to Customer. For the purposes of this Exhibit A, Customer's Guestroom Reservation cancellation policy overrides any Hotel policies concerning the cancellation of rooms by Attendees.

16.   Reservation Cut-off Date: Monday, January 20, 2020

17.   Function Space.

Snell Isle Ballroom

18.   Food and Beverage.

Catered dinner, menu TBD.

19.   Comp Room Ratio: No Change

20.   Staff and Speaker Rooms.

2 staff rooms, 1 speaker room, and 3 talent rooms

21. **Rewards Program.** Unless indicated "Not Applicable," Hotel shall award any rewards associated with Hotel's reward program to Customer's membership account, as follows: Not Applicable

22. **Hotel Termination Period.** As specified in the Agreement.

23. **Additional Concessions.** Unless indicated "Not Applicable," Hotel shall provide the following concessions:

    Hotel shall provide free table centerpieces.

24. **Prepared By.**

    Hotel: Mr. Mineaux, Director of Sales, 813-555-1212, mineaux@oldnehotelandspa.com

    Customer: Carrie Browning, Meeting Planner, 703-555-1212, carrie.browning@guthventures.com

Executed on the dates set forth below by the undersigned authorized representatives of the parties to be effective as of the later of the dates below.

GUTH VENTURES LLC ("Customer")	OLD NORTHEAST HOTEL AND SPA ("Hotel")
By: _____	By: _____
Name: Stephen R. Guth	Name: Ronald J. Guth
Title: Chief Corporate Counsel	Title: General Manager
Date:	Date:

Appendix II ~ MHSA Defined Terms

The following terms are defined to have a specific meaning by the MHSA contained in *Appendix I ~ Master Hotel Services Agreement.* In some cases, the meaning of a certain term as defined herein and by the MHSA may be different than the industry-recognized definition.

Additional Concessions – An enumerated list of concessions made by Hotel that are in addition to any other concessions described in the Agreement. More specifically described in an Exhibit A to the Agreement.

Agreement – The Master Hotel Services Agreement executed between Customer and Hotel, as well as all exhibits, schedules, and addenda.

Attendees – Any individual, group or entity associated with a Meeting, including Customer and its directors, employees, associations members, representatives, agents, speakers, exhibitors, members, delegates, guests, invitees, contractors, and subcontractors with reservations at Hotel, regardless of how the Guestroom Reservations were made or accepted by Hotel, including, without limitation, Guestroom Reservations accepted through Customer's designated Housing Coordinator, if any, any Web sites and e-commerce sites on the Internet / World Wide Web, travel agents and corporate travel departments, or any other reservation portals.

Check-In Time – The time at which Attendees are guaranteed to be able to check-in to a Guestroom. If not otherwise specified in an Exhibit A to the Agreement, the Check-In Time shall be 3:00 P.M. Hotel local time.

Check-Out Time – The time at which Attendees are required to check-out of a Guestroom. If not otherwise specified in an Exhibit A to the Agreement, the Check-Out Time shall be Noon Hotel local time.

Claims – Collectively refers to those categories of liabilities subject to the obligation of indemnification. A list of Claims is enumerated in the Agreement.

Comp Room Ratio – See *Comp Room*.

Comp Room(s) – Sleeping rooms provided by Hotel on a complimentary basis in the ratio of Comp Rooms to Room Nights described in the Agreement or as otherwise specified in an Exhibit A (described therein as "Comp Room Ratio") to the Agreement. Included as a part of the Room Pick-Up.

Construction – Construction, remodeling, or renovation to a Hotel facility that is not a part of normal maintenance.

Customer – The customer entity described in the preamble of the Agreement.

Customer Meeting Manager – The group representative who is typically an employee of Customer, or, someone else responsible for representing Attendees to Hotel on behalf of Customer. More specifically described in an Exhibit A to the Agreement.

Effective Date – The date that the Agreement was executed by both Customer and Hotel, and the date that the Agreement becomes effective.

F&B – Food and beverage, if so specified in an Exhibit A (described therein as "Food and Beverage") to the Agreement, to be provided by Hotel.

Force Majeure Event – Collectively refers to those events beyond the control of Customer or Hotel making it inadvisable, impractical, or impossible for a party to perform. A list of Force Majeure Events is enumerated in the Agreement.

Function Space – Meeting or other function space, equipment, telephony, and / or telecommunication, if so specified in an Exhibit A (or in an attachment thereto) to the Agreement, to be provided by Hotel.

Guestroom – The types of sleeping rooms described in an Exhibit A to the Agreement.

Guestroom Reservations – Reservations, regardless of how made, for Guestrooms by Attendees.

Hotel – The hotel described in the preamble of the Agreement.

Hotel Name – See *Hotel*. Also described in an Exhibit A to the Agreement.

Housing Coordinator – The third-party entity, if so specified in an Exhibit A to the Agreement, which is acting on behalf of Customer to manage Guestroom Reservations and the rooming list with Hotel.

Indemnitee – Collectively refers to those parties benefiting from the other party's obligation of indemnification. A list of Indemnitees is enumerated in the Agreement.

In-House Dates – The dates described in an Exhibit A to the Agreement that contractors and / or staff of Customer will be "in-house" at Hotel in order to open, conduct, or close the Meeting. The In-House Dates may be the same as the Official Dates.

Intermediary – The third-party entity, if so specified in an Exhibit A to the Agreement, that is acting on behalf of Customer to book a Meeting with Hotel.

Master Account – Account at Hotel established by Hotel on behalf of Customer under which all authorized charges are to be posted.

Meeting – The meeting that will be hosted by Hotel that is described in an Exhibit A to the Agreement and is referred to in an Exhibit A as "Meeting Name."

Meeting Location – The location of the Meeting. More specifically described in an Exhibit A to the Agreement.

Meeting Name – The name of the Meeting. More specifically described in an Exhibit A to the Agreement.

Net Inventory – Total number of sleeping rooms at Hotel excluding the total of: (a) all sleeping rooms "out of order," being renovated, or repaired; (b) sleeping rooms held for last sale to Hotel's preferred customers; (c) sleeping rooms "comped" to third-parties; and, (d) any unsold suites.

Occupancy Fee – Occupancy associated with a Guestroom. More specifically described in an Exhibit A to the Agreement.

Official Dates – The dates described in an Exhibit A to the Agreement over which the Meeting will be held and during which Attendees will be in attendance.

Other Fees – Any fees that are not otherwise named or categorized in the Agreement or in an Exhibit A to the Agreement. More specifically described in an Exhibit A to the Agreement.

POE – See *Program of Events*.

Prepared By – The Customer individual who prepared an Exhibit A to the Agreement. More specifically described in an Exhibit A to the Agreement.

Program of Events – A list of basic information associated with each event / function for the Meeting—such as event name, date / day, times, food and beverage, audio-visual, number of attendees, and room set—that is either included in or attached to an Exhibit A to the Agreement.

Representative – The director-level staff appointed by Hotel and by Customer for purposes of informally resolving a dispute.

Reservation Cut-Off Date – The date, if so specified in an Exhibit A to the Agreement, after which Hotel is no longer required to accept Guestroom Reservations.

Reservation Procedures – The procedures by which Attendees will reserve Guestrooms. More specifically described in an Exhibit A to the Agreement.

Review Dates – The dates, if so specified in an Exhibit A to the Agreement, that Customer is entitled to review and adjust the Room Block without liability.

Rewards Program – The identification of the rewards or loyalty program, if any, associated with Hotel and the account information of Customer to which any reward or loyalty points will be directed. More specifically described in an Exhibit A to the Agreement.

Room Block – The Guestrooms required for a Meeting and for the Official Dates and In-House Dates as described in an Exhibit A to the Agreement.

Room Night(s) – The night(s) in which Guestrooms have been reserved. Also refers to the number of sleeping rooms described in an Exhibit A to the Agreement.

Room Pick-Up – Total of Guestrooms actualized (in terms of Room Nights) following a Meeting, whether reserved before or after the Reservation Cut-Off Date, calculated by adding all of the following: (a) Guestrooms used by Attendees; (b) Guestrooms canceled by Attendees, where the Attendee has paid an "early departure" or other such fee for the cancellation; (c) displaced Guestrooms resulting from Hotel's over-booking; (d) Comp Rooms; (e) Staff Rooms; and, (f) Dishonored Reservations. Where a Guestroom consists of more than one room, each room is counted as a separate Guestroom for the purposes of the Room Pick-Up calculation (for example, a Guestroom consisting of a sleeping room and a parlor shall be counted as two Guestrooms).

Room Rate(s) – The room rate(s) for the types of Guestrooms described in an Exhibit A to the Agreement.

Sales Tax – Sales tax associated with a Guestroom. More specifically described in an Exhibit A to the Agreement.

Services – All lodging and hospitality-related services to be provided by Hotel under the Agreement.

Staff and Speaker Rooms – Guestrooms needed, if any, for staff and / or speakers associated with a Meeting. More specifically described in an Exhibit A to the Agreement.

Staff Room(s) – Sleeping room(s) for staff (contracted or otherwise) of Customer if so specified in an Exhibit A to the Agreement. Included as part of the *Room Pick-Up*.

Glossary

The following terms and phrases are commonly used in the hospitality industry specific to group business and contract negotiations. Terms that are defined in the MHSA and described in *Appendix II ~ MHSA Defined Terms* are *not* duplicated here. For a more expansive glossary of terms, acronyms, and abbreviations developed by the Convention Industry Council's Accepted Practices Exchange, visit the APEX Industry Glossary website at the following link: www.conventionindustry.org/StandardsPractices/APEX/glossary.aspx

24-Hour Space Hold – A reservation on function space that allows a group representative exclusive use and access of such function space for a period of 24-hours, usually midnight to midnight.

ADR – See *Average Daily Rate*.

Airport Hotel – A full-service hotel in close proximity to a major airport, typically used for small groups where attendees are arriving primarily by air.

Ancillary Revenue – Revenue to a hotel generated from categories other than sleeping rooms, food and beverage, and audio-visual services such as hotel restaurants, Internet access, and parking.

ARR – See *Average Room Rate*.

Attrition – Used in two contexts: sleeping room attrition and food and beverage attrition. Sleeping room attrition: the difference between the room block (the number of sleeping rooms contracted for) and the room pick-up (the sleeping rooms actually used). Food and beverage attrition:

the difference between the food and beverage actually contracted for and the food and beverage actually consumed.

Attrition Damages – In the context of sleeping room attrition, liquidated damages that a group representative may be required to pay in the event that minimum room block commitments in the contract are not met.

Average Daily Rate (ADR) – The total sleeping room revenue for a given period (day, week to date, week, month to date, month, year, year to date) divided by the number of paid-for sleeping rooms occupied for the same period. Used by hotels as a measure of economic performance.

Average Room Rate (ARR) – Synonymous with *Average Daily Rate.*

Banquet Event Order (BEO) – Document prepared by hotel or facility staff describing an event / function and outlining all logistical details to ensure successful execution of the event including day, date, start and end time, timeline, customer contact, event type, number of attendees, function space name / location, food and beverage, audio-visual, entertainment, room set, and labor and staffing.

BEO – See *Banquet Event Order.*

Big Box – A large (200+ sleeping rooms), full service hotel with extensive function space that is either physically connected to, or located adjacent to, a large venue such as a convention center. Large groups holding meetings and / or events at a convention center will seek to contract a room block at a big box for convenience. Big boxes have more negotiation leverage because of their location and are more sophisticated in their negotiation ability. Big boxes have higher room rates than other, more distant hotels but the room rates must be evaluated against transportation costs that may be incurred with the more distant hotels. They are also likely to demand high food and beverage minimums.

Block of Business – The amount of potential revenue represented by a group's meeting, including room block, food and beverage, and ancillary revenue.

Book(ing) Around the Block – The action of an attendee intentionally or mistakenly booking a sleeping room through a reservation procedure other than through the designated reservation procedure.

Book(ing) Through the Block – The action of an attendee booking a sleeping room through the designated reservation procedure.

Booking – A synonym for making a reservation for either a sleeping room or for a venue, such as convention center space.

Boutique Hotel – A full-service hotel, typically less than 200 sleeping rooms and with limited function space, with a themed design in an intimate luxury environment.

Brand Operator – See *Flag*.

Business Hotel – Full-service hotel located in a city center or in close proximity to a business district, with services and accommodations (including limited function space) oriented to business travelers and small- to mid-size groups. Also called "corporate hotels."

Citywide – A large meeting that requires the use of multiple hotels in the host city and likely requires the use of a convention center or other function space venue.

Convention and Visitors Bureau (CVB) – A destination and tourism marketing organization specializing in bringing conventions, meetings, conferences and visitations to a city, county, or region. Convention and Visitors Bureaus can be a resource to group representatives, such as by consolidating proposals from multiple hotels in response to a lead sheet. Convention and Visitors Bureaus are membership-based, funded by the businesses (such as hotels) they represent.

Convention Hotel – See *Big Box*.

Count – See *Guarantee*.

CVB – See *Convention and Visitors Bureau*.

Director of Sales (DOS) – The individual at a hotel responsible for overseeing and meeting the hotel's annual sales objectives. The DOS may have responsibility for managing a sales team (such as sales managers, coordinators, and assistants) as well as serving as an individual contributor by working closely with preferred and large accounts to book business.

DOS – See *Director of Sales*.

Early Departure Fee – A fee charged to a hotel guest who checks out of a hotel earlier than the original departure date indicated in the reservation or verified at check-in.

Event – An organized occasion, such as a meeting or an exhibition, that is often comprised of multiple functions.

Fam – A trip attended by a group representative or other industry participants (such as intermediaries) to familiarize an attendee with a site (and its destination) as a possible site for a future meeting or event. All or part of the travel expenses are paid for by the site or by another entity, such as a convention and visitors bureau. A fam trip typically includes some sort of entertaining or socializing.

Fam Trip – See *Fam.*

First Option – A group that has a tentative hold on a hotel and has yet to enter into a formal contract with the hotel.

Flag – A prominent hotel ownership or management company, such as Hilton, Marriott, Hyatt, or Starwood, which owns or manages more than one brand of hotel.

Full-Service Hotel – A hotel with lounge facilities, attached restaurant, room service, function space, and other services and amenities such as bell service, fitness center, and pool. The quality of a full-service hotel can range from mid-price to luxury.

Function – A scheduled occasion, that, when combined with one or more scheduled occasions, contributes to an event.

Group – A grouping of at least ten attendees.

Group History – See *History.*

Group Profile – A description of attendees which comprise a group and which typically contains demographic information such as gender and age make-up, travel-type ratios (e.g., how many attendees will use ground versus air transportation), and spending habits. Frequently used by a group representative as a part of an RFP.

Group Rate – The negotiated sleeping room rate for a group and its attendees (including guests, contractors, exhibitors, et al). *Room Rate* is also frequently and commonly used to mean the group rate.

Group Representative – The individual, such as a meeting planner, or the organization, such as an intermediary, collectively representing a group.

Guarantee – A final attendee count for a food and beverage function provided by a group representative to a hotel prior to the function.

Guest Room – See *Sleeping Room*.

Head in a Bed – Occupied sleeping room.

Headquarters Hotel – Where a group is using multiple hotels, the headquarters hotel is the center of operations and where the staff of the group representative typically is located. Frequently, a headquarters hotel contains the registration area and most functions associated with a meeting.

History – A record of a group's room pick-up performance (contracted room block versus pick-up) for a prior meeting. Used by a group representative to demonstrate to prospective hotels the value of the group's business and that the size of the room block being requested is reasonable. If the size of the requested room block is materially higher than the history, a prospective hotel will likely challenge the increase and / or decline to book the requested room block (instead offering a smaller room block).

Hold All Space – A request made by a group of a hotel for the hotel to tentatively hold all of its available sleeping rooms and function space in anticipation of entering into a contract. Sometimes used as an informal pre-cursor to a *first option*.

In-House – See *On Property*.

Intermediary – A company that provides site selection services to a group and that negotiates the room rate and other deal points on behalf of a group for a commission. The commission is based on the negotiated room rate. Also referred to as a "ten-percenter" due to the typically commission being ten-percent of the room rate.

Lead Sheet – A form used by a Convention and Visitors Bureau to communicate a sales lead (for example, an RFP from a group representative) to prospective hotels and to consolidate the hotels' responses for review by the sales lead (e.g., a group representative).

Limited-Service Hotel – A budget or economy hotel that provides sleeping rooms with no or very few amenities. Typically has no attached restaurant and no function space.

Multi-Year (Contract) – A contract between a group representative and a hotel for room blocks over more than one year. The contract can be for contiguous or non-contiguous years and can involve different meetings with varying-sized room blocks. While a group representative is committing his or her meetings to the same hotel for multiple years, the group representative typically receives the benefit of preferred dates, better room rates, and additional concessions.

Occupancy (Level / Rate) – The percentage of available sleeping rooms occupied in a hotel for a given period (day, week to date, week, month to date, month, year, year to date). Calculated by dividing the number of sleeping rooms occupied over a period by the number of sleeping rooms available for the same period and expressed as a percentage. Used by hotels as a measure of economic performance.

On Property – A group that is "on property" at a hotel, conducting its meeting.

Over-booking – The practice of a hotel confirming more sleeping rooms or function space than actually available.

Overflow Hotel – A hotel needed to accommodate attendees who cannot be accommodated in a headquarters hotel.

Pattern – The number of sleeping rooms blocked represented on a per-night basis over the in-house dates of a meeting. Numerically depicts (in units of sleeping rooms) the arrival and departure pattern of attendees and defines shoulder nights and peak night(s).

Peak Night(s) – The night (or nights) within a pattern over which attendees occupy the greatest number of sleeping rooms.

Pick-Up – Also called "room pick-up." Pick-up is used in two different contexts: pre-meeting and post-meeting. In the pre-meeting context, pick-up refers to the number of sleeping rooms in the contracted room block that have been reserved. In the post-meeting context, pick-up refers to the number of sleeping rooms actually occupied. Frequently, a hotel contract defines how post-meeting room pick-up is calculated. For example, an "occupied" sleeping room included for the purpose of determining room pick-up may in fact be an unoccupied sleeping room for which an early departure fee was charged.

Pick-Up Report – This type of report informs a group representative of the number of sleeping rooms reserved prior to a meeting as compared to the room block (pre-meeting pick-up report) or, after the conclusion of a meeting, the number of sleeping room actually picked-up out of the room block (post-meeting pick-up report).

Planning Meeting – A meeting conducted by a group representative at a contracted hotel, and typically involving contractors of the group representative and key hotel staff, for purposes of planning the future meeting including, for example, reviewing the program of events, function space assignments, food and beverage, audio-visual, and signage placement.

Post-Con (Meeting) – A meeting between a group representative, contractors of the group representative, and key hotel staff that occurs after or in conjunction with the official end date of the meeting in order to discuss an evaluation of the meeting and, if available, review various post-meeting documents such as banquet event orders, other billing documents, and room pick-up reports. See also *Pre-Con*.

Pre-Con (Meeting) – A meeting between a group representative, contractors of the group representative, and key hotel staff that occurs before or in conjunction with the official start date of the meeting in order to make introductions, coordinate efforts, review the program of events and associated needs such as room sets and food and beverage, discuss the meeting, and make any adjustments. See also *Post-Con.*

Property – See *Hotel.*

Rack Rate – A hotel's full, undiscounted published rate for sleeping rooms.

Request for Proposal (RFP) – A process by which a group representative communicates his or her documented meeting requirements to one or more hotels in order to obtain a written proposal. When more than one hotel is requested to provide a proposal, the hotels are competing with each other for a meeting. In that case, the term "competitive bid" is also used to refer to the Request for Proposal process.

RevPAR (Revenue Per Available Room) – The total sleeping room revenue for a given period (day, week to date, week, month to date, month, year, year to date) divided by the number of available sleeping rooms for the same period. Used by hotels as a measure of economic performance.

RFP – See Request for Proposal.

Room List – See *Rooming List.*

Room Rate – May have a variety of meanings based on the context. Prior to negotiations, the room rate represents the proposed room rate. Following negotiations, the room rate represents the *Group Rate.* May also refer to *Rack Rate.*

Room Set – The specified physical arrangement of function space, such as a ballroom, including the layout of chairs, tables, and audio-visual equipment.

Rooming List – A list of attendee reservations gathered by a group representative or a housing coordinator and used to communicate reservation requirements to a hotel which then makes the reservations of the requested sleeping rooms (and for which the hotel often provides a corresponding confirmation number).

Run of House – A flat room rate for any sleeping rooms available at a hotel (excluding suites) that are assigned to a group, with the final assignment of sleeping rooms being at the discretion of the hotel.

Second Option – A group that is wait-listed for a hotel and that has the option to enter into a formal contract with the hotel should the first option held by another group fall through.

Select-Service Hotel – A hotel oriented to address the market demand for a level of service and amenities beyond limited-service hotels, but less than full-service hotels. Amenities of select-service hotels typically include 24-hour food service and snacks, wireless Internet in the common areas, a business computer center, and a lounge. Function space tends to be limited.

Shoulder Night – A night in a room block and pattern that is either before or after the peak night(s).

Site – A facility associated with a meeting, such as a convention center or hotel.

Site Inspection – Inspection of a site, such as a hotel, by a group representative (who has either already contracted with the site or there is a strong intention to contract with the site) to assess the site's layout, services, amenities, quality, and physical condition as compared to the needs and requirements of the group. Travel expenses may or may not be funded in part or in whole by the site.

Site Visit – See *Site Inspection.*

Sleeping Room – Hotel room with bed and bathroom; intended to be occupied by a hotel guest.

Slippage – The difference, usually expressed as a percentage, between the contracted room block (as adjusted, if permitted) and the room pick-up. "Permitted" slippage refers to sleeping rooms not picked-up but which do not trigger attrition damages.

Space Hold – A request made by a group of a hotel for the hotel to tentatively hold the specified number of its available sleeping rooms and specified amount of function space in anticipation of entering into a contract. See also *All Space Hold.*

Ten-Percenter – See *Intermediary.*

Total Room Nights – The total number of sleeping room nights represented by a room block and pattern.

Transient – Hotel guests not associated with a group, such as individual business travelers. Sometimes referred to as "transient travelers," "transient business," or "transient traffic."

Walk – A "walk" or a "walked" attendee is a person holding a confirmed sleeping room reservation but who is denied accommodation by the hotel. Also referred to as a "dishonored reservation."

Index

D

E

N

O

P

S

Acknowledgements

There were a number of people and experiences that were key in enabling me to write this book. First and most obvious are the hoteliers. There were a number of hoteliers with whom I had unfortunate experiences with and who are directly responsible for my beefing up (and continuing to beef up) the MHSA. I thank you because, without you, I wouldn't have become the hotel negotiator I've become and I wouldn't have been able to share some of the experiences that I describe in this book. Note: your fellow hoteliers with whom I negotiate with might not be as thankful as I. In contrast, there are many more hoteliers with whom I've had extremely positive experiences such as Adriana Molina with Starwood and Jayne Carmona with Marriott.

There is one hotelier who deserves special recognition, who took me under his wing even though we represented different interests, who showed me the ropes in the hospitality industry and gave me insight into the inner workings of the hotel business, who introduced me to hotel insiders, who gave me access to Hilton execs, and who advocated for me with fellow hoteliers when the dreaded "A" word came up: David Giger with Hilton. Thank you, David, for being a consummate professional, a true gentleman, a mentor, and a valued business partner. Hilton is lucky to have you. P.S. Hi, Mary!

Particular and effusive thanks to my editor-in-chief and mother-in-chief, Barbara Talbot, for all of the work that she does and has done for me without charge. Barbara has the ability to find errors in my work even after I've proofed that same work more than once—I don't know how she does it. In life, however, she's let me discover mistakes on my own and has never been critical. I'm who I am because of her. Thanks, Mom!

Much appreciation to my meeting planning staff and my procurement staff, who have, at my side, endured (or enjoyed) many of the hotel experiences I describe in this book. Thank you (especially Jean Johnson) for bearing with me whenever I've given you a hard time for increasing a room block or for bringing me an overflow contract. A big thanks also to Robin Slye, who does a terrific job of managing my meeting planning team and keeping everything running smoothly.

Many thanks in particular to Mike Burke, one of my awesome meeting planners, who reviewed this book in his personal time and provided me with his important and valuable insight.

LaVergne, TN USA
12 January 2011
212043LV00001B/1/P